The Guide to
BLACK WASHINGTON

The Guide to
BLACK WASHINGTON

Places and Events of
Historical and Cultural Significance
in the Nation's Capital

SANDRA FITZPATRICK
MARIA R. GOODWIN

HIPPOCRENE BOOKS
New York

Revised Illustrated Edition, 2001.
Revised Edition, 1999.

For information, address:
Hippocrene Books, Inc.
171 Madison Avenue
New York, NY 10016

Library of Congress Cataloging-in-Publication Data
Fitzpatrick, Sandra.
A guide to Black Washington: a directory of places of Black historic and cultural significance in Washington, D.C. / Sandra Fitzpatrick, Maria R. Goodwin. p. cm.
Includes bibliographical references.
ISBN 0-7818-0871-5
1. Afro-Americans—Homes and haunts—Washington (D.C.)—Guide-books. 2. Washington (D.C.)—Description—1981—Tours. 3. Historic building—Washington (D.C.)—Guide-books. I. Goodwin, Maria R. II. Title.

Printed in the United States of America.

Contents

Chapter 11—U Street and Strivers' Section: 161
A Walking Tour

Foreword

As a federal district, Washington, D.C. is neither a state, nor part of one. In this respect, our nation's capital differs from every other city in the country. The immense federal presence contributes to the duality of our city, with its complex layering of official Monumental Washington downtown around the Mall and the numerous neighborhoods that constitute the local community. There are also two levels of government. The federal, executive and legislative branches exert control over much of the city's affairs from Capitol Hill and the White House, and the District of Columbia government administers the city with limited authority derived from the District's recently acquired home rule in the 1970s. And recently, during the mid 90s, broad areas of the city's responsibilities have been placed under the authority of a federally-appointed Control Board. Finally, the city's population of fewer than 550,000 consists of both long-time residents who consider Washington their permanent home and a large group of transient citizens, whose government-related employment brings them to the city for shorter stays, often only until the next presidential election.

For two hundred years the threads of two distinct communities have been woven through the intricate web of federal and local interests in Washington—the traditionally dominant white population and a vibrant, thriving black community which attained majority status during the past four decades. Although the city is now almost three-quarters black, Washington's black residents were, until fairly recently, rigidly separated socially, economically, politically, and even geographically from the city's white community. Washington's black neighborhoods were for years called a "secret city," a term popularized by Washington's late historian laureate Constance McLaughlin Green. Forced to overcome the barriers imposed by segregation and discrimination, black Washingtonians created a vital social and economic culture within their carefully delineated neighborhoods. This is, in essence, the silver lining to those difficult years for black Americans, and it is this legacy, this cultural, entrepreneurial, and artistic heritage, that this book seeks to illuminate.

The *Guide to Black Washington* will serve as a guide to many of the persons and places of historical significance within the "secret city." It attempts to highlight the struggles and accomplishments of black Washingtonians and to chronicle the institutions that have, for over a century, made Washington's black community one of the nation's most influential, and Washington itself one of this country's unique metropolitan areas.

Like other American cities, Washington is undergoing dynamic change with each passing year; buildings are torn down, neighborhoods are changing through gentrification and shifting demographics, and families and institutions continue to seek out the comforts of suburban Maryland and Virginia. Before they are lost to the inevitable and transforming forces, *The Guide to Black Washington* endeavors to document these historic sites and those black personalities that inhabited them. For all Washingtonians, one hopes this material serves to uncover more fully the rich and proud, if shrouded, history of the city's black community; for black Washingtonians, one hopes this guide further opens the doors to their own heritage.

Whether exploring the city by automobile or on foot, this guide provides a wealth of information about the rich and varied neighborhoods in the community. Two specific walking tours are provided through the Shaw neighborhood, located north of M Street between 7th and 15th Streets. The guide can also be kept in the glove compartment of your car, providing clues to the rich history behind a particular and intriguing home or building spotted while at a stoplight. The journey through our city begins downtown, moving to those two important neighborhoods at the eastern end of the Mall—Capitol Hill and Anacostia. It then passes through Northeast, Shaw and Georgetown, leading one on an arc north and west of the Capitol, ending at the Lincoln Memorial at the west end of the mall.

*   *   *

The authors wish to extend their appreciation to the following: the staff of Howard University's Moorland-Spingarn Research Center Reading Room; Marcia Battle, formerly of Prints and Photographs, Moorland-Spingarn Research Center; Marv Ternes, Photo Librarian, and Mr. G.R.F. Key, Washingtonian Division, Martin Luther King, Jr. Public Library; the late Robert Scurlock; Margaret Burri, Librarian, The Historical Society of Washington, D.C.; Adele Logan Alexander; and Michael Fitzpatrick for his insight and assistance in editing the manuscript and in selecting photographs for the first edition. Special thanks to Washington historian Kathryn S. Smith whose skills and energies on behalf of the historical heritage of the nation's capital are an inspiration to both of us.

Introduction

Long before history became my vocation, my late mother enthralled me with stories about her youth. She had grown up in black Washington, not "official" Washington. During World War I, her family was able to buy their first home on Seaton Place in Le Droit Park only because the property had been confiscated from a German national whom the federal government had designated an "unfriendly alien." On Saturdays, she and her pals roller-skated down Ninth Street, Northwest to the old central library on K, and then on Sundays, her family motored across town to attend Rev. Bennett's Episcopal church. Girls in her dancing class walked up Georgia Avenue to the former residence of Gen. O. O. Howard on Howard University's campus where they stood on sheets of paper while their teacher carefully traced outlines of their feet to order new ballet slippers from New York City. They attended the "colored" schools and patronized segregated restaurants, movie houses, and amusement parks. Sometimes, however, they also attempted to circumvent the city's degrading Jim Crow restrictions by claiming that they were "of foreign extraction."

I first learned about the glorious legacy of Paul Laurence Dunbar High School from my mother. Her illustrious contemporaries there included the young men who later became Federal Circuit Judge William Hastie and Robert C. Weaver, the nation's first black Cabinet member. Inspirational black female teachers brought their Ph.D.'s to that school because they had so few other career opportunities. In 1922, a group of her girl friends who referred to each other by secret names (derived from their initials) such as "Jumpy Dumpy Dog" and "Catty Batty Eel," formed a club they called the Mignonettes. Even today surviving members of the group still meet quarterly to reminisce and share recent events in their lives. Many of my mother's classmates attended the all-black Miner Teachers College and went on to teach in the District's segregated school system. Mother also regaled me with stories about their summers at the Highland Beach enclave on Chesapeake Bay where young people picnicked, swam, and boated with such distinguished members of the "colored" community as Mary Church Terrell, known by others of her social set as "Lady Mollie." Washington's entrenched African American community holds so strongly to its traditions of "who knows whom" that when I came to Washington in 1963 as a married woman, some people still introduced me by my mother's maiden name.

My husband and I moved into what was then called the "New Southwest," a neighborhood that became home to many young black professionals in the Kennedy administration who were newcomers to the District of Columbia. Much of the "Old Southwest" had been demolished in the name of "urban renewal" and "progress." The redeveloped area emerged as one of the few places in the city that did not retain the legacy of segregated living. My mother, however, remembered the dubious reputation that Southwest carried from her childhood. Mother told me that she did not think that anyone "respectable" lived there. My first August in Washington, pushing my baby in a stroller, I walked down toward the Lincoln Memorial to participate in the memorable March on Washington where more than a quarter of a million demonstrators of all races, economic levels, and walks of life peacefully protested the political, social, and economic injustices that the United States still imposed on its black citizens.

My acquaintance with "black Washington" long predates my own arrival and extends back to the time before 1920 when my mother first came here, and her stories still live vividly in my memory. In recent years, however, I have learned about the city's more inclusive history dating back more than two hundred years.

Many Africans were brought as slaves to the first settlements in this region that was destined to become the nation's capital. They provided much of the labor force that laid out the city's early, narrow streets, and they worked on the Georgetown wharves and constructed many of the oldest private and public buildings. As early as the end of the eighteenth century, however, a free black man named Benjamin Banneker helped survey the territory to create a master plan for the new Federal City.

By 1800 slaves comprised about eighty percent of the black population of Washington and adjoining Georgetown, but gradually that balance shifted. In 1830 the city included equal numbers of bondsmen and free people of color, and by the start of the Civil War, nearly eighty percent of local people of African ancestry were not enslaved. In absolute numbers, the slave population swelled from about 3,200 in 1800 to 6,100 in 1830, then declined again to 3,200 at the start of the Civil War. During those same years, however, the city's free black population expanded from 800, to 6,200, to 11,100. For the nonenslaved people of color, restrictive and discriminatory laws stringently inhibited their economic, social, educational, and political activities, but despite those restrictions, free status was far preferable to enslavement, and life in the nation's capital seemed less demeaning than life in the slave states to the south.

During the War of 1812, free people of color responded to the same patriotic impulses that motivated whites who fought to defend the capital. Following the burning of Washington by the British army in 1815, slaves (most of whom lived in wretched alley dwellings behind their masters' homes) did most of the city's physical reconstruction. During the ensuing decades, African Americans began to establish their own small schools and independent churches, and most free people of color found employment as domestics, service workers, and artisans. Some owned small businesses, and a few even defied the barriers of law and prejudice and became successful entrepreneurs.

Through the 1830s slavery remained firmly entrenched in Washington despite the growing debate between pro-slavery advocates and abolitionists (black and white) focusing on the institution's continued existence in the nation's capital. That decade also saw intensified anti-black activity. In 1835, during the "Snow riots," mobs of whites destroyed schools, churches, and businesses in the African American community in an attempt to intimidate the city's blacks. Legal sanctions followed and further curtailed commercial endeavors and civil liberties. Nonetheless, runaway slaves and freed people anxious to escape the Deep South swelled Washington's black population. Prior to the Civil War, African Americans in Washington probably had developed the most cohesive community in any southern city.

Throughout the Civil War, Washington's black population increased dramatically as freed slaves who were refugees from the Confederate states streamed into the city, and in 1862, Congress emancipated the capital's remaining bondsmen. Between 1860 and 1870, the number of African American residents more than tripled, until they comprised almost one-third of the city's total population. At least partially as a result of that rapid influx of needy people, living conditions for blacks in the city deteriorated rapidly. Many members of the white community lashed out in fear and anger against the burgeoning black population that the bonds of slavery no longer constrained.

During the 1860s, African Americans in the capital city achieved some measures of equality. The war years had seen the advent of the District's first public schools for blacks — segregated and unequally supported though they were. Starting in 1866, all adult men could exercise the franchise, regardless of race. Some black Washingtonians were elected or appointed to public office, and laws enacted around 1870 prohibited segregation in public accommodations. Reconstruction also brought a number of African American representatives to the halls of congress. A few blacks in the city taught in the public schools, started newspapers, and entered the legal and medical professions, and Howard University was founded in 1867.

BLACK WASHINGTON

By the mid-to-late 1870s, however, the United States Congress, which retained constitutional authority over the District of Columbia, used local political turmoil, mismanagement, and corruption as excuses to snatch away the limited self-government that it previously had granted the city. The congress thus alleviated any apprehensions about possible political control by Washington's increasing black population which by 1875 approached forty percent. Three white, federally appointed commissioners replaced the locally elected officials. Segregation of most public accommodations became common practice during the 1870s and 1880s, and in the century's final decades black Reconstruction members of congress from the southern states gradually were removed from office.

By the turn of the century, Washington's black people had lost many of their struggles for civil rights, and housing and health conditions in black neighborhoods compared poorly with those in most white areas. Still, a number of "colored" Washingtonians managed to succeed economically and professionally. Educated black people from around the country gravitated to Howard University and the M Street High School — Dunbar's predecessor — which provided an education equal to (or better than) that available in the white public schools.

By the early twentieth century, blacks held few jobs in the government of the District of Columbia, and most of those were at the lowest levels. Their numbers decreased in federal service as well, though Republican administrations continued to appoint a few token blacks to selected government posts. For example, until his death in 1896, Frederick Douglass had held both local and diplomatic posts, and Robert Terrell ("Lady Mollie's husband) was appointed as the nation's first black federal judge. Those Washingtonians, however, were notable exceptions. The city which once held such promise for its African American citizens, hardened its lines of segregation both in public accommodations and in government, and interracial relations deteriorated. Economic success proved increasingly elusive for all but a few black people. By 1920, "colored" people comprised only twenty-five percent of the total population, and for the most part, black Washington constituted a separate and very unequal city.

World War I brought a few increased opportunities for black Washingtonians, but at its end, white Americans were disinclined to acknowledge or appreciate the contributions that African Americans had made to the war effort. In 1919, bands of soldiers and civilians, incensed by rumors about attacks on white women and fears of "black criminality" and "Bolshevism," rampaged through "colored" neighborhoods and triggered a period of racial strife and tensions that culminated in the governmentally sanctioned Ku Klux Klan parade in 1925, highlighted by the Klan's ceremonies that convened at the Washington Monument.

The small number of "colored" Washingtonians who managed to acquire a better education, professional status, and decent housing, distanced themselves from the hostile white community, but also had conflicting relationships with the disadvantaged majority of their own race. They wanted to avoid the insults of everyday life in the segregated city, but sometimes turned deaf ears to the distress of the black lower classes. Nonetheless, most members of that privileged group devoted themselves to their work as the community's physicians, lawyers, merchants, teachers, and ministers that benefited all members of the race. Some evidences of class schisms, however, surfaced along the "color line" between dark-skinned and light-skinned African Americans. For example, while both Dunbar High School and Howard University accepted and embraced anyone who qualified for admission, any astute observer could see that an unusually high percentage of Washingtonians associated with those institutions had lighter complexions. A deep abyss existed between the black and white communities — discrimination wounded all African Americans — but the city was also subjected to some uncomfortable social and economic tensions within the "colored" community itself.

The Great Depression generated disproportionate distress for black people throughout the country, although Washington, which was less dependent on the vitality of private industry, may have suffered less than other communities. The New Deal, faith in Franklin Delano Roosevelt himself, his creation of a "Black Cabinet," and the slackening of discrimination in some federal employment policies and facilities, gave a bit of hope to black Washingtonians during that period of economic despair. The 1930s also saw a few chinks in the barriers of Washington's segregated educational institutions when the graduate schools of Catholic and American Universities admitted the first, few black students. And then in 1939, the internationally famed black contralto Marian Anderson was denied permission to sing at DAR Constitution Hall. That widely publicized rebuff, only partially negated by her glowing performance (arranged by Eleanor Roosevelt) before a massive audience at the Lincoln Memorial, thrust the shame of segregation in the nation's capital onto the national scene.

By the beginning of the following decade, the United States entered World War II to help defeat Nazism — grounded, as it was, on myths of Aryan racial supremacy. At the war's end, however, the nation's capital still treated its black people as second class citizens, and the walls of segregation had only begun to crack. In 1947, a committee studying segregation in Washington issued a report that iterated and exposed many of the city's discriminatory policies and practices. Efforts — including demonstrations, boycotts, and courtroom struggles — spearheaded by Washington's African American citizens finally removed many restrictive barriers in housing, employment, recreation, movie houses, and restaurants. Nonetheless, those changes that were brought about through nonviolent "revolution," did little to ameliorate economic inequalities or create a unified city free from racial bias. Following the public schools' relatively peaceful desegregation in 1954, the "white flight" that typified and accompanied such changes elsewhere in the country, quickly transformed Washington's demography. The capital city's population dropped, and it soon became predominantly black. Public schools (once such a source of pride) more and more became the province of the black and the disadvantaged.

Events of the 1960s and early 1970s substantively altered Washington's political face. The president appointed the District's first black commissioner in 1961. In 1964 a constitutional amendment gave the city's residents the right to vote for president, and an elected school board came into being in 1968 — the same year that urban riots following the assassination of Rev. Martin Luther King, Jr. vividly exposed the pent-up frustrations of so many black Americans. The year 1970 saw the first election of a non-voting delegate from the District to the House of Representatives, and in 1974, voters finally had the opportunity to elect a mayor and city council under provisions of new Home Rule legislation. Nonetheless, the congress still retains strong control over the District's purse strings as well as legislative veto power over local political actions. In the mid-1990s it has usurped local citizens' power and appointed federal overseers to reestablish its own hegemony and correct what it considers the failures of local government.

Today, Washington includes many beautiful and historic neighborhoods — some integrated, some predominantly black, others mostly white. It is home to the nation's leading historically black university, fine hospitals, and a cultural life that often reflects the richness of the black experience. The District of Columbia still has the highest percentage of African American college graduates of any major city in the nation, yet our public school system suffers from high dropout rates and far too many students perform poorly on standardized tests. Washingtonians have exquisitely restored numerous old homes, but the city also has embarrassing pockets of abandoned and dilapidated housing, while drugs and drug-related crime plague some neighborhoods. Shamefully, Washington's infant mortality and black male death rates are among the highest in the nation. These are but a few of the less fortunate legacies of contemporary urban life, and the District of Columbia has not escaped them.

Sandra Fitzpatrick and Maria Goodwin first provided this fine book for the inquisitive visitor in 1990. They offered profuse information and intimate details about many aspects of the political and economic history of Washington's "Secret City," its cultural life, its neighborhoods, and the variety of people who created and lived in them. Once again, they have vividly brought bricks, mortar, and paving stones to life with stories about the African American Washingtonians who, through more than two centuries, have traversed the grand avenues, walked down the alleyways, and contributed to all aspects of this city's life.

For the curious traveler, this revised guide provides an accessible conduit into aspects of the District that run-of-the-mill tourist information usually ignores. For the one-time or frequent visitor, even the long-time resident, it offers material that answers many questions and provides unexpected insights into the fascinating history of black Washington.

— Adele Logan Alexander
Washington, D. C.
(Revised, May 1998)

CHAPTER 1

Downtown Washington

Slavery in the District of Columbia was always a very fuzzy business. Although the importation of slaves was constitutionally abolished in 1808, Washington remained an active center for the domestic slave trade, due in large part to its geographic location. The Potomac River was tidal to Great Falls above Georgetown, making Washington a significant port for the coastal shipment of slaves. Because of the city's strategic location between the North and South, Washington was a center for the overland coffles—large slave gangs—traveling to the South. "The auction block, the lash, and the manacled gangs on their way to the South" were, according to historian David Lewis, a way of life in Washington before the Civil War.

Antebellum Washington was also an attractive center for free blacks. Fugitive slaves came through the city on their way to the North and many stayed. Newly freed slaves were allowed to remain in the District, whereas in Virginia and other border states slaves were required to leave immediately upon emancipation. Many found their way to the nation's capital. The 1830 census figures counted 6,152 free blacks and 6,119 slaves in the District. By 1850, the year of the Great Compromise and the abolition of slave trading in the District, these figures were dramatically altered to 11,131 free blacks and 3,185 slaves.

Prior to the 1830s and the influx of Irish and German immigrants, slaves made up the major part of Washington's labor market. Slaves owned by District citizens were generally considered "better off" than their counterparts in the South, but life in the nation's capital was strictly regulated through a system of rigid codes.

These laws, known as Black Codes, controlled the movement and behavior of free blacks and slaves in Washington. As early as 1808 a $5 fine was imposed if a black person was found on the street after 10 p.m. Two years later the punishments were increased to a six-month jail term for a free black or forty lashes for a slave. Emancipated blacks were required to carry their certificates of freedom at all times.

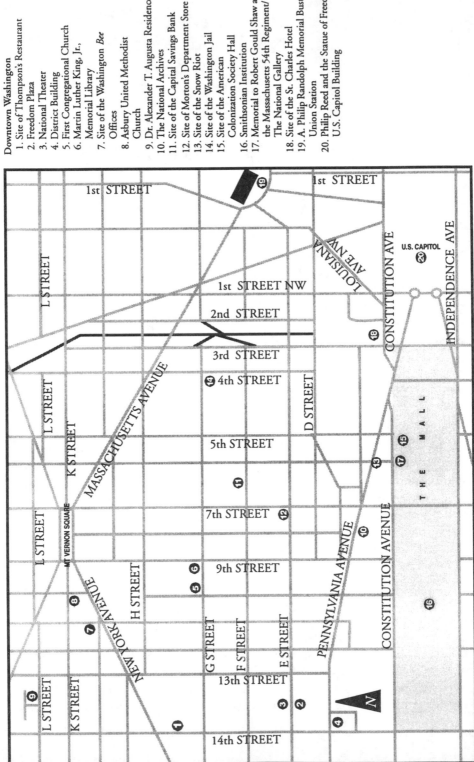

Downtown Washington
1. Site of Thompson's Restaurant
2. Freedom Plaza
3. National Theater
4. District Building
5. First Congregational Church
6. Martin Luther King, Jr.,
   Memorial Library
7. Site of the Washington *Bee*
   Offices
8. Asbury United Methodist
   Church
9. Dr. Alexander T. Augusta Residence
10. The National Archives
11. Site of the Capital Savings Bank
12. Site of Morton's Department Store
13. Site of the Snow Riot
14. Site of the Washington Jail
15. Site of the American
    Colonization Society Hall
16. Smithsonian Institution
17. Memorial to Robert Gould Shaw and
    the Massachusetts 54th Regiment/
    The National Gallery
18. Site of the St. Charles Hotel
19. A. Philip Randolph Memorial Bust/
    Union Station
20. Philip Reed and the Statue of Freedom/
    U.S. Capitol Building

By 1827 fines had increased, a blanket curfew had been imposed, and the cost of a freedman's bond had risen from $20 to $500.

Free blacks could obtain a license "to drive carts, drays, hackney carriages or wagons," although existing law prohibited them from operating any other business. However, enforcement was lax and numerous black artisans successfully plied their trades, especially those of carpenter, bricklayer, stone mason, painter, blacksmith and shoemaker. These black "mechanics" comprised a large portion of the labor market in pre-Civil War Washington. After the war, hostility toward blacks becoming members of the local unions that controlled these trades made earning a living much more difficult.

Nonenforcement of the licensing regulations which forbade blacks to sell liquor or to operate eating establishments permitted several black-owned hotels and restaurants to prosper in downtown Washington prior to the Civil War. "Aunt" Lettie Thompson owned a famous eatery on F Street near the Ebbitt House hotel between 14th and 15th Streets; John Kugjohn operated an oyster house on the northeast corner of Pennsylvania Avenue at 15th Street. The nearby Hope Club Hotel on F Street had black management as early as 1845. And Lynch Wormley, the father of the proprietor of the famed Wormley Hotel, not only owned a livery stable but also operated the Liberia Hotel on E Street between 14th and 15th Streets.

Dr. Robert T. Freeman, the first black to practice dentistry in the city of Washington, maintained offices on the north side of Pennsylvania Avenue between 11th and 12th Streets. An 1868 Harvard University graduate, Dr. Freeman practiced in Washington until his death in 1873.

In 1892 Frederick Douglass' grandson, Joseph H. Douglass, advertised the "Finest Crayon Portraits" and violin instruction at his 934 F Street studio. By the turn of the century he was sharing space in the Capital Savings Bank (609 F Street, NW) with his uncle, Lewis Douglass, a notary public and real estate agent.

Site of Thompson's Restaurant

725 14th Street, NW

Segregation in Washington's public accommodations was a national disgrace, according to Mary Church Terrell, the black community's tireless leader in the struggle for equal rights and a leader in bringing the test case to desegregate Washington's restaurants in 1953. In 1907 she wrote: "For fifteen years I have resided in Washington, and while it was far from being a paradise for colored people when I first touched these shores, it has been doing its level best ever since to make conditions for us intolerable." Blacks were either excluded entirely from hotels, places of entertainment, and eating establishments, or were directed to a separate and inadequate section. "As a colored woman," she continued, "I may walk from the Capitol to the White House, ravenously hungry and abundantly supplied with money with which to purchase a meal, without finding a single restaurant in which I would be permitted to take a morsel of food, if it was patronized by white people, unless I were willing to sit behind a screen."

Nearly half a century later conditions had not improved. In 1950 the only places in Washington where blacks could be seated to eat were the cafeterias at Federal office buildings, the 17th and K Streets YWCA, Union Station, National Airport, The Methodist Building Cafeteria, Hains Point Tea House, and the American Veterans Committee Club on New Hampshire Avenue. The hard-hitting report issued by President Truman's Committee on Civil Rights in 1947 declared that the "shamefulness and absurdity of Washington's treatment of Negro Americans is highlighted by the presence of many dark-skinned foreign visitors." The city's racial customs not only humiliated our own citizens but "foreign officials are often mistaken for American Negroes and refused food, lodging, and entertainment."

In 1950 the Coordinating Committee for the Enforcement of the D.C. Anti-Discrimination Laws, headed by octogenarian Mary Church Terrell, selected the 14th Street restaurant owned by the John R. Thompson Co., Inc., as their test case to desegregate Washington's restaurants after "Miss Mollie," as Terrell was affectionately known, and three others respectfully asked for and were denied service. They immediately filed suit against Thompson's for violating the "Lost-Laws" of 1872-73, rarely-enforced statutes mandating equal treatment in public accommodations. As the Thompson case dragged through the courts on appeal, the committee simultaneously launched the Dime Store Campaign aimed at desegregating the Jim Crow stand-up lunch counters at G.C. Murphy's downtown stores and the Hecht Company department store at 7th and F Streets, NW. After sixteen weeks of picketing, G.C. Murphy announced on September 3, 1952, that they would serve all citizens. The Hecht store capitulated soon after.

In 1953, the committee unanimously won the landmark Supreme Court case, *District of Columbia v. Thompson Co.* Justice William O. Douglas declared that the so-called "Lost Laws" had never been repealed and were therefore still enforceable. The anticipated mass closing of the city's restaurants or the use of evasive tactics never took place. After the victory, 90-year-old Mary Church Terrell, having devoted her life to equal rights, was triumphant. "We will not," she declared, "permit these laws to become lost again."

Freedom Plaza

Pennsylvania Avenue between 13th and 14th Streets, NW

On January 15, 1988, a time capsule was planted under Freedom Plaza containing the Bible, robe and other relics of assassinated civil rights leader, Dr. Martin Luther King, Jr. The capsule is scheduled to be reopened twenty years later on his birthday, in 2008.

National Theater

1321 Pennsylvania Avenue, NW

Nowhere in Washington was there a more visible symbol of the city's rigid segregation than the National Theater. When the theater opened in 1835, blacks were permitted to sit in the upper balcony. In 1838 the theater refused to permit black patrons to attend the run of *The Gladiator* after receiving anonymous and threatening letters. Fearing that the content of the play in which slave gladiators were incited to revolt against their masters might cause trouble, the theater advertised in the local newspaper that "On this occasion colored persons cannot be admitted to the gallery." The seating of blacks in the balcony policy remained in effect until 1873 when black patrons were refused entrance to any section of the theater.

By the 1920s and 1930s the National Theater was a focal point of antisegregation protest in Washington. The arrival of Marc Connelly's successful Broadway production, *The Green Pastures,* starring the distinguished black actor Richard B. Harrison as "de Lawd," threw the black community into turmoil. The National adopted a box office-only ticket policy to prevent blacks from securing tickets. The local Scripps-Howard newspaper printed a letter from the playwright denouncing the theater's racial policy; in response, the theater dropped its advertising in that newspaper. Finally, the National conceded a "Jim Crow" evening, staging one special performance for a black audience.

These so-called "Black Days" continued when other plays were performed with black cast members. Ralph Bunche recalled how disturbed Todd Duncan was at the prospect of playing the lead in *Porgy and Bess* to a Jim Crow audience in his hometown. "I got together a committee from the teachers' union and we went down to see the manager," Bunche remembered. "At first he was very tough—said it wasn't a personal policy, it was economic: white patrons wouldn't come if Negroes were admitted. He tried to pacify our committee by offering us complimentary tickets—said we could come to represent the community. We didn't like that, either, so we threatened him.... I told him I could get a good many pickets out. He finally agreed to change the policy for that one production; but just for that one. As soon as Porgy left, Jim Crow came back in."

In 1947 a Presidential Advisory Committee on Civil Rights termed the racial policies of Washington's theaters "ludicrous extremes....Constitution Hall, owned by the Daughters of the American Revolution, seats concert audiences without distinctions of color, but allows no Negroes on its stage....On the other hand, the commercial legitimate theater has had Negro actors on its stage, but stubbornly refuses to admit Negro patrons."

After local pressure, Actor's Equity Association issued an ultimatum to the National's management in 1947: It would not book productions there unless the theater's policy changed. Refusing to do so, the National closed its doors as a legitimate theater on July 31, 1948, opening shortly after as a movie house.

At the same time, racial barriers at other theaters in Washington began to fall. The newly organized Arena Stage opened to integrated audiences. When the new Lisner Auditorium on The George Washington University campus opened, picket lines formed immediately to protest the theater's segregated policy. Performing in one of the auditorium's early productions, actress Ingrid Bergman refused to go on stage until the seating policy was changed.

In 1952 the National Theater capitulated. That year at her 90th birthday celebration at the Statler Hotel (now the Capital Hilton), Mary Church Terrell jubilantly announced that Washington's theaters were finally open to all citizens.

District Building

(The Wilson Building)
14th Street and Pennsylvania Avenue, NW

The impressive Beaux Arts-style District Building has housed the municipal government of the District of Columbia since it was completed in 1908. Although those planning the monumental complex of neo-classical buildings known as the Federal Triangle during the 1920s envisioned the demolition of the District Building and its neighbor, the Old Post Office, both have survived. Now closed for extensive renovations, the District Building, named after the late Council Chairman, John Wilson, will reopen as home to the District's City Council and other Federal government tenants.

Among the first challenges facing Congress when the capital was moved to Washington in 1800 was the organization of the city's government. The municipal charter granted in 1802 provided for limited home rule—the mayor was appointed by the president and the city council could levy real estate taxes to raise revenue for city services. However, by the end of the Civil War there were strong pressures for a new and more responsive form of local government.

In 1871 the city's three jurisdictions—Washington County, the city of Washington, and Georgetown—were united under a territorial government in which the governor and council continued to be appointed by the president. The franchise was extended to all male residents, including blacks, and the city gained a non-voting representative in the Congress. Due to a variety of events and factors, Congress took back its power over the capital's affairs in 1878, establishing a presidentially-appointed commission system of local government. Although the citizens lost their right to self-rule, they gained a federal subsidy payment equal to half the city's expenses.

For nearly a century the debate over Home Rule ebbed and flowed, gaining strength after World War II with slogans such as "Washington, D.C.—America's Last Colony." By the early 1960s Washingtonians were granted the right to vote for president and vice president, followed by an elected school board in 1968. With the passage of the Home Rule Act of 1973, the city gained an elected mayor and city council, but Congress retained veto power over city laws and authority over the city's budget.

The nation's capital was among the first major cities in the country to be governed by a black mayor when Walter E. Washington was elected in 1974. (Washington had previously served as mayor under the appointment of Presidents Lyndon B. Johnson and Richard M. Nixon.) The mayor, city council and other government departments maintained offices here in the District Building until recently. Former Mayor Sharon Pratt Kelly relocated the Mayor's Executive Offices to the new One Judiciary Square Building several years ago. The move sparked a great deal of controversy, and angered then Council Chairman John Wilson, who called the action expensive and wasteful and refused to move the Council to Judiciary Square.

First Congregational Church

Northeast corner of G and 10th Streets, NW

First Congregational's history as an integrated congregation makes it unique among Washington's churches. General Oliver O. Howard, head of the Freedmen's Bureau and founder of Howard University, was one of the organizers of First Congregational in 1865. When Howard, a white, fought for and achieved a racially integrated congregation, the minister and many members left to join a nearby church. The popularity of the second pastor, Dr. Jeremiah E. Rankin, greatly increased the church's membership. Rankin, a white minister, later became the president of Howard University, and the chapel on the campus bears his family name.

For many decades First Congregational was a lively center of the city's artistic and intellectual life. Frequent concerts featured well-known musical artists, including contralto Marian Anderson in her first Washington concert in 1920.

As the congregation fled to the suburbs, the building was demolished in 1959 and was replaced by a smaller contemporary church building (1961).

Martin Luther King, Jr., Memorial Library

901 G Street, NW

The Martin Luther King, Jr., Memorial Library opened in 1972, replacing the Carnegie Library on Mt. Vernon Square as the central library of the District of Columbia. The brick, matte black steel, and bronze-tinted glass structure was designed by internationally-acclaimed architect Ludwig Mies van der Rohe.

Dominating the lobby, a remarkable mural depicting the life and times of Dr. Martin Luther King, Jr., commemorates the most successful black leader in post-World War II America and traces the important events and leaders of the civil rights movement. The viewer will recognize the Ebenezer Baptist Church in Atlanta; Mohandas K. Gandhi, the leader of India whose nonviolent philosophy influenced King; Rosa Parks, whose arrest triggered the Montgomery, Alabama, bus boycott; leaders of the Southern Christian Leadership Conference founded by Dr. King; the Birmingham protest demonstrations; the award of the Nobel Peace Prize; and Dr. King delivering his great "I Have a Dream" address at the Lincoln Memorial in 1963. The mural is the work of artist Don Miller.

The library's Washingtoniana Room contains one of the city's most comprehensive collections of books, photographs, maps, directories, and memorabilia relating to the history of Washington, D.C.

In 1996, Washingtoniana Room reference librarian G.R.F. Key celebrated his 100th birthday. Key, an African American, was born in a Georgetown row house the same year that the D.C. Library came into existence. He worked at the Library for thirty years and at the time of his century birthday was considered to be the oldest D.C. government employee.

Site of the *Washington Bee* Offices

1109 I Street, NW

One of the most significant black journals of the era, the *Washington Bee* newspaper "stood guard here at the nation's capital, shelling the citadel of prejudice with facts and figures." Vigilant, brilliant, bold, and outspoken, William Calvin Chase published the weekly for nearly forty years. Taking over as editor and proprietor in 1882, Chase was true to the *Bee's* masthead motto: "Honey for Our Friends, Stings for Our Enemies." Chase and the *Bee* voiced the protests of the black community against the outrages of segregation and discrimination. The *Bee* fearlessly attacked discrimination as practiced by the Federal government (especially during the administration of President Woodrow Wilson), and condemned racial violence, lynchings, and riots. A loyal member of the Republican Party, Chase protested its support of segregation. On the other hand, stressing the need for blacks to control their own education, the *Bee* editorially supported a dual school system in Washington.

Chase was educated at John F. Cook's school in the basement of the 15th Street Presbyterian Church before he assumed the care and support of his mother and five sisters after his father's death. Soon after taking over the *Bee*, Chase enrolled in Howard University's law school and conducted a legal practice at the *Bee* offices for years. He died at his office desk in 1921.

Asbury United Methodist Church

11th and K Streets, NW

Dissatisfied with the discriminatory practices of Foundry Methodist Church, seventy-five black parishioners, some still slaves, split from the church to establish Asbury Methodist in 1836. While still members of Foundry Methodist, these "breakaway" communicants formed the Asbury Aid Society to help families displaced after the serious racial violence during the 1835 Snow riot that destroyed many black homes, schools, and businesses. They erected a frame church on a field at 11th and K Streets, NW, naming it Asbury in honor of British Bishop Francis Asbury, who had sent Methodist missionaries to convert Georgetowners well before the Revolutionary War. The small wooden church was replaced by a larger brick building in 1845. In 1915 the present imposing neo-Gothic church was built.

Called in the press "the national church of Negro Methodism," Asbury has been important as an educational institution as well as a place of worship. The Reverend John F. Cook, founder of the 15th Street Presbyterian Church, conducted Sunday school classes for black youth here. During the Civil War, Asbury was the site of a school operated by two teachers sponsored by the National Freedmen's Relief Association of the District of Columbia and was the largest all-black congregation in the city.

Today Asbury is the oldest Methodist Church in the District of Columbia to continue on its original site. It was placed on the Register of Historic Places in 1986.

Dr. Alexander T. Augusta Residence

1319 L Street, NW

Born in 1825 in Virginia, the young Alexander Augusta was taught to read by Daniel Payne, later a bishop of the African Methodist Episcopal Church. At the time, teaching a Negro to read was illegal. Denied admission to the University of Pennsylvania Medical School, Augusta studied in the office of one of the professors, and later, after leaving his own country, received a degree from the University of Toronto Medical College.

In 1863 Dr. Augusta was one of eight black doctors commissioned in the U.S. Army. His rank of major as surgeon of colored troops made him the highest ranking black officer in the armed forces. In 1869 Freedmen's Hospital became the teaching hospital for the Howard University Medical School. Dr. Augusta was offered a place on the faculty—the first black to hold such a position at any medical school in the United States. His exemplary record notwithstanding, he and two other Howard faculty members were denied membership in the Medical Society of the District of Columbia.

During the Civil War Washington's numerous streetcar lines were segregated. As the charters of the various companies came up for renewal, U.S. Senator Charles Sumner attempted to add anti-discriminatory clauses to the contracts. In 1864, Major Augusta was traveling by streetcar to a court-martial proceeding where he was an important witness. He wrote a letter to the judge-advocate explaining his late arrival:

> *Sir: I have the honor to report that I have been obstructed in getting to the court this morning by the conductor of car No. 32 of the Fourteenth street line of the city railway.*

I started from my lodgings to go to the hospital I formerly had charge of to get some notes of the case I was to give evidence in, and hailed the car at the corner of Fourteenth and I Streets. It was stopped for me and when I attempted to enter, the conductor pulled me back and informed me that I must ride on the front with the driver as it was against the rules for colored persons to ride inside. I told him I would not ride on the front, and he said I should not ride at all. He then ejected me from the platform, and at the same time gave orders to the driver to go on. I have therefore been compelled to walk the distance in the mud and rain, and have also been delayed in my attendance upon the court.

Sumner read this letter to the U.S. Senate introducing a resolution to instruct the District of Columbia Committee to introduce legislation banning discrimination on the District's public transportation. Such a law was passed in 1865.

Dr. Augusta resigned from the Howard University faculty in 1877 and practiced privately until his death at home in 1890. He is buried in Arlington National Cemetery.

The National Archives

7th Street and Pennsylvania Avenue, NW

Along with the Declaration of Independence and many other treasured documents of American history, the Emancipation Proclamation is stored with more than 3 billion other records at the National Archives. Periodically, it is placed on temporary display, often during February, Black History Month.

Alex Haley, the noted African American author of *Roots: An American Saga*, spent many hours here researching his ancestry back to its African origins.

The Harmon Foundation which purchased and exhibited paintings, prints, and sculpture by African American artists from 1928 to 1945, donated photographic copies of this important collection to the Archives when it ceased activities in 1967, thus providing access to this important visual history. The records of the Freedmen's Bureau may also be found at the National Archives.

Site of the Capital Savings Bank

609 F Street, NW

A group of black businessmen met in 1888 to create the Capital Savings Bank, prompted, it is said, by an insulting charge made by a U.S. Senator on the Senate floor, "With all of their boasted progress, the colored race had not a single bank official to its credit." The bank's president and founding member, Leonard C. Bailey, had been a member of the first racially-mixed jury empaneled in the District of Columbia.

From its original location at 804 F Street, NW, Capital Savings moved into its own building at 609 F Street in the summer of 1893. With its substantial assets the bank was able to withstand the financial strain of the panic of 1893 "without asking a quarter from anyone, paying every obligation on demand," as the Union League directory admiringly pointed out. Other black businesses—the real estate office of Lewis Douglass, son of the famous abolitionist; the Benevolent Investment and Relief Association; and the National Benefit Association insurance firms—occupied the floors above the bank. The only black member of the U.S. House of Representatives from 1896 to 1900, George White, practiced law for a few years in the building.

Closed in 1902, the bank had provided the opportunity and experience for black involvement in the banking profession. The Capital Savings Bank building continued to be used as an office building for black businesses for many years.

Site of Morton's Department Store

7th and D Streets, NW

In 1933 during the bleakest days of the Depression, Mortimer C. Lebowitz opened his first department store on this corner. What made the Morton's store special was its policy of welcoming black customers. In Washington, "retailers had separate fitting rooms and toilets for blacks," Lebowitz reminisced in 1993. "They were treated very cruelly and clearly were not made to feel welcome. Everyone at the time felt they would lose white customers if they catered to black customers." Morton's, which became a very popular store for much of black Washington, had dressing rooms and rest rooms shared by both white and black customers. These policies angered many of Morton's white staff members. Lebowitz simply replaced them with black employees and soon most of his staff was black.

During the riots of 1968, two Morton's stores were burned and vandalized. Lebowitz told reporters at the time that he was certain the rioters did not know him and he did not take it personally. The newspaper interview continued:

> Everything in the two stores was destroyed except for his layaway records. He and his clerks took the records to another store and began contacting customers telling them that they could still pick up Easter outfits they had been paying for. After the riots, he remained loyal to his customers in Washington as he expanded into Maryland...."

As he reached the age of 80, Lebowitz closed his stores in 1993 after sixty years of successful merchandising.

Site of the Snow Riot

6th Street and Pennsylvania Avenue, NW

At the corner of 6th and Pennsylvania stood the Epicurean Eating House, a popular restaurant owned and operated by an African American, Beverly Snow. In 1835 Snow's Eating House became the target of local rioting.

The Nat Turner Plantation Uprising in Virginia, the growing number of blacks in the nation's capital, and the increasing militancy of abolitionist literature produced conditions in which an isolated occurrence sparked widespread violence in Washington. An alleged assault by a slave on Mrs. William Thornton, widow of the famous architect of the U.S. Capitol Building and Octagon House, was that catalytic event.

According to the newspapers this incident caused great excitement among the citizenry and "menacing assemblages" gathered in the streets. Rumors spread that Snow had made disparaging remarks about the "wives of white mechanics who worked at the Navy Yard." Denying that he had used such language, Snow escaped with the help of white friends to Canada where he remained.

The initial wrath of the white crowds centered on the looting and vandalizing of Snow's popular restaurant. Ostensibly looking for abolitionist literature, the rioters then attacked black homes, businesses, and churches. But most especially, the roving bands vandalized all black schoolhouses, destroying completely those operated by Mary Wormley and John F. Cooke. Cooke escaped to Pennsylvania on a horse provided by an abolitionist white supporter. He stayed there for three years before returning to Washington.

Despite a new city ordinance that blacks could no longer operate their own businesses, Snow's restaurant reopened within a year under the ownership of Absalom Shadd, a black man. Twenty years later Shadd liquidated his business for the handsome sum of $25,000.

Site of the Washington Jail

Judiciary Square
Southwest corner of G and 4th Streets, NW

Washington's first two jails served as storehouses for the District's slave traders who operated quite profitably in the nation's capital. The original jail, built in 1801 on Judiciary Square, became the Washington Infirmary in 1844 and was destroyed by fire in 1861. The second jail, located at the southwest corner of G and 4th Streets, NW, was erected in 1839 to alleviate overcrowding at the original jail; it was demolished in 1874.

Any black person who ran afoul of any of the city's numerous Black Codes was sent to Washington Jail. Visiting Washington in 1815, European writer Jesse Torrey described the dreadful conditions at the jail where "several hundred people, including not legal slaves only, but many kidnapped freemen ... are annually collected at Washington (as if it were an emporium of slavery) for transportation to the slave regions." Notices were published in the local newspapers requesting slave owners to appear to pay not only the fine but also the costs of incarceration. Free blacks able to prove their status but unable to pay the expenses for their stay in prison were sold into slavery, often by the city's presidentially-appointed U.S. Marshall or his staff.

In the late 1820s Congressman Charles Miner of Pennsylvania decried the "gross corruptions" of Washington's slave laws in which federal jails were blatantly used as warehouses by slave dealers. He found that during a five-year period, 452 slaves and 290 free blacks, arrested as runaways, were lodged in the Washington Jail. Fifteen of the nonslave prisoners had been able to prove their free status but five had been sold into life slavery.

Site of the American Colonization Society Hall

Pennsylvania Avenue and 4th Street, NW

The first and only permanent home of the American Colonization Society, built in 1860, stood on the southwest corner of the intersection of Pennsylvania Avenue and 4th Street. Often called the Back to Africa movement, colonization attempted to quicken the process of emancipation by providing the means for free blacks to emigrate to Africa. The Society was created in 1817 by leaders and politicians from both the North and the South, including Henry Clay, Daniel Webster, and Georgetown attorney Francis Scott Key.

The state of Liberia was formed in 1822, and from that year to 1867 the Society sent more than 6,000 American blacks to resettle there on the African west coast. By the 1830s the Back to Africa movement was severely split between moderates and more radical abolitionists who favored immediate emancipation rather than resettlement. Colonization never gained popular support among free black citizens who considered themselves Americans rather than Africans.

The headquarters building was razed in the 1930s when Constitution Avenue was cut through from 6th Street to Pennsylvania Avenue.

The Smithsonian Institution

The Mall

One of the world's largest museum complexes, the Smithsonian Institution consists of sixteen museums and galleries and the National Zoo. Artifacts of major African American significance are part of the Smithsonian's vast collections which make up the extensive resources available to the public.

Of particular note at the **National Air and Space Museum**, dedicated to the history of the science, technology and culture of aviation and space flight, is an exhibition entitled "Black Wings: The American Black in Aviation." It focuses on the progress made by African Americans in overcoming racial barriers in both commercial and military aviation. The Museum's World War II gallery has a special section on black military pilots. The inflight suit of the first African American astronaut in space, Guion "Guy" Bluford, is part of the museum collection.

The **Hirshhorn Museum and Sculpture Garden**, devoted to modern and contemporary art, owns over 130 works by 24 African American artists including Romare Bearden, Robert Colescott, David Hammons, Jacob Lawrence, Betye and Alison Saar, and Washingtonians Sam Gilliam, Alma Thomas, and Lois Mailou Jones.

The **National Museum of American Art** located off the Mall at 8th and G streets, NW, includes nearly 2,000 artworks by more than 140 black artists. It is especially strong in 19th century works by Edward Mitchell Bannister, Henry Ossawa Tanner, and Robert Duncanson. Artists active during the Harlem Renaissance and the WPA programs of the 1930s include William H. Johnson, Palmer Hayden and Joseph and Beauford Delaney. The sculpture collection contains significant works by Edmonia Lewis, Elizabeth Catlett, Sargent Johnson, and

Richard Hunt. Folk artists William Edmondson, James Hampton, Mose Tolliver and Bill Traylor are well represented. The museum also houses the photographic documentation of Harlem during the 1930s and 1940s by white photographer Aaron Siskind.

In the same building, the **Archives of American Art**, the world's largest collection of materials documenting the visual arts in the United States, holds the personal papers of over eighty African American artists.

Sharing the historic Patent Office Building with the NMAA, the **National Portrait Gallery** collects likenesses of those who have contributed to the historical and cultural development of the United States. In 1944 a portrait of George Washington Carver, painted only months before his death by Betsy Graves Reyneau, was presented to the Smithsonian. It was the first portrait of a black American to enter this national collection.

One of many, the History of Jazz Collection at the **National Museum of American History** includes the Duke Ellington archives of more than 200,000 pages of music manuscripts, newspaper clippings and photographs. A special treasure that is often displayed at the Museum is the "Bible Quilt" made by former slave, Harriet Powers, around 1886. The Museum's Division of Social History contains artifacts representing civil rights leader Roy Wilkins, presidential campaign items from the Reverend Jesse Jackson's candidacy, and memorabilia of Nannie Helen Burroughs, who established the National Training School for Women and Girls in Washington, D.C.

One of Washington's newer museums, the **National Postal Museum** in the old Main Post Office at 2 Massachusetts Avenue, NE, houses a vast collection of 16 million stamps and postal history artifacts. "The relationship between the U.S. Postal Service and African Americans is a significant one," according to the Smithsonian. "For years the Postal Service was the only federal agency that employed African Americans. Today, the Postal Service is the largest civilian employer of minorities, with 21 percent of its 680,000 employees being African American."

Memorial to Robert Gould Shaw and the Massachusetts 54th Regiment

The National Gallery of Art, The Mall

Monumental in size, vision, and message, the original plaster version of one of America's major 19th century sculptures, the Shaw Memorial, was installed at the National Gallery of Art in September 1997. A master work of Augustus Saint-

Gaudens, the foremost American sculptor in the post-Civil War period, the Shaw Memorial was commissioned in 1884 to commemorate the first African American unit in the Union Army, the Massachusetts 54th Regiment commanded by Colonel Robert Gould Shaw, a white officer.

For twelve years the sculptor worked on the tribute in his New York studio before the bronze cast was dedicated on the Boston Common in front of the State Capitol in 1897. Booker T. Washington was the principal speaker at the Dedication banquet. A year later, Saint-Gaudens made this plaster version and it was exhibited in Paris in 1898 and 1900 and at the 1901 Pan-American Exposition in Buffalo, NY. It was moved in 1949 to the late sculptor's home in Cornish, New Hampshire, where it rested under a pavilion in the open air.

The sculpture depicts the 26-year-old Shaw, the son of Boston abolitionist parents and already a wounded war veteran, leading his troops on horseback. After training his 1000 recruits, they marched through Boston's streets passing poet and pacifist, John Greenleaf Whittier and Frederick Douglass whose sons had joined the regiment and who had lobbied President Lincoln for the inclusion of black soldiers in the Union Army. Five months later the 54th was the lead regiment in the assault on the ramparts of Fort Wagner which defended the harbor of Charleston, SC. Shaw and 281 of his men were fatally wounded. Clara Barton and Harriet Tubman were eyewitnesses to the battle that was celebrated in the recent movie *Glory*.

Saint-Gaudens used living African Americans as models for the soldier's heads. More than twenty of the soldiers and Colonel Shaw are recognizable portraits of real persons. An angel hovers above the marching column. Art critic Robert Hughes talked of the work's great humanity: "In the 1880s nearly all images of African Americans by white American artists were either crude racist stereotypes ... or else merely generic .... These studies neither mock nor condescend, but set before you a fellow human being in his own vitality and presence." And the conservator who conducted the final restoration was impressed by the detailing of the sculpture, declaring that "that there are things that are amazing. There's an insignia on top of Shaw's hat ... and some of the soldiers' brims are tipped up. The horse's tail is untamed, the creases in Shaw's gloves and boots hang like leather. Shaw and the soldiers look ready to wave and wink as they pass by in parade formation...and the soldiers on foot look as though the winds of Boston are at their backs."

The sculpture which is 15 feet high and 18 feet wide and almost a yard deep was transported to Washington in 21 pieces which were reassembled and the completed work was recessed in an original Gallery wall. The installation appears to be a permanent one although it is technically on a ten-year renewable loan.

The National Gallery's Curator of American Art declared that the Gallery had added "one of the greatest pieces of sculpture of the 19th century. We have nothing like it at all, certainly in size and significance."

Site of the St. Charles Hotel

3rd Street and Pennsylvania Avenue, NW

Facing 3rd Street, the St. Charles Hotel was a major Washington hostelry from 1820 to 1926. In antebellum Washington the St. Charles had a distinctly Southern clientele. Wealthy plantation owners visiting Washington favored the hotel because the basement contained six 30-foot-long arched cells equipped with heavy iron doors and iron wall rings. Recessed grills in the sidewalks provided light and air. Slaves purchased at the District's auction houses stayed here while their masters were in residence upstairs.

So secure were these cells that the hotel posted the following notice:

> *The Proprietor of this hotel has roomy underground cells for confining slaves for safekeeping, and patrons are notified that their slaves will be well cared for. In case of escape, full value of the negro will be paid by the Proprietor.*

Auctions ceased in 1850 when slave trading was abolished in the District of Columbia. However, Southern visitors still used the hotel, which accommodated their accompanying slaves.

The St. Charles declined in importance after the Civil War. During the last decades of the 19th century, the hotel was the primary residence for American Indians brought to the nation's capital to sign treaties with the United States government. Known later as the Capital Hotel, it was demolished in 1924.

A. Philip Randolph Memorial Bust

Union Station, Massachusetts Avenue, NE

Born in Crescent City, Florida, Asa Philip Randolph (1889-1979) is best remembered as the most significant black figure in the U.S. labor movement and as one of the most important civil rights leaders of this century. His achievements were many—co-founder in 1917 of a Socialist weekly, *The Messenger*, and organizer of the first trade union, the Brotherhood of Sleeping Car Porters and Maids.

Believing that organizing was the best and swiftest way to economic opportunity, Randolph spent twelve difficult years organizing the sleeping car porters in the notoriously anti-union Pullman Company. Ultimately, New Deal legislation forced the company to negotiate with its porters and a contract was signed. A labor organizer during that time remembered, "When the Brotherhood won the agreement from the Pullman Company, I thought my heart would burst."

Randolph was a persistent, driving force in 1941 to pressure and persuade President Franklin D. Roosevelt to develop the Fair Employment Practice Commission (FEPC) and to prohibit, by Executive Order, racial discrimination in the defense industry. Randolph had been concerned during the early years of World War II that blacks would not receive their share of the newly-created war jobs. One of his colleagues remembered him declaring that "We've got to do something about these jobs .... I think we ought to get 10,000 Negroes and march down Pennsylvania Avenue and protest." Such a march was averted when the President signed Executive Order 8802. Following the war, Randolph again threatened to march in protest over continued segregation in the military. In 1948 President Truman signed Executive Order 9981 which led to the integration of the armed forces.

By 1963 Randolph was the elder statesman of the civil rights movement and the leader, with Dr. King and Roy Wilkins, of the NAACP and the March on Washington (his idea of twenty-two years before). In his address at the March, Randolph declared:

> *"Let the nation and the world know the meaning of our numbers. We are not a pressure group; we are not an organization or a group of organizations; we are not a mob. We are the advance guard of a massive moral revolution for jobs and freedom...."*

When he introduced Dr. Martin Luther King, Jr. "there were no dry eyes. Symbolically, it was like passing the torch from one generation of fighters to a new generation of fighters."

In 1968, he retired from the Sleeping Car Porters union, which is now part of the Transportation Communications Union. A. Philip Randolph died in Harlem in 1979. The following year he received the Presidential Medal of Freedom, the nation's highest honor for its citizens.

Philip Reed and the Statue of Freedom

U.S. Capitol Building

The son of sculptor Clark Mills, who created the statue of freedom atop the dome of the Capitol Building, published in the 19th century the following account of black slave Philip Reed's role in the creation of this historic figure:

Before the statue was cast, the several large sections of the plaster model were put together so nicely by an adroit Italian employed about the Capitol, that no crevices were perceptible at the places of joining—the bolts were all firmly riveted inside, and where they were placed concealed by coverings of plaster. In this condition the model was for some time on exhibition.

At length the time arrived when the figure was desired to be cast, and the Italian was ordered to take the model apart. This he positively refused to do, unless he was given a large increase in wages, and secured employment for a number of years. He said, he alone "knew how to separate it," and would do so only upon such conditions.

Mr. Mills at that time owned a highly intelligent mulatto slave named Philip Reed, who had long been employed about his foundry as an expert and admirable workman.

Philip undertook to take the model apart without injury, despite the Italian's assertion, and proceeded to accomplish his purpose. His plan of working was this: a pulley and tackle was brought into use, and its hook inserted into an iron eye affixed to the head of the figure—the rope was then gently strained repeatedly until the uppermost joining of the top section of the model began to make a faint appearance. This gave some indication as to the whereabouts of its bolts inside, and lead to their discovery; and thus, finally, one, after another of the sections was discovered, their bolts unloosed, and the model, uninjured, made ready for the foundry.

CHAPTER 2

Southwest

Many northern cities experienced the flood of black migration and the resulting formation of housing ghettos during World War I and the Great Depression. Washington's black population increased much earlier. Although more than a quarter of its population had been black since 1800, Washington's black population grew from 14,000 to more than 60,000 persons between 1860 and 1880. In 1880 the largest residential concentration of black citizens was in Southwest.

Prior to the Civil War, the Southwest area, only a half mile from the Capitol Building, was the location of at least two of Washington's infamous slave pens and auction sites. This shameful history of the nation's capital during the first half of the 19th century was lamented by an early observer:

> You call this the land of liberty, and every day that passes things are done in it at which the despotisms of Europe would be horror-struck and disgusted .... In no part of the earth—not even excepting the rivers of the coast of Africa—was there so great, so infamous a slave market as in the metropolis, in the seat of government of this nation which prides itself on freedom.

During the early 20th century Southwest became a densely populated, racially "mixed," low-income neighborhood. One of the city's most notorious alleys, Willow Tree Court near 4th and B Streets, housed hundreds of impoverished residents. By the post-World War II years the sea-level and swampy Southwest area along the Potomac River became a slum. In the 1960s one of the nation's first programs of urban renewal leveled blocks of Southwest housing, replacing them with townhouses and architect-designed high-rise apartment buildings. This redevelopment included no low-cost housing for the displaced black families. Urban renewal, in this case, meant black removal. Today, Southwest, with little housing for the poor, is a bustling waterfront community for black and white professionals.

Southwest
1. Benjamin Banneker Circle and Fountain
2. Site of Anthony Bowen Residence
3. Site of William's Private Jail
4. Robey's Tavern and Slave Pen

Benjamin Banneker Circle and Fountain

L'Enfant Plaza

This memorial park commemorates the contributions of Benjamin Banneker, a remarkable black mathematician and astronomer who assisted in the survey and planning of the federal city.

Banneker, the son of a former slave and an English indentured servant girl, was born in 1731 and raised on a farm near Baltimore, Maryland. He learned to read and write and, as a young man, amazed his neighbors by constructing a wooden clock even though the only timepiece he had ever seen was a pocket watch. When the white Ellicott family moved into the area and shared their scientific interests and knowledge with their black neighbor, Banneker taught himself astronomy and mathematics from borrowed books and instruments. In 1791 he published an almanac, an astounding project for someone with no formal education.

In the same year the boundaries of the federal capital were defined. Appointed to survey the territory, Major Andrew Ellicott recommended that his friend and neighbor Benjamin Banneker assist him. However, Banneker's failing health forced him to return home after a short time. Historian David Lewis observed that Banneker's "intrinsic significance to the Federal City was not his arguable accomplishments as Major Ellicott's assistant, but the symbolism of his presence ... a gifted black man in attendance at the creation of the nation's capital."

Site of Anthony Bowen Residence

85 E Street, SW (L'Enfant Plaza)

The Southwest home of Anthony Bowen, founder of the first YMCA in the District of Columbia, was one of several Washington stations on the Underground Railroad. Bowen often met incoming boats from the South at the 6th Street Wharf on the Potomac River, leading the fugitives to the sanctuary of his residence.

When President Lincoln authorized the enlistment of black troops during the Civil War, Bowen, John F. Cook, Jr., and the Reverend Henry McNeal Turner served on a committee to recruit black Washingtonians for the Union forces and presented 800 names to the President on May 8, 1863. These recruits, the First U.S. Colored Troops unit, later suffered severe casualties in the attack on Petersburg, Virginia.

Site of William's Private Jail

"The Yellow House"
Corner of 7th Street and Independence Avenue, SW

On this corner William H. Williams, a prosperous trader in slaves and owner of two slave ships, the *Tribune* and the *Uncas*, which regularly supplied slaves to New Orleans and the Mississippi market, conducted his private jail. During the 1830s Williams purchased slaves from a downtown lottery office—losers were often anxious to sell their slaves in order to buy more chances. By December 1836 Williams was advertising to offer "cash for Four hundred Negroes" and was considered the city's most successful trader.

The Yellow House, so named because of its painted exterior, was a two-story home located in a tree-shaded garden. The actual jail was an adjacent detached building, although slaves were often housed in a room off the kitchen where "staples" for the shackling of slaves were found in the walls by a subsequent owner.

Mr. William's Yellow House "had a virtual monopoly of the private-jail business" before slave trading was abolished in 1850 in the District.

Robey's Tavern and Slave Pen

7th Street between B Street and Maryland Avenue, SW

Just across the street, one of several active competitors of Mr. Williams and his private jail, Washington Robey, operated a popular tavern with a slave pen adjacent where a lively slave trading business was conducted. A prominent slave firm, Neal and Company, could "at all times be found at Robey's Tavern" where they could keep their many purchases in his pen.

In 1833 an English visitor to the nation's capital and Mr. Robey's tavern described the place surrounded by "wooden paling fourteen or fifteen feet high, with the posts outside to prevent escape, and separated from the building by a space too narrow for ventilation. At a small window above he saw two or three sable faces wistfully looking out.... In this wretched hovel all colors except white, both sexes, and all ages, are confined, exposed indiscriminately to the contamination which may be expected...."

CHAPTER 3

Anacostia and Southeast

When the nation's capital was established in 1800, a tiny Indian settlement existed in what is now Anacostia. Inhabited by the Nacotchtank Indians, this area near the confluence of the Anacostia and Potomac rivers was visited by Captain John Smith in 1608. During the early 19th century the village, which derived its name from the Indians known as Anacostians, attracted traders, tobacco farmers, and a small community of free blacks.

In 1854 the Union Land Company began the earliest "suburban development" in the District of Columbia on a 240-acre site in Anacostia. The "Homes for All" advertisement that was aimed at the employees of the nearby Navy Yard in Southeast Washington did not, however, extend to prospective black or Irish buyers. Successful for a few years, the uncertainty of the impending civil conflict caused property sales to lag. Such fears were later realized as much of the land in Anacostia was confiscated for the defense of the capital during the Civil War. The Union Land Company never recovered from the war years and declared bankruptcy in 1877. That same year statesman Frederick Douglass purchased Cedar Hill, which had served as the company's headquarters and the home of one of the partners.

The Anacostia neighborhood thrived after the 1870s due in large part to city improvements undertaken during the administration of "Boss" Alexander Shepherd, the head of the Board of Public Works. The city paved the streets, introduced public transportation, and built the 11th Street bridge linking "the village at the edge of the city" with the "mainland."

Although predominantly white, Anacostia was home to a small, hard-working black middle class community at the turn of the century. A former president of the Washington school board recalled growing up in the tight-knit community during the 1930s and 40s. Her Anacostia was "built around the churches ... and our school—the only one we had, the old Birney Elementary ... and the old Barry

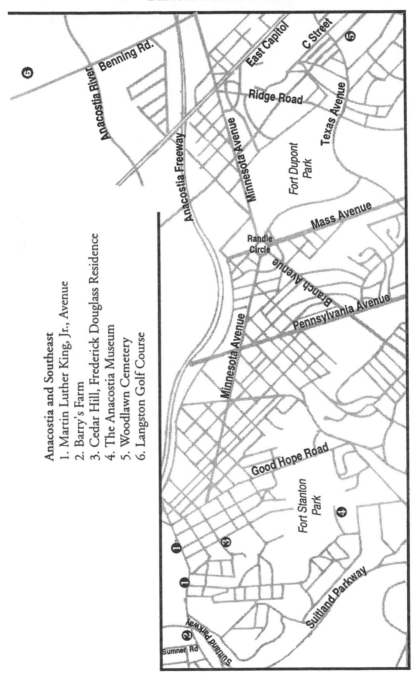

Anacostia and Southeast
1. Martin Luther King, Jr., Avenue
2. Barry's Farm
3. Cedar Hill, Frederick Douglass Residence
4. The Anacostia Museum
5. Woodlawn Cemetery
6. Langston Golf Course

Farms playground." Douglass Hall, meeting place and social center for the black community, stood on the corner of Howard Road and Nichols Avenue across the street from Birney School. A drugstore and several black-owned shops on the street level served the local black residents.

Spurred by school desegregation and suburban expansion, whites began leaving Anacostia in the 1960s. In the thirty years from 1940 to 1970, Anacostia experienced an almost total reversal of its population. Twenty percent of Anacostia's 26,000 residents were black in 1940; by 1970, blacks constituted 96 percent of the population of 126,000. Washington's 1968 riots devastated the commercial avenues of Anacostia and further damaged the neighborhood's reputation.

A scenic contrast between urban blight and suburbia, Anacostia is frequently referred to as the city's "forgotten" neighborhood. Construction of the long-awaited Metro Green Line subway will, it is hoped, bring the economic development to transform Anacostia into a thriving neighborhood.

Martin Luther King, Jr., Avenue

Anacostia, Southeast

Stretching from the District line that runs from Prince George's County in Maryland through Anacostia's historic district to the 11th Street bridge and Interstate 295, Martin Luther King, Jr. Avenue honors the slain civil rights leader. Originally called Asylum Road because it bisected the St. Elizabeth's Hospital (for the mentally ill) property, it was renamed Nichols Avenue in 1872 after a previous hospital superintendent, Charles Henry Nichols.

Together with Good Hope Road, the Avenue was the major commercial strip for thriving Anacostia at the turn of the century. Today the Avenue is the parade route for Washington's annual Martin Luther King, Jr. Day celebration in January.

Barry's Farm

Southeast Washington

Barry's Farm is a public project, housing many of the city's lowest income residents. The original community of Barry's Farm was created in 1865 by the Bureau of Refugees, Freedmen and Abandoned Lands, commonly known as the Freedmen's Bureau. During the Civil War freedmen and black refugees poured into the city. Many former slaves arrived as "contraband," confiscated by the

Union armies as a means of disrupting the Southern economy and way of life. Temporary barracks and tents were erected to shelter the new arrivals. By the end of the war General O.O. Howard of the Freedmen's Bureau had used government and private charitable funds to purchase the Talbert, Barry and Stanton farms for permanent housing. The Talbert tract was set aside for settlement by whites, while the Barry and Stanton farms were reserved for Negro freedmen.

Barry's Farm was a self-help community. The freedmen laid roads and cleared the densely wooded area into one-acre lots which were sold for $125 to $300. Each owner was allotted enough lumber to construct a small house. The adjoining military barracks were renovated into low-cost rental units. Housing codes were strictly enforced and policed by the residents themselves. One hundred eighty lots were sold during the first year and the waiting list grew quickly. "In order to purchase property," writes historian Louise Hutchinson, "entire families worked in the city all day and walked at night to Barry's Farm to develop their land and construct their homes by lantern and candlelight."

Two churches, an infirmary, and the Hillsdale School (1871), the first school for blacks in Anacostia, were built. Hillsdale, located at Nichols (Martin Luther King, Jr., Avenue) and Sheridan Avenues, remained the only public school in the area until the James G. Birney School opened in 1889.

Construction of the Suitland Parkway in the 1940s physically divided the Barry's Farm and Hillsdale communities, disrupting the "small town" ambiance and stability of the neighborhood. Shortly thereafter the single family houses were demolished to make way for public housing units.

Cedar Hill, Frederick Douglass Residence

14th and W Streets, SE

Located in the historic district of Old Anacostia with a spectacular view of the city, Cedar Hill was the beloved home of Frederick Douglass. Now owned and operated by the National Park Service, the 1850s Gothic revival and Italianate-style residence was part of Uniontown, the first suburban development outside the original town of Washington. Originally, "any Negro mulatto, or person of African blood" was prohibited from purchasing land or residences in the neighborhood. But after the demise of the Union Land Development Company in 1877, the racial ban was broken when Cedar Hill was sold to Frederick Douglass, Old Anacostia's first black resident.

Douglass purchased this home the same year that he became U.S. Marshall for the District of Columbia. Here he spent his final eighteen years and wrote his third autobiographical volume, *Life and Times of Frederick Douglass*. On February 20, 1895, the 78-year-old Douglass suffered a fatal heart attack while waiting for a carriage to take him to a lecture at the nearby Campbell AME Church. Private services for the Sage of Anacostia were held at Cedar Hill; his body was then placed on a horse-drawn hearse and carried on its final ride across the Anacostia River to a "state" funeral at Metropolitan AME Church, attended by government dignitaries and the city's black community.

The Anacostia Museum

1901 Fort Place, SE

One of the nation's first neighborhood museums was created by the Smithsonian Institution in 1967. Originally called the Anacostia Neighborhood Museum, this storefront museum in the old Carver movie theater was, according to its longtime director John Kinard, "a combination museum, cultural arts center, meeting place for neighborhood groups and a skill training facility. The museum's role is to enliven the community and enlighten the people it serves."

The Anacostia Museum is a forceful community institution. Exhibitions such as "Blacks in the Westward Movement" and "The Frederick Douglass Years" are representative of its expertise in black history and culture. "The Evolution of a Community" focused on the history of Anacostia from its 16th century Indian days to the present, while "The Rat: Man's Invited Affliction" addressed urban problems of immediate concern. The museum's educational outreach program transports condensed exhibitions on buses to schools and community groups.

Twenty years after its founding, the museum moved to its new park site on land donated by the National Park Service and dropped the word "Neighborhood" from its name. On the occasion of its 10th anniversary in 1977, the Washington *Post* declared that the museum and its many activities "have been a success—and a blessing...."

Woodlawn Cemetery

4611 Benning Road, SE

Woodlawn Cemetery was the first non-segregated cemetery within Washington's city limits. When the cemetery was founded in 1895, there were approximately fifty burial locations in Washington, but most of them were in the Northwest section of the city. Residents living in predominantly black Northeast had only two choices—Payne's or Graceland cemeteries. When city expansion forced the closure of Graceland in 1895, the Woodlawn Cemetery Association was established.

Many African Americans of local and national acclaim are interred at Woodlawn: the Reverend Sterling Brown, Jesse Lawson, Wilson Bruce Evans, John Wesley Cromwell, Dr. John R. Francis, Daniel Payne Murray, Nelson E. Weatherless, Winfield Scott Montgomery, Will Marion Cook, and John Mercer Langston among others.

Beginning in the 1930s, conditions at the cemetery began to deteriorate dramatically; the 22-acre cemetery, surrounded by apartment buildings, houses and commercial establishments, stood abandoned, a victim of contemporary negligence, political and jurisdictional disputes, and a lack of financial support.

However, there is now a five-year restoration plan and the cemetery is being cleaned up by volunteers and members of Americorps, the national service organization.

Langston Golf Course

Anacostia Park north of Benning Road, SE

Before 1939 when Langston Golf Course opened, blacks could only play golf at a nine-hole course near present-day Constitution Gardens on the Mall. Golf has historically been considered a white, and often upper-class, sport, although blacks have a long tradition as caddies. In 1926 a group of Washingtonians were active in the creation of the United Golfers Association (UGA) which encouraged the establishment of black golf courses across the country. Two doctors, Albert Harris and George Adams, founded Washington's first black golf club called the Royal Golf Club. In 1937 the wives of members established the first black women's golf club in the U.S., the Wake Robin Golf Club. Their long campaign for first-class facilities were successful with the construction of Langston Golf Course in 1939. It was not until 1955 that the course was expanded to 18 holes.

Although golf facilities were desegregated in the 1950s, Langston continues to be the home course for Washington's black golfers. In the 1990s they mounted a fierce campaign to keep the city from allowing Redskins owner Jack Kent Cooke to gain access to a portion of the Langston Course to build a new football stadium.

CHAPTER 4

Capitol Hill

Site of Duff Green's Row

1st Street, between East Capitol Street and Independence Avenue, SE

On the site now occupied by the Library of Congress, an imposing row of five brick townhouses (c.1801) commanded the site east of the U.S. Capitol Building until they were torn down in 1887, when the Library was built. Originally known as Carroll Row, then later as Duff Green's Row, the houses were used variously as residences, hotels, and boarding houses. The young congressman from Illinois, Abraham Lincoln, lived here with his wife and son Robert during his first term in the House of Representatives.

During the first months of the Civil War, Washington was in chaos, swelling with troops, refugees, and runaway slaves. At that time slavery had not yet been abolished in the District and bounty hunters scoured the streets looking for fugitive slaves. Once detained, they often were returned to their owners for a reward. Union soldiers, however, frequently protected them from these unscrupulous characters. The military governor of the District, General James Wadsworth, gathered over 400 of these new arrivals, most of whom were ill, hungry, and desperate, and sheltered them in the houses of Duff Green's Row.

After a smallpox epidemic wiped out many residents in Duff Green's Row, the houses became an annex to the government's prison located across the street in the Old Brick Capitol Building (now the site of the U.S. Supreme Court). The remaining black inhabitants were removed to barracks at Camp Barker, located at 12th and Q Streets, NW, in the present Shaw neighborhood.

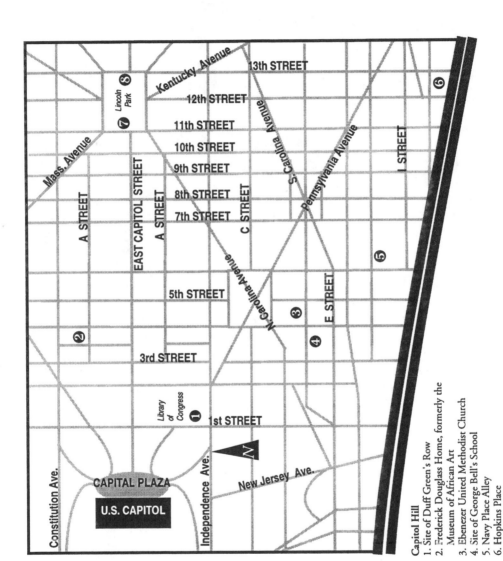

Capitol Hill
1. Site of Duff Green's Row
2. Frederick Douglass Home, formerly the Museum of African Art
3. Ebenezer United Methodist Church
4. Site of George Bell's School
5. Navy Place Alley
6. Hopkins Place
7. Emancipation Memorial

Frederick Douglass Home

316-318 A Street, NE

The handsome rowhouse at 316 A Street was the first Washington residence of Frederick Douglass when he moved to the city in 1870. From 1964 to 1987 the Douglass home and a number of adjoining rowhouses housed the National Museum of African Art which is now part of the Smithsonian Institution and is located on the Mall.

Abraham Lincoln once said that Frederick Douglass was the "most meritorious man of the 19th century." Frederick Augustus Washington Bailey was born about 1817 to a slave mother and an unknown white father in Talbot County on Maryland's eastern shore. Although mostly self taught, the young Douglass was instructed in reading and writing by his master's wife. With forged papers, he escaped to Massachusetts at the age of 21, changing his surname to Douglass to avoid capture. During the 1840s he was a frequent lecturer for the Anti-Slavery Society and completed his popular autobiography, *Narrative of the Life of Frederick Douglass, An American Slave* (1845). After the book's publication, he was subject to arrest as a fugitive slave. Douglass fled to England, where he raised the funds to return and buy his freedom. In 1847, while living in Rochester, New York, Douglass founded an antislavery newspaper, *The North Star*, named after the star used by fugitive and runaway slaves as a beacon in their flight to freedom. During the Civil War Douglass urged President Lincoln to enlist blacks in the Union Army. After issuing the Emancipation Proclamation on January 1, 1863, the United States armed forces were opened to former slaves and free blacks; Douglass helped recruit the distinguished 54th and 55th Massachusetts Regiments. The 55th Massachusetts Colored Infantry was instrumental in liberating Charleston, South Carolina, in February 1865. By the end of the war, over 200,000 black recruits had served in the army and navy.

Frederick Douglass moved to Washington, D.C. in 1870 to become the editor of the *New Era* newspaper, later called the *New National Era*. Accompanied by his wife, daughter, and three grandchildren, Douglass resided at 316 A Street, NE, for several years before moving in 1878 to his Anacostia home, Cedar Hill. The adjoining home at 318 A Street was purchased soon after his arrival and was used by other members of the family.

During his later years Douglass served as a U.S. Marshall, Recorder of Deeds for the District of Columbia (1881-1886), and United States Minister to Haiti (1889-1891).

In 1964 the residence became the home of the Museum of African Art, the first museum to house and promote the artistic heritage of Africa in this country.

Ebenezer United Methodist Church

4th and D Streets, SE

The Ebenezer United Methodist Church is the oldest black congregation on Capitol Hill. The original church was founded by 61 white and 25 black residents in 1805, only a few years after the seat of government had moved to Washington. In 1811 the congregation built the first Methodist church building in Washington, called the Fourth Street Station.

Although many early church congregations were integrated, discriminatory practices (such as white ministers refusing to hold a black child during baptism) were a fact of religious life. The most common practice was to segregate the worshipers; black members sat in the balcony. These churches often contained an outside stairway which led to the gallery, frequently referred to as "the niggers' back stairs to heaven."

In 1827 the black worshipers of the original church withdrew, forming their own congregation named Little Ebenezer. The church's historian has noted that the "colored membership had outgrown the galleries which were reserved for them in the Mother Church." A small frame church was immediately erected on the newly purchased lot at the corner of 4th and D Street, SE. The white congregation—later called Trinity Methodist Church—continued to send their clergy to minister to Little Ebenezer. In 1864 the Reverend Noah Jones became the first black minister to serve Little Ebenezer.

Little Ebenezer was also the site of the first public school for blacks in the District of Columbia. From May 1864 to May 1865 black students were taught in this church by teachers paid with federal funds. Miss Frances W. Perkins was dispatched by the New England Freedmen's Aid Society and was assisted by Mrs. Emma V. Brown, "a prominent colored worker," who was paid $400 per year by the District of Columbia.

The second church, a brick building, was completed in 1870, but was irreparably damaged in a severe storm twenty-six years later. Within a year (1897) the present church was built. Ebenezer United Methodist Church has been recently designated a Historic Landmark.

Site of George Bell's School

3rd and D Street, SE
(formerly site of Providence Hospital)

During the early years of the 19th century, Washington's white children either paid tuition to attend small schools or studied at home with a tutor. In 1804 public monies provided free schooling for poor white children; black students were excluded not by legislation, but "as a matter of course," according to historian Constance McLaughlin Green.

In 1807, three former slaves—George Bell, Moses Liverpool, and Nicholas Franklin, all of whom worked as caulkers at the nearby Washington Navy Yard, organized the city's first school for black students in a small frame schoolhouse on this site. Initially, the school employed a white teacher, Mr. Lowe, who was paid with the students' meager tuition fees.

George Bell had been the slave of the Addison family of Oxen Hill, Maryland. He became a free man through the industry and devotion of his wife, Sophia Browning Bell, who secretly saved $400 from the sale of her garden produce. He then purchased her freedom and that of their two sons. However, he was unable to purchase that of their daughter, who remained a slave until her master's death many years later. Black education in early Washington was a risky business, and Bell feared that his school might be abolished at any time simply because he educated young black students. To allay white apprehension, Bell placed a newspaper advertisement stating that "no writings are to be done by the teachers for a slave, neither directly or indirectly, to serve the purpose of a slave on any account...." However, after Bell and his colleagues established their school, numerous private academies for the education of free black children were established in Washington and Georgetown during the years prior to the Civil War. Among the most successful were those of Mrs. Mary Billings on Dumbarton Street in Georgetown (1810) and the Columbian Institute, renamed Union Seminary by its director, John F. Cook, Sr., in 1834.

Navy Place Alley

Bounded by 6th and 7th Streets,
G Street and the Southeast Freeway, SE

At the end of the 19th century, New York City might have been described as a city of tenements; by contrast, the District of Columbia was a city of inhabited alleys. Historian Constance Green declared that there was "an inadequacy of words to convey a vivid picture of Washington's inhabited alleys. No other city in America had their like." Disease, crime, and fire were normal features of life in these overcrowded alleys—the shame of Washington for nearly one hundred years.

As late as 1927 Capitol Hill's Navy Place, SE, was rated at the top of a worst-alleys survey. That report listed seventy dwellings housing 280 persons in this alley. Described by the Washington *Tribune* as a Washington landmark to poor housing, unsanitary conditions, vice, crime, prostitution and juvenile delinquency, Navy Place became a byword for the indescribable conditions of alley life in the city.

The population explosion during and after the Civil War strained the limits of this pedestrian city. More intensive land use became essential. Many residential lots were subdivided. At the rear of many properties modest two-story brick rowhouses were built; stables and outbuildings were converted for use as housing.

Conditions in these alleys were indeed deplorable. Louse Alley and Slop Bucket Row on Capitol Hill were aptly named. Many dwellings did not have water; those that did received it from pumps or hydrants in the tiny backyards or on the outside of the block. Sanitation consisted of communal outhouses; tuberculosis, the most common cause of death for those living in alleys, was rampant. Washington still ranks at the top nationally in the incidence of tuberculosis. With little water and limited accessibility, the alleys were a fire hazard. Most of the alleys were blind alleys—a "T" or a "H" configuration with only one entrance which was also the exit.

In 1892 Congress passed legislation, seldom enforced, halting alley construction. Five years later the police department conducted a special alley census, finding 237 blocks in the District with one or more inhabited alleys. The alley population in the federal city (excluding Georgetown) was 17,244, or 11 percent of the population. Of those residents, 16,046 were black; thus, one quarter of the city's black population resided in alleys. These special 1897 census figures were no doubt very conservative and extremely suspect. The census takers were not only unwelcome in these alleys, but many question whether they actually ventured into many of them in the first place.

In the early years of this century Congress summoned reformers such as Jacob Riis to report on alley conditions. Their shocking findings convinced President Theodore Roosevelt of the need to eliminate alley dwellings. Charles Weller's widely-read book of 1909, *Neglected Neighbors in the National Capital,* contributed to the public outcry.

Mrs. Woodrow Wilson, an outspoken critic of housing conditions in the District, led tours of Washington's inhabited alleys to draw public attention to their miserable condition. It is city legend that Mrs. Wilson's dying wish in 1914 was that Congress respond and enact legislation to eliminate the nightmare of alley housing in the nation's capital.

Finally, in 1939 the shacks of Navy Place were torn down. Following government policy not to disrupt existing racial housing patterns, the sprawling Ellen Wilson Dwellings, consisting of approximately 218 houses and apartments, were opened in 1941. Because the immediate neighborhood surrounding the project was white, the units were open only to white residents. The displaced black alley families were not eligible for housing in the complex bearing the First Lady's name.

Hopkins Place

12th and K Streets, SE

Public concern over the city's deplorable housing conditions gained impetus at the turn of the century. "Good homes make a good community" was a slogan adopted by many of the District's charitable organizations.

Among the most committed crusaders for the elimination of the city's slums and inhabited alleys was a formidable Washingtonian, Mrs. Archibald Hopkins. A behind-the-scenes organizer who "incessantly prodded and encouraged the men who took charge," Mrs. Hopkins was a strong proponent of low-cost public housing for evicted black alley dwellers. She was credited with focusing the attention and energies of Mrs. Woodrow Wilson on the need to eradicate these alley slums.

In 1934 Congress created the Alley Dwelling Authority, later renamed the National Capital Housing Authority. The Authority's director and housing planner, John Ihlder, was an early advocate of public housing for all income levels. Empowered to demolish the worst of the alley slums and to construct new public housing, Ihlder was largely responsible for Hopkins Place, the first major public housing project in Washington.

Built by relief labor in 1936, eleven reconditioned and twelve new homes were opened to low-income black families. Eleanor Roosevelt sent a telegram from her husband's presidential campaign train expressing her support of the project named for Mrs. Hopkins. She "should have all the credit and honor that any of us can bring to her memory because of the wonderful work she did for better housing in Washington ...," Mrs. Roosevelt wrote.

Lincoln Park

North Carolina Avenue, NE, and Massachusetts Avenue, SE,
between 11th and 12th Streets

Emancipation Memorial

Lincoln Park was sited exactly one mile east from the center of the U.S. Capitol Building on L'Enfant's original plan for Washington. By the time of the Civil War this still-undeveloped area was a campground teeming with Union soldiers. Lincoln Hospital, a temporary war facility, was also located in the square.

Today Lincoln Park retains both the scale and ambience of the late 19th century. Most of the homes and rowhouses surrounding the park were built between 1890 and 1895.

The Emancipation statue, located at the west end of Lincoln Park, was the principal tribute to President Lincoln in this city until the dedication of the Lincoln Memorial in 1922. Fundraising for a memorial to the president began immediately after his assassination. The Emancipation Memorial was financed almost entirely from money contributed by freed men and women, including nearly $12,000 from black soldiers headquartered in Natchez, Mississippi. It is noted on the pedestal that the first gift was a $5 donation by a Virginia free woman, Charlotte Scott.

The two-figure grouping was carved in marble by sculptor Thomas Ball, who was working in Italy after the Civil War. This work served as the model for the monument, which was cast in bronze in Munich, Germany. The kneeling slave is the likeness of Archer Alexander, the last man captured under the Fugitive Slave Law. From a photograph of Alexander, Ball created an assertive black figure who is physically breaking the chains of slavery as President Lincoln holds the Emancipation Proclamation in his outstretched hand.

John Mercer Langston of Howard University invited President Ulysses S. Grant to unveil the monument on April 14, 1876, the fourteenth anniversary of emancipation in the District of Columbia and the eleventh anniversary of Lincoln's assassination. Thousands of black Washingtonians, representing the Masons, the military, and numerous clubs and organizations, heard Frederick Douglass read the Emancipation Proclamation and deliver an eloquent oration. Douglass later wrote that participating in the ceremonies on that grand occasion "takes rank among the most interesting incidents of my life." He noted that not only the President of the United States, but also his cabinet, Justices of the Supreme Court, and members of Congress were there to hear his address about "the illustrious man to whose memory the colored people of the United States had, as a mark of their gratitude, erected that impressive monument." Douglass, who once referred to Abraham Lincoln as the only white man who did not make him feel that he was colored, talked frankly in his speech of the relationship of Lincoln to both the white and black citizens of this country:

> *Abraham Lincoln was not, in the fullest sense of the word, either our man or our model.... I concede to you, my white fellow citizens ... you are the children of Abraham Lincoln. We are, at best, only his stepchildren by force of circumstances and necessity.... We have done a good work for our race today. In doing honor to the memory of our friend and liberator, we have been doing the highest honor to ourselves.*

Mary McLeod Bethune Memorial

The first memorial to a woman in a public park and the first honoring a black American in the District of Columbia is that of Mary McLeod Bethune at the east end of Lincoln Park. Resting on a cane given to her by President Roosevelt, Mrs. Bethune passes on her legacy to two black children. Dedicated on the ninety-ninth anniversary of Mrs. Bethune's birth, July 10, 1974, the sculpture is the work of black artist Robert Berks, whose large sculpture of the head of President John F. Kennedy dominates the lobby of the Kennedy Center for the Performing Arts. The New York sculptor also executed a bust of the slain president's brother Robert, located in the courtyard of the Justice Department on Pennsylvania Avenue.

The fifteenth of seventeen children born to former slaves and sharecroppers in Florida, Mary McLeod was fortunate to attend a missionary school at the age of 11. Later her Quaker teachers helped her attend a small college, followed by a year's study at the Moody Bible Institute in Chicago. Mrs. Bethune was committed to the idea of organizing a school for young black women. In 1904 in one room furnished with orange crates, a budget of $1.50, and five female students, she founded the Daytona Normal and Industrial Institute for Negro Girls in Florida. The school, where she served as president until 1947, became Bethune-Cookman College in 1923.

Mrs. Bethune was a recognized national leader during the years between the world wars. In 1924 she was elected president of the National Association of Colored Women, and a decade later she was founder and president of the National Council of Negro Women. In 1934 she became Special Advisor for Minority

Affairs to President Franklin D. Roosevelt and was instrumental, with Mrs. Roosevelt, in establishing the informal "Black Cabinet" that met and consulted with the president during the Depression. Mary McLeod Bethune became the first black woman to head a federal office when she was appointed Director of Negro Affairs in the National Youth Administration in 1936.

Washington historian Constance Green described Mrs. Bethune at the time of the appointment:

> *Consensus, however, was general that Mary McLeod Bethune ... was the person to take charge of the NYA Negro Division. Although nuances indicated a faint irritation among some of Washington's colored elite that she kept herself somewhat apart from the local community, they quickly realized that her breadth of knowledge, her perceptiveness, her political finesse and her direct access to the President were invaluable to the Negro cause. In dealing with her white associates, as one young man recalled, her pronouncedly Negroid appearance in itself helped. With her deep chocolate-colored skin, her heavy build, and rather pronathous jaw, she seemed like a product of darkest Africa—until she spoke. Then the exquisitely musical voice, offering sagacious counsel in a perfect Oxford accent, carried an impact that left no one in doubt that here was an extraordinary woman to whom any sensible person would listen with respectful attention.*

Mary McLeod Bethune died in Florida on May 18, 1955. Engraved on the stone pedestal base of this 17-foot high statue is an excerpt from her will. Her final words were directed to America's black youth:

> *I leave you love. I leave you hope. I leave you the challenge of developing confidence in one another. I leave you a thirst for education. I leave you respect for the use of power. I leave you faith. I leave you racial dignity. I leave you a desire to live harmoniously with your fellow man. I leave you, finally, a responsibility to our young people.*

CHAPTER 5

Northeast and Brookland

Northeast

National Training School for Women and Girls

50th and Grant Streets, NE

Born in Virginia and educated in Washington, D.C., Nannie Helen Burroughs fulfilled a childhood dream by founding an industrial school for girls in 1909. The school, established with the aid of the National Baptist Convention, offered practical training in gardening, domestic work, interior decorating and vocational skills. Concentrating on the spiritual character of her students, Burroughs often referred to the school as the "School of the 3 B's—the Bible, bath, and broom." Founded with 31 students, the school had graduated more than 2,000 young black women by 1935.

This unique institution, "the only boarding school for Negro girls north of Richmond, and ... the only school ever established by a national organization of [black] women," continued to operate until Burroughs' death in 1961. It then became the Nannie Burroughs public elementary school; today, the building complex is a religious retreat.

Nannie Burroughs was deeply concerned about the plight of black working women. In the 1930s she organized the National Association of Wage Earners to address their problems. A tireless advocate of black cultural heritage, Burroughs was a lifelong supporter of Carter Woodson's Association for the Study of Negro Life and History and worked zealously for the memorialization of Frederick Douglass' home, Cedar Hill.

BLACK WASHINGTON

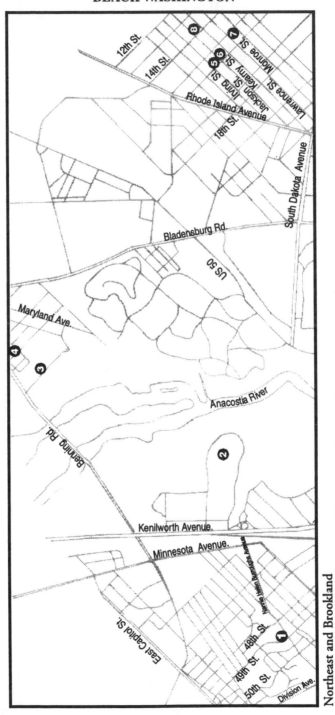

Northeast and Brookland

1. The National Training School for Women and Girls
2. Mayfair Mansions
3. Spingarn High School
4. Langston Terrace Dwellings
5. Rayford Logan Residence
6. Ralph Bunche Residence
7. Robert Weaver Residence
8. Sterling Brown Residence

Directly across the street from the school was Suburban Gardens, an amusement park for blacks that was the counterpart to the whites-only Glen Echo, just over the District line in Maryland.

Mayfair Mansions

West of Kenilworth Avenue between Hayes and Jay Streets, NE

The legend of Mayfair Mansions is often repeated: flamboyant radio evangelist and pastor of the Temple of Freedom Under God, Elder Lightfoot Solomon Michaux talked a Congressman out of buying the old Benning Race Track in Northeast, arguing that the property's use had been the work of the devil. Michaux then purchased the sprawling 34-acre site in 1942 and built Mayfair Gardens on the Parkway, as it was originally called. Mayfair was one of the earliest efforts to provide decent housing to Washington's black population during this period of rigid segregation and discrimination in the housing industry.

The 595 units in 17 three-story suburban-type buildings were a luxury housing development for nearby black families uprooted by the demolition of their homes for new federal buildings. As the first federally-subsidized black housing in the nation, Michaux and the developers, in order to qualify for a government loan, had to guarantee that middle class black families could afford the rents.

The project was designed by Albert I. Cassell, who established Howard University's School of Architecture, the first fully-accredited Architecture Department in a black university. Today Mayfair Mansions is one of the District's largest apartment complexes for low-to-moderate income families.

Spingarn High School

24th and Benning Road, NE

Spingarn High School's name pays tribute to Joel E. Spingarn (1875-1939), a literary critic and head of the department of comparative literature at Columbia University. A founder and chairman of the board of the National Association for the Advancement of Colored People, Spingarn established the Spingarn Medal in 1914 to be awarded to "the man or woman of African descent and American citizenship, who shall have made the highest achievement during the preceding year or years in any honorable field of human endeavor."

Langston Terrace Dwellings

Near 21st Street and Benning Road, NE

"Washington soon will witness a wild scramble among thousands of prospective tenants at Langston Terrace to take advantage of rents which the government assures will be the lowest for any Federal housing in the country," predicted the Washington *Evening Star* in 1936. With few public housing alternatives at that time, Washington's citizens flooded Langston Terrace rental offices with applications for the 274 family units.

The Federal government undertook the $1.8 million project to provide housing for Depression homeless and former alley dwellers living in the adjoining Marshall Heights shantytown. Langston Terrace, one of the earliest federally-sponsored public housing projects in the nation, rented to those just above the public relief category who could afford the $6 per room monthly rate ($4.50 without utilities).

The project's black architect, Hilyard Robinson, was a pioneer and innovator in the field of government housing for the poor. The Langston Terrace complex, the first of eight housing projects designed by Robinson, received architectural acclaim when a model of the project was exhibited at the Museum of Modern Art in New York City.

Born on Capitol Hill and graduated with the final class at M Street High School, Hilyard Robinson studied in Europe with Bauhaus master Walter Gropius after completing his architectural training at Columbia University. Upon his return to the U.S. in 1932, Robinson established a busy practice with a racially mixed firm. After completing his second major project, the 303-unit Frederick Douglass Dwellings at Alabama Avenue and Stanton Terrace, SE, Robinson received commissions for private homes and several buildings on the Howard University campus where he became dean of the School of Architecture.

However, Langston Terrace, named after John Mercer Langston, was his masterpiece. The clean, straightforward, International Style lines of the buildings reflect the influence of both Gropius and Marcel Breuer. The two-, three-, and four-story units of two-colored brick were designed around a central commons area of gardens and playground. Bas-relief, or flat sculpture decorations, on the buildings distinguished the development. The dramatic signature work that stretched across the front building, entitled "The Progress of the Negro Race," depicted the migration of blacks from the rural south to the urban north. (All of the terra-cotta frieze work was done by Dan Olney as a commission of the New Deal Treasury Art Program.) Writing in *The New Yorker* magazine, historian Lewis Mumford praised the "high standard of exterior design" and the use of sculpture against the flat facade that "looks better than the best modern work in Hamburg and Vienna that I can recall ...."

In 1986 former residents of the Dwellings gathered for a "family" reunion. "Langston was a close-knit community," reminisced one longtime resident. "There were hundreds of youngsters and we all knew each other. There were two recreation centers. There was a co-op store. They had speaker forums on Sunday ... it was a Utopia."

Brookland

Established in 1887, Brookland followed the earlier LeDroit Park suburban expansion of the 1870s. And like LeDroit Park, Logan Circle and Shaw, Brookland's population shifted from white to black. However, unlike those areas, Brookland has remained economically stable and solidly middle class. Black professionals began building homes and moving into the white neighborhood during the Depression; soon after World War II, Brookland was predominantly black. Former Brookland residents have included U.S. Senator Edward Brooke and singer Pearl Bailey.

Black architects Hilyard Robinson and Howard Mackey were commissioned to design approximately thirteen houses in the Brookland neighborhood. Robinson designed residences for Ralph Bunche and Howard University historian Rayford Logan at 1510 and 1519 Jackson Street; Mackey's commissions included houses at 1214 Franklin, 1232 Girard, 1300 Lawrence, 1217 Hamlin and 1509 Newton. In 1924 Mackey joined the Howard University architectural program, the first at a black college in America. Both Robinson and Mackey later headed the university's school of architecture.

To meet the need for a Sunday school in Brookland's black community, Brookland's black residents established the Brookland Union Baptist Church (3101 14th Street, NE) in 1945, the only black church in the community until the 1960s.

Rayford Logan Residence

1519 Jackson Street, NE

Rayford Logan was one of a distinguished group of black historians who came to prominence in the 20th century. After earning degrees from Williams College and a Ph.D. from Howard University, Logan assisted Carter G. Woodson at the Association for the Study of Negro Life and History. In 1942 he became head of the history department at Howard where he authored *The Negro in American Life and Thought* and a centennial history of the university.

Ralph Bunche Residence

1510 Jackson Street, NE

The Ralph Bunche (1904-1971) story almost parallels Booker T. Washington's *Up from Slavery*. The grandson of slaves and the son of a struggling barber in Detroit, Bunche was orphaned at age 11. He and his sister were raised in Los Angeles by his grandmother, the inspiration of his life. Selling papers and shining shoes to support his family, Bunche excelled in the classroom and as an all-state high school basketball player. He was refused membership, however, in the Honor Society even though he was class valedictorian. A Phi Beta Kappa scholarship student at UCLA, Bunche went on to graduate studies at Harvard University where his Ph.D. dissertation won the prestigious Tappan Award. After post-doctoral work at Northeastern University and the London School of Economics, Bunche created and became chairman of the political science department at Howard University, a department that consisted of Bunche and Emmet E. Dorsey.

During the late 1930s Bunche was an assistant to Swedish sociologist Gunnar Myrdal. Together they toured the South collecting data for Myrdal's study on race relations in the United States, *An American Dilemma: The Negro Program and Modern Democracy.* As chief of the African Section of the Office of Strategic Services (OSS) at the beginning of World War II, Bunche greatly impressed the director, General William J. Donovan, who swore that Bunche was a "walking colonial institute." In 1944 Bunche became the first black desk officer at the State Department. There he drafted three chapters on trusteeships and colonies for the United Nations charter. At the end of the war, Bunche went to Palestine as the U.N. Secretary General's personal representative. After the assassination of his friend and mentor, Swedish Count Folke Bernadotte, he took over as the key mediator in the negotiations that led to the settlement of the 1948 Arab-Israeli War. For these remarkable achievements, in 1950 Bunche was the first black awarded the Nobel Prize for Peace. President John F. Kennedy conferred on Dr. Bunche the nation's highest civilian award, the Medal of Freedom.

Dr. Bunche reminisced about Brookland and his home: "It was in a section of the city in which the whites predominated at that time. The architect and the builders and I spent eighteen months going over plans and putting it up. When we moved in, my daughters had to go three miles to school—I had to hire a driver to take them—even though there was a school for white kids just around the corner." Efforts to integrate the local school were unsuccessful; Brookland's Slowe School was opened in 1948 for black students.

At the time of his death in 1971, *Crisis* magazine declared that it was Bunche's "unfailing love of people" that was the "great motivating force in his life."

Robert Weaver Residence

3519 14th Street, NE

Native Washingtonian and Dunbar High School graduate, Robert Weaver became the first black to head a Cabinet department in the federal government. Appointed by President Lyndon B. Johnson in 1965, Weaver was the first secretary of the newly created Department of Housing and Urban Development (HUD).

Robert Weaver grew up in Brookland. After earning three degrees from Harvard University, Weaver came back to Washington during the Depression to serve as an advisor on minorities to Secretary of the Interior Harold Ickes. The young New Dealer was also a leader of President Franklin Roosevelt's informal "Black Cabinet."

Positions on the War Production Board during World War II, Rent Commissioner for New York State in the 1950s, and Director of the Housing and Home Finance Agency during the Kennedy Administration preceded Weaver's cabinet-level appointment. In 1969 Weaver left government service to become president of Bernard Baruch College of City University of New York.

Sterling Brown Residence

1222 Kearney Street, NE

The son of the pastor of the Lincoln Memorial Congregational Temple on 11th Street, Brown was born in 1901 at 6th and Fairmont Streets in the "Collegetown" community next to the Howard University campus. Educated at Williams College and Harvard University, Brown taught English at Howard, was a mentor of poet Amiri Baraka (LeRoi Jones), and served as editor of Negro affairs for the Federal Writers' Project (1936-1939), part of the WPA program. In 1941, Brown was senior editor of *The Negro Caravan*, an important anthology that has become a standard reference work.

Railroad workers, chain gangs and field hands dominate Brown's 1932 collection of poems, *Southern Road.* Brown translated the culture of the Southern Negro into a prose that one critic described as the "racy idiom of humble workers." Coming to prominence during the Harlem Renaissance years, Brown was considered by many as the dean of American black poets until his death in 1989.

CHAPTER 6

North Capitol Street

Al Walker Bootblacking Stands and Messenger Service

Union Station

In 1901 the Union League directory described the Al Walker Bootblacking Stands and Messenger Service as "probably the most unique, and at the same time successful business enterprise, conducted by a man of our race in Washington." The main stand was located outside the B & O Railroad Station on the site of the present Union Station. Alfred H.T. Walker was a College of Pharmacy (New York City) graduate and utilized his knowledge of chemistry to manufacture his best-selling shoe dressings, dyes, and colorings. As a successful businessman, Walker had, according to the directory, a "dignified calling heretofore not consid ered proper for a man of education."

Bible Way Church of Our Lord Jesus Christ World Wide

1130 New Jersey Avenue, NW

The Bible Way Church of Our Lord Jesus Christ celebrated its 50th anniversary in 1977. The youngest minister ever ordained in the Apostalic Faith, the Reverend Smallwood E. Williams began his ministry in 1925 on the streets of Washington where, as he recalls, "the fireplug was my pulpit, the curbstone my altar, and passersby were my congregation."

The Bible Way Church has evolved "From Tent to Temple." After several years in a storefront, from 1931 to 1947 the church held services in giant tents to overflow crowds at its present church site. Today the large building complex consists of the Bible Way Church, the adjacent educational and recreational

North Capitol Street Neighborhood
1. Al Walker Bootblacking Stands and Messenger Service
2. Bible Way Church of Our Lord Jesus Christ World Wide
3. M Street High School
4. Site of Dunbar High School
5. Armstrong Technical High School
6. Barnett-Aden Gallery

addition, and the recently-completed Bible Way Temple, seating 3,000 people. The free-standing bell tower is crowned by an 80-foot stainless steel cross inscribed "GOD." Now a bishop, Williams has been active in Washington's civic, political, and economic life, serving as chairman of the Democratic Central Committee and on the Board of Directors of the NAACP. In 1952 Williams conducted Washington's first "sit-in" demonstration. With his 6-year-old son, Wallace, Williams refused to leave the Wheatley Elementary School's first grade classroom, protesting that his son was not permitted to attend this all-white school only one block from his home.

Bible Way has been a primary force in the economic revitalization of its inner city neighborhood. In 1973 the church financed and built the Golden Rule Apartments and Supermarket, a 10-story housing complex for low- and moderate-income families occupying the 900 block of New Jersey Avenue.

M Street High School

M Street between New Jersey Avenue and 1st Street, NW

Education is central to any look at black Washington. Stories abound of middle class families that moved to Washington from the South and elsewhere for the sole purpose of educating their children in the District's quality schools. These schools were, of course, segregated. Proclaiming that "the separate school is not equivalent," Senator Charles Sumner introduced legislation in 1872 that prohibited racial discrimination in hiring teachers and admitting students in the District's schools. After its defeat, the District of Columbia maintained two separate school systems for the following 82 years—one for white students and one for blacks.

J. Ormand Wilson, Washington's white superintendent of schools, declared in 1877 that "the educational ladder was too short" and needed to be extended at both ends with the addition of a high school and kindergarten level. But Washington's black citizens had had a high school for seven years when the superintendent made that statement. The Preparatory High School for Negro Youth, the first public high school for black students in the U.S., began modestly in 1870 in the basement of the 15th Street Presbyterian church, then moved to the Sumner and Stevens School buildings and to the Myrtilla Miner Building at 17th Street, between P and Q Streets, NW. In 1891 the school relocated in a brick building at the intersection of 1st and M Streets and New Jersey Avenue, NW. Taking its name from its location, M Street High School was the precursor to the equally eminent Dunbar High School (1916).

When the frequently asked question arises—what made M Street so great?—the almost unanimous response is: The administrators and faculty. It certainly was not the physical facilities or equipment. M Street High School had neither gym nor lockers for physical education, no pool or track, nor even a yard or grass outside. Science laboratories were too few and inferior to those in white schools. Thus, impressive faculty credentials, coupled with ambitious and progressive direction provided by a succession of distinguished principals, helped explain the high standards of excellence achieved by this high school.

Between the years 1870 and 1890, the Preparatory High School was headed by Emma Hutchins, the only white administrator of those early years; Richard T. Greener, the first black graduate of Harvard University; and Mary Jane Patterson, considered to be the first black woman to receive a college degree in this country (Oberlin College, 1862).

The talented Francis Cardozo, Sr., was the first principal at the M Street site. During his tenure, enrollment more than doubled—from 172 to 361 students—and, more importantly, the rigorous classical curriculum was expanded to a full four-year program including four years of Latin. The high school program was strongly college preparatory. (Almost all of M Street/Dunbar's graduates went on to higher education even though most of this country's students did not.)

Cardozo was followed by Dr. Winfield Scott Montgomery, Robert Terrell, and skilled educator Anna J. Cooper. The major issue during Cooper's term at the turn of the century concerned maintaining an equal academic curriculum with that of white students. Many in the black community agreed with Booker T. Washington that blacks must advance through self-reliance, hard work, and tenacity, and thus advocated an agricultural, technical, and business training program. (Vocations and skills, not the study of the arts and humanities were the ticket for racial progress.) College preparatory institutions such as M Street High School came under attack from Washington's supporters as well as the District's director of high schools who suggested that black students not pursue an academic curriculum as rigorous as that for white students as they were not suited to it. Supported by most of the city's black middle class community, Anna J. Cooper successfully resisted the pressure to turn M Street into a trade school.

Site of Dunbar High School

West side of 1st Street, between N and O Streets, NW

Dunbar was one of the premier black high schools in America. With a strong liberal arts and college preparatory curriculum, Dunbar was among the few black high schools in the nation whose students could enter major northern colleges and universities without a special entrance examination.

The handsome brick and stone Tudor Collegiate style school drew its student body from across the city and Georgetown. A great majority of the students came from the long-established, best-educated and wealthiest of Washington's black families. However, Dunbar and Armstrong Technical (1902), the city's only black high schools, were open to any black child desiring a secondary education.

The academic credentials of the Dunbar faculty compared favorably with those of professors at many U.S. universities. In 1921, for example, three black women on the staff held Ph.D. degrees—Georgiana Simpson, University of Chicago; Sadie Tanner Mossell, University of Pennsylvania; and Eva B. Dykes, Radcliffe College.

Although Dunbar was still considered a very good high school by the end of the 1940s, the facility had deteriorated considerably. A faculty of 45 taught a student body of over 1,500 and per-pupil appropriations for black high school students ($120.52) were much less than those for white students ($160.21).

With school desegregation in 1954, Dunbar became a neighborhood school. Although the school's alumni bitterly opposed its demolition, the historic old Dunbar building was torn down in 1977. A new inner-city-style school building was constructed around the corner at 1st and N Streets, NW.

Dunbar educated generations of students who provided the city's black leadership. Former student Robert Weaver, Secretary for Housing and Urban Development in President Johnson's administration, declared that "the efficacy of this high school is certainly expressed in the success of its graduates." Or, as historian David Lewis stated, "the Dunbar degree was not always a guarantee of brilliant success, but it was very seldom a passport to failure."

Armstrong Technical High School

O Street, between 1st and 2nd Streets, NW

In the late 1890s Congress authorized the construction of two technical training high schools in the District of Columbia. The one for black students was designed by the famous Washington architect, Waddy B. Wood, and was named in honor of General Samuel Chapman Armstrong, a white commander of a freedmen's Civil War regiment and the founder of Virginia's Hampton Institute. Appropriately the speaker at the 1902 Dedication was Booker T. Washington, who had been both a student and teacher at Hampton Institute.

An experiment in vocational education, Armstrong evolved from attempts by proponents of Booker T. Washington's educational philosophy to convert M Street High School to a trade school. By incorporating M Street's recently instituted business and technical courses, Armstrong's course of study appeased the advocates for technical training at M Street.

The success of Armstrong was largely attributable to the zeal and talent of its first principal, Dr. Wilson Bruce Evans, the father of Mme. Evanti, the first black professional opera singer. Evans was educated in Washington's public schools, at Oberlin College, and received a Doctor of Medicine degree from Howard University. He assembled an outstanding faculty and his dynamism permeated the school. Beginning with sixteen students, Dr. Evans nurtured Armstrong into a student body of more than 700 at the time of his retirement in 1912. The outstanding educators who followed Dr. Evans—Garnet C. Wilkinson, Dr. Carter G. Woodson, Arthur C. Newman, and Dr. Benetta B. Washington, the wife of the city's first mayor—continued his legacy of strong leadership at Armstrong.

The handsome 28-room building was designed for 300 students. By the 1950s, after three additions, Armstrong accommodated nearly 1,300 students. In 1964 it was designated an adult education center until it closed in 1996.

Site of Barnett-Aden Gallery

127 Randolph Street, NW

The first black privately owned and operated art gallery in the United States opened in October 1943 on the first floor of the modest rowhouse at 127 Randolph Street, NW. It was the residence of the gallery's owners, Howard University Professor James V. Herring and Alonzo Aden. Herring founded Howard's fine arts department in 1922. Aden had served as the first curator of the university's Gallery of Art, founded by Herring in 1930.

By establishing the gallery (named after Aden's mother's family) in their home, the partners literally brought art into the neighborhood. After the government's WPA programs dried up at the end of the 1930s, few exhibition venues for black artists survived. Barnett-Aden exhibited both black and white artists; talent was the only criteria for selection at Barnett-Aden. Herring, in particular, felt strongly that blacks could not fight segregation and then advocate separate galleries for black artists.

Aden and Herring were strongly committed to collecting and preserving the work of black artists. Since their only sources of income were Herring's faculty salary and the gallery's unpredictable sales, they devised a unique system to form a collection. Rather than taking a commission on sales, the traditional gallery procedure, Aden and Herring selected the best work from each exhibition for their collection.

On Saturday evenings, Barnett-Aden became a mingling place for artists, art lovers, Howard faculty, and curators from the Phillips, Corcoran, and National Gallery of Art. "We all wore our version of evening clothes," artist Therese Schwartz recalled. These evenings were among the few racially integrated social events in the city at that time.

After Lonnie Aden's untimely death in 1961, the gallery never regained its dynamic direction. Professor Herring died eight years later. The gallery's splendid collection of African American art was dispersed, much of it going to Herring's protégé Adolphus Ealey. In 1989 the collection was sold for nearly $6 million to a Florida educational institution.

CHAPTER 7

Florida Avenue and LeDroit Park

Florida Avenue

In the early decades of the twentieth century, Florida Avenue, near the entrance gate to LeDroit Park, was an enclave of doctors' offices, small businesses, drugstores, funeral homes, and cafes. Three of Washington's most interesting citizens—Emmett Scott, Dr. John Washington and Dr. Ionia Whipper—lived on this section of Florida Avenue near Harrison's Cafe, one of the black community's most popular restaurants. At one time or other physicians Sidney Sumby, Edmund Wilson, Charles A. Tignor and Algernon B. Jackson were located on the avenue near the pharmacies of Leo Williams and George Butcher (501 Florida Avenue, NW). If all else failed, there were two nearby funeral homes—McGuire's and Frazier's.

Emmett J. Scott Residence

239 Florida Avenue, NW

Emmett J. Scott (1873-1957) lived at this address while he was special assistant for Negro affairs to Secretary of War Newton D. Baker during World War I. He served as an effective liaison between the government and the black community during this period of lynchings, riots, and racial hostility toward black soldiers.

BLACK WASHINGTON

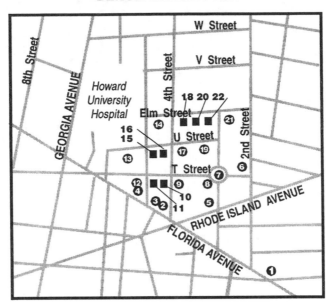

Florida Avenue and LeDroit Park

1. Emmett J. Scott Residence
2. Harrison's Cafe
3. Dr. John Washington Residence
4. Dr. Ionia R. Whipper Residence
5. Site of David McClelland Residence
6. Anna J. Cooper Residence
7. Anna J. Cooper Memorial Circle
8. Robert and Mary Church Terrell Residence
9. Fountain Peyton Residence
10. Walter E. Washington Residence
11. Dr. Ernest E. Just Residence
12. Major James E. Walker Residence
13. Montgomery Apartments
14. The Honorable Oscar DePriest Residence
15. John H. Smyth Residence
16. Dr. Garnet C. Wilkinson Residence
17. Octavius Augustus Williams Residence
18. Site of Alice Moore and Paul Laurence Dunbar Residence
19. John and Julia West Hamilton Residence
20. Site of Christian Fleetwood Residence
21. Lucy Diggs Slowe Hall
22. Senator Edward Brooke Residence

Scott established his reputation earlier as Booker T. Washington's private secretary and confidant from 1897 until Washington's death in 1915. Scott's close relationship with his employer prompted Washington to write in his autobiography:

> ... *Scott understands so thoroughly my motives, plans and ambitions that he puts himself into my own position as nearly as possible for one individual to put himself into the place of another, and in this way makes himself invaluable not only to me personally but to the institution.*

Beginning as a janitor-messenger for the Houston *Post* newspaper, Scott later became editor of the *Texas Freeman*, one of the most influential publications in the state. After his government service, Scott served as secretary and treasurer of Howard University, the most powerful black administrator of that institution until Mordecai W. Johnson was appointed the university's first black president in 1926. Scott was the first black elected to a vice-presidency of the national council of the YMCA. Active in Republican Party politics, he served as an advisor on Negro affairs to the Republican National Committee from 1939 to 1942. Scott died at Freedmen's Hospital in 1957.

Harrison's Cafe

455 Florida Avenue, NW

Harrison's Cafe, the creation of Robert Hilliard Harrison, was a city institution for nearly half a century. At the age of 13, Harrison left school and his poor working-class family to work for a wealthy employer in Cambridge, Ohio. There he learned social graces and the art of fine cooking. Later, as the valet of a rich Englishman, Harrison traveled to Europe, absorbing the world of continental cuisine. After returning to the States, Harrison spent six years with the B & O Railroad and then clerked for the government. Within a short period of time he quit his job to devote his full energies to the successful candy store business which he had established at 467 Florida Avenue, NW. Then in 1920 he opened the Robert Harrison Cafe down the street at 455 Florida Avenue, NW.

Harrison's was a first-class dining establishment, its menu selection ranging from lobster to the best 20¢ hamburger in Washington. Washington's black elite, Howard faculty, students, and working-class citizens patronized the restaurant. The cafe expanded next door and opened its Gold Room for banquets and special occasions.

Robert Harrison died in 1957, leaving the cafe to his two longtime employees, Manager "Miss Nealy" Boone, who began as a waitress in 1923, and "Miss Willie" Campbell. As co-owners, they operated the restaurant until 1962.

Dr. John Washington Residence

463 Florida Avenue, NW

In 1947 Dr. John Washington (1880-1964) was honored by the Library of Congress for his collection of Abraham Lincoln memorabilia. For more than 35 years, Washington pursued his avocation, interviewing and recording the recollections of elderly blacks who had known Lincoln, his presidential aides, and former members of the White House staff. In 1942 Washington published this material as a book, *They Knew Lincoln*, with an introduction by Carl Sandburg. Dr. Washington's passion for the life and times of the martyred president was passed on to him by his grandmother, who revered the Great Emancipator. Her own Lincoln scrapbook was the cornerstone of Washington's collection.

A man of many talents and interests, Dr. Washington was an artist, a practicing dentist, and an instructor of commercial art and civics for 26 years in the high schools. He coached track and basketball in the city leagues and became the first athletic coach at Cardozo High School.

Dr. Ionia R. Whipper Residence

511 Florida Avenue, NW

Dedicating her life to aiding others, Ionia R. Whipper was a pioneer in providing health care services for more than forty years to the District's black unwed mothers.

Concerned about the plight of young mothers she delivered at Freedman's Hospital, Dr. Whipper provided care in her home for many of these women during and after their pregnancies. In the 1930s she raised funds through the Lend-A-Hand Club to provide a permanent building on East Capitol Street for the Ionia R. Whipper Home for Unwed Mothers. It was the only such home for young black mothers in segregated Washington until the 1960s.

Ionia Whipper was the third generation of her family committed to moral and social progress. Her grandfather, moral reformer William Whipper, was a conductor on the Underground Railroad. A delegate to South Carolina's State Constitutional Convention, her father, in 1868, founded the first black law firm in the

United States—Whipper, Elliott & Allen. That same year, using the pseudonym Frank A. Rollin, Ionia's mother, Frances, wrote *The Life and Public Services of Martin R. Delany*, a biography of her contemporary, the fiery spokesman for black liberation.

In the 1880s, after moving to Washington with Ionia, Frances Rollin Whipper became one of the first black female physicians in the United States. Following in her mother's footsteps, Ionia graduated in obstetrics from Howard University Medical School in 1903. Her brother, Leigh Whipper, was a famed stage and movie actor.

Dr. Whipper's mission was recalled simply in the 1953 death notice appearing in the St. Luke's Episcopal Church bulletin: "Her aim was to rehabilitate the unwed mothers upon whom society had placed a great stigma."

LeDroit Park

Tiny LeDroit Park, one of the oldest neighborhoods outside the original city of Washington, is less than one square mile in size. Located north of Florida Avenue (formerly Boundary Street) and Rhode Island Avenue, and south of W Street between 2nd and 6th Streets, LeDroit Park is noteworthy for its architecture and for its stature as one of the city's political and cultural black residential centers during the first decades of the 20th century.

Washington's white middle class, its ranks swollen by large numbers of government workers during the Civil War, filled available housing in the District and then pushed Washington's residential areas beyond the city's boundaries. Responding to the need for new housing, developers built new neighborhoods, such as LeDroit Park, Brookland, Mt. Pleasant, and Columbia Heights.

An architect-designed and planned suburb, LeDroit Park was developed by Amzi L. Barber, a white ministry graduate of Oberlin College, who became a faculty member at Howard University a year after its founding in 1867. Desperately needing funds during the 1873 Depression, the university sold two parcels of land, one to the city for a reservoir, and the other of more than 40 acres to Barber and his LeDroit Park partners. The neighborhood was named for Barber's father-in-law, New York real estate developer LeDroit Langdon.

The original residents of LeDroit Park were white. Most were members of nearby Howard University's faculty and administration. Among the first to live in this exclusive suburb was explorer and geographer Henry Gannett (1902 Harewood Street), who, as creator of most of the maps of the American West, is considered the "Father of American Mapmaking."

The basic design for the neighborhood was a grid pattern with a circle at the eastern end. Reminiscent of the circles on L'Enfant's original plan for Washington, the LeDroit circle is off axis to the city plan, making access to the neighborhood somewhat difficult.

Following the era's desire for the rural and picturesque, the neighborhood was developed as a park. Wishing to achieve a feeling of openness, the developer permitted no fences between homes. Most of the neighborhood streets were named for trees. "The gardens were wonderful," remembered a former resident who delivered newspapers at the turn of the century. "You could smell the flowers the minute you crossed 6th Street."

Separated by a fence from the nearby unkempt vacant lots and shanty towns, LeDroit Park projected a sense of privacy, a place away from the rest of the city. Entry to the neighborhood was gained only through gates in the "unpainted and unsightly" wooden fence to the north and the ornamental iron and wood fence to the south. The fence became a racial wall which effectively "kept out the dogs and the Negroes"—in the words of one old resident—and closed direct access to downtown Washington for Howard's students.

In July 1888 an angry mob of blacks tore the fence down, only to have it rebuilt four days later. After several more attempts and a series of lawsuits, "the most famous fence in the country" was finally demolished in 1901.

Developer Barber hired architect James H. McGill to design more than 60 individual homes in LeDroit Park. Sadly, only about 30 survive today. True to late Victorian taste and eclecticism, McGill worked in all of the architectural styles popular at that time—Gothic Revival, Italianate, Second Empire, and Queen Anne. He designed his homes with large rooms equipped with the most up-to-date conveniences: closets, pantries, cellars, bathrooms, Latrobe stoves, marble mantels, and call bells for the servants. An 1877 brochure advertised that the houses in LeDroit Park had "velvet wallpaper and gilt picture frames" and "no cheap structures will under any circumstances be permitted." Developed for the "merchant, professional man, or government clerk," LeDroit Park advertised its privacy and country atmosphere. Amenities such as private trash collection, a security watchman, and easy access to the downtown city on the nearby 7th Street streetcar line were stressed.

LeDroit Park's rowhouses came later. As lots were subdivided in the late 1880s and 1890s, they were filled in with impressive rows of brick townhouses. A few black families moved into LeDroit Park in the 1890s. Most were connected in some way with Howard University and the nearby Collegetown neighborhood. By World War I LeDroit Park had become one of the most desirable black neighborhoods in the city. One of the first black residents, poet Paul Laurence Dunbar, wrote that in LeDroit Park "comes together the flower of colored citizenship from all parts of the country." By 1915 there were 5,000 black residents; LeDroit Park had experienced a reversal of racial composition in less than ten years.

The deterioration of LeDroit Park began after World War II and accelerated in the 1950s and 60s. Middle class families left for newer integrated neighborhoods—the "Gold Coast" of 16th Street and the suburbs of Maryland. By 1971 the average per capita income of LeDroit's 6,500 residents was $2,000— $4,000 below the city median. Many of the original McGill houses became apartments or boarding houses owned by absentee landlords. Howard University, owner of nearly 40 percent of LeDroit Park's houses, permitted most to fall into disrepair. Confrontations between the university and local residents over plans to tear down many of these properties were common during the 1970s.

Today, through the dedicated efforts of its residents, LeDroit Park is a historic district. Howard University has sold several houses to community-based organizations to be restored as family dwellings, but the pace of development and restoration has been slow.

Site of David McClelland Residence

Northwest corner of Rhode Island Avenue and 3rd Street, NW

Where the Safeway store now stands, one of the original white partners in the development of LeDroit Park, David McClelland, lived at the main entrance to the neighborhood in a grand Italianate mansion surrounded by beautifully landscaped grounds.

The home was purchased by a black organization, the Elks Columbian Lodge No. 85, in 1925. The lodge sponsored the popular Elks parades on U Street that terminated at this corner. The mansion was demolished for construction of the present Safeway store in 1968 and the new Elks Lodge building at 1844 3rd Street.

Amzi Barber, the developer of LeDroit Park, built his home across the street at 1801 Harewood. Later, Barber developed another suburban community, Columbia Heights, where he built his splendid castle, "Belmont," on the present site of the Clifton Terrace Apartments at 13th and Clifton Streets, NW.

Anna J. Cooper Residence

201 T Street, NW

The picturesque residence on the corner of T and 2nd Streets, NW, was for decades the home of author and educator Anna Julia Cooper (1858-1964). Cooper purchased this Victorian home with its unique chalet-style bargeboard trim and hexagonal gazebo at the corner of the porch in 1916 for $5,000. The home is missing its distinctive iron fence which she donated to the 1942 War Scrap Drive.

Born into slavery, Cooper was widowed at the age of 21 in 1879. She never remarried. In 1884 Cooper graduated from Oberlin College where she also received her master's degree. At the age of 67 she finished her doctoral degree at the Sorbonne, defending in French her dissertation, "The Attitude of France in Regard to Slavery [American] During the Revolution."

A Latin teacher for nearly forty years at M Street/Dunbar High School, Cooper served as principal of M Street from 1901 to 1906. When she was notified that her students at M Street were ineligible for college scholarships, Cooper immediately secured assurances from Harvard, Yale, Brown and other Ivy League universities that her students would be considered for admittance if they passed a rigorous entrance examination. With Anna Cooper's guidance, two M Street students were the first to enter Harvard without having studied at an academy or preparatory school. Cooper stressed self-improvement, racial pride, and scholarship to her students and for this she is still remembered.

For many years her home was also the site of Frelinghuysen University. Originally founded in 1906 by Dr. Jesse and Rosetta E. Lawson as the Bible Educational Association, the school's name changed in 1917 to honor F.T. Frelinghuysen, Secretary of State under President Chester Arthur, who had rendered "great service to the cause of the colored people while a member of the U.S. Senate ...." As the university's president, Cooper offered evening adult education classes to "employed colored persons" during the Depression and war years, until its demise in the 1950s. Although never accredited, Frelinghuysen offered hundreds of working black Washingtonians a chance for an education and self-improvement.

After a life filled with accomplishments and many honors, Anna J. Cooper died at the age of 105 in 1964.

Anna J. Cooper Memorial Circle

3rd and T Streets, NW

Named in honor of one of the neighborhood's most illustrious citizens, the restored circle is the heart of LeDroit Park. With no existing explanation for the circle's unusual placement in relation to the street grid pattern, one can theorize that the 19th century developers wanted to discourage additional traffic through their neighborhood while the McMillan Reservoir was being constructed to the north. In any case, the circle, originally landscaped with a fountain and flowers, fell into disrepair during the 20th century. Its final desecration occurred when Harewood Avenue, now 3rd Street, was cut through the circle for car and bus traffic. In 1982 the circle was filled in and returned to its former beauty.

The largest and most opulent of the neighborhood's original McGill-designed homes faced the circle. Only two of these houses remain. The impressive Second Empire structure on the northeast corner of the circle was the home of Civil War General William Birney and his son Arthur A., a professor of law at Howard University.

Robert and Mary Church Terrell Residence

326 T Street, NW

Robert and Mary Church Terrell were among the first black families to buy into the exclusively white LeDroit Park neighborhood during the late 1890s. Mrs. Terrell recalled the difficulties they encountered:

> *...when the woman who owned the house which we had selected learned that colored people wanted it, she refused to sell it to us. Since it was so near a settlement of colored people, I had no idea there would be the slightest objection to selling it to us.*
>
> *It reached the ears of an old, well-established real estate firm that we wanted this piece of property. Both father and son came to see us one evening. After I had given a detailed account of the prolonged strenuous efforts I had made to find a house, the elder of the two men said, "Do you want that house in LeDroit Park?" I assured him that I wanted it very much. "Well, you shall have it," he declared. "I'll be damned if you shan't."*

The real estate agent convinced a wealthy friend who employed a black secretary, a unique situation at the time, to purchase the home and resell it immediately to the Terrells. Today the "half" house at Number 326 has been designated a Historic Landmark.

Robert Terrell (1857-1925) came to the District of Columbia from Virginia as a boy of ten. Educated in the city's public schools and at Groton Academy in Massachusetts, he was one of seven *magna cum laude* graduates in Harvard's class of 1884. Returning to Washington, Terrell taught and served as principal of the M Street High School, earned a law degree at Howard University, and practiced law for several years. In the 1890s he was appointed to the powerful, white-dominated Washington Board of Trade. In spite of vigorous opposition by its Southern members, the U.S. Senate confirmed Terrell's nomination to the Municipal Court of the District of Columbia, making him its first black judge. The Terrells were among the most prominent social leaders of Washington's black community until Terrell's death in 1925 from the complications of a stroke suffered several years earlier.

Mary Church Terrell (1863-1954) had few peers in the struggle for civil rights and equal opportunity in the nation's capital. Her life spanned the history of that struggle for freedom—from the Emancipation Proclamation in 1863 to the 1954 *Brown v. Board of Education* Supreme Court decision, desegregating the nation's public schools.

Born in suburban Memphis, Mary Church's Tennessean father became wealthy through shrewd real estate investments after Reconstruction. The Churches sent their young daughter north to Ohio's Antioch College Model School for her elementary and secondary education. She continued at Oberlin College, taking the four-year classical curriculum rather than the more usual two-year course. Returning to Memphis after earning a master's degree in 1888, she argued with her father over her desire to pursue a career; he wanted her to remain in Memphis to be his hostess.

But Church persevered, accepting a position teaching Latin at the M Street High School in Washington, D.C. She traveled to Europe for two years studying languages and, upon her return in 1891, married Robert Terrell, her former supervisor at M Street. Marriage ended her teaching career. Under the District's Board of Education "Rule 45," married women were not eligible for full-time teaching positions. In 1895 Mary Church Terrell was appointed to the D.C. School Board, becoming, it is believed, the first black to serve on a school board in the United States. She served 6 four-year terms. Always active in club work, she was pivotal in the establishment of the National Association of Colored Women in 1897, becoming the organization's first president. She worked for almost three decades with Susan B. Anthony in the women's suffrage movement, marching and picketing for the 19th Amendment. Nationally, during these years, she lectured and delivered her well-known speech, "The Progress of Colored Women." In 1909 Mrs. Terrell served on the Committee of Forty which laid the foundation for the organization of the National Association for the Advancement of Colored People and for years she was vice-president of the NAACP's local chapter. During these difficult times and well into the 1920s she lectured frequently against lynching.

During World War I, "Lady Mollie," as she was affectionately called, focused her energies on organizations that met the needs of black servicemen who were refused service in the capital city's public places. After the war she attended the 1919 Peace Congress.

Racial struggles and confrontation played a major role in Mary Church Terrell's life. Having allowed her membership in the American Association of University Women to lapse for several decades, Mrs. Terrell attempted to renew that membership in 1946. The District of Columbia chapter refused to reinstate her, although the national organization had no racial requirements. After a three-year battle that included court litigation, her membership was restored by a vote of 2,168 to 65 at the Association's national convention.

In 1940, at the age of 76, Mary Church Terrell wrote her autobiography, *A Colored Woman in a White World.* Her good friend, British novelist H. G. Wells, wrote the preface.

Nine years later Mrs. Terrell began her last fight—an assault on segregation in the restaurants of the nation's capital. As chairman of the Interracial Coordinating Committee for the Enforcement of District of Columbia Anti-Discrimination Laws, Terrell and others chose their field of battle: Thompson's Restaurant. When they were denied service the committee sued. After years of court defeats the committee won in a landmark 1953 Supreme Court decision prohibiting segregation in public places in the District of Columbia.

Buoyed by that victory, Mrs. Terrell mounted a defense campaign on behalf of a Georgia sharecropper, Rose Lee Ingram, who was sentenced to death for killing a white man. On her way to Georgia to help Ingram, Lady Mollie collapsed at her summer home at Highland Beach and died in nearby Annapolis, Maryland, at the age of 91.

Fountain Peyton Residence

330 T Street, NW

As a youngster, Fountain Peyton (1861-1951) sold newspapers. Among his customers was President Ulysses S. Grant who always gave him an "extra tip." An 1886 graduate of Howard's Law School, Peyton was one of Washington's earliest black attorneys. The 1896 Union League directory listed sixteen black attorneys practicing in Washington, including the partnership of Peyton and Renfro at 505 D St., NW. Peyton also was a member of the District's Board of Education with his neighbor, Mary Church Terrell.

The handsome white brick home at the corner of 4th and T Streets (400 T Street, NW), was purchased in the mid-1980s by the Reverend Jesse Jackson, well-known civil rights leader and 1984 presidential candidate.

Walter E. Washington Residence

408 T Street, NW

After the nation's capital was granted Home Rule on January 2, 1975, Walter E. Washington became the city's first elected mayor in more than 100 years. His longtime residence at 408 T Street, NW, was a familiar sight to District citizens.

Born in Georgia in 1915, Washington grew up in Buffalo, New York. Upon the death of his mother when he was 6 years old, the young Washington was raised by his laborer father. Washington saved for a college education and, in 1934, took the train to Washington, D.C. to enter Howard University. While studying public administration, Washington was active in the New Negro Alliance, which picketed and boycotted white-owned businesses that catered to black patrons but refused to hire black employees.

Washington began his professional career at the Alley Dwelling Authority, later called the National Capital Housing Authority, an organization he headed 20 years later. He brought many blacks into the pre-World War II "white plantation government" of this city. While chairman of the New York City Housing Authority, Washington was appointed mayor of the nation's capital in 1967 by President Lyndon B. Johnson prior to his election under Home Rule several years later.

In 1918 the Reverend George O. Bullock, influential pastor of the Third Baptist Church, moved into this house. Daughter Benetta Bullock married Walter Washington in 1941. A graduate of Dunbar High School and Howard University, Dr. Benetta Washington served as principal of Cardozo High School and director of the federal government's Women's Job Corps.

Mrs. Washington, who lived in this house since she was an infant, observed:

> *In my mind's eye—even as a child—I feel (my father) wanted one of his children to be here, to keep the family homestead .... I could never reproduce this anywhere else.*

Dr. Ernest E. Just Residence

412 T Street, NW

Longtime Howard University faculty member and world-renowned scientist Dr. Ernest Just (1883-1941) was another of LeDroit Park's distinguished residents. Just's mentor, Professor Frank R. Lillie of the University of Chicago, called him "the best investigator in the field of biology" that black America had produced.

Leaving his native South Carolina for a New England education, Just graduated Phi Beta Kappa from Dartmouth College in 1907 as a history and biology major. He joined the Howard faculty in the same year as an instructor of English and, with Benjamin G. Brawley, organized the first drama club at the university.

After graduate training at the prestigious Marine Biological Laboratory in Woods Hole, Massachusetts, Just began a teaching and research career in science. Much of the latter was conducted in Europe, where he felt much "freer" as a black man and gained a solid "sense of dignity." Writing to Professor Lillie in 1936, Just lamented that there was little opportunity for him to join a "real university" and that he was compelled to use his first years in the best possible way—"to keep aglow the flame within me, which in my particular circumstances as a Negro I am not allowed to nourish in America."

Major James E. Walker Residence

502-504 T Street, NW

James Edward Walker (1874-1918) was a teacher, principal, and administrator in the Washington Public Schools for 24 years. He moved to D.C. with his family in 1880 where his father, a former slave, earned his living as a butler and waiter. A graduate of M Street High School and Miner Teachers College, Walker moved to this address in 1909. An avid tennis player, Walker organized a private tennis club at the courts at 13th and T Streets, NW. When the Whitelaw Apartments were built on that site, he moved the club to courts next to Freedmen's Hospital.

Major James E. Walker, however, is best remembered for his service in the U.S. Army and with the First Separate Battalion, a local National Guard unit. The battalion was what its name implied—separate from the white National Guard units. Walker joined the battalion in 1896, became commander of Company B in 1909, and succeeded the respected Major Arthur Brooks as commander of the battalion in 1912. His unit policed the Mexican border in 1916. The following year, the battalion, the first unit activated prior to the U.S. entry into World War I, was directed to defend the nation's capital. As a result, Walker spent a great deal of time in the swampy areas near the Potomac River where he contracted tuberculosis. Without their commander, the First Separate Battalion left in March 1918 for combat in Europe as part of the 372nd Regiment. Shortly after, Major Walker died on April 4, 1918, and was buried in Arlington Cemetery. American Legion Post 26 was named in his memory and Walker Jones Elementary School honors his years of service to the school system.

Walker's brother-in-law, Arthur C. Newman, lived around the corner at 504 T Street, NW. A principal of Armstrong Technical High School, Captain Newman served in World War I and later commanded the First Separate Battalion. Major Walker's son and namesake continued to reside at No. 502.

Montgomery Apartments

512 U Street, NW

During the years of World War I, Willis Richardson, an important playwright of the Harlem Renaissance period, resided in the now-abandoned Montgomery Apartments at 512 U Street. Richardson is considered to be the first black American to have a serious play produced on a Broadway stage. A North Carolinian, Richardson was educated at M Street High School and secured a clerkship at the U.S. Bureau of Printing and Engraving which he held for 43 years. But his great interest was the theater; his first play was performed in Minnesota in 1921. His second effort, The *Chip Woman's Fortune*, was performed by the Ethiopian Art Players in Chicago, Washington and New York with great success. In 1925 *The Broken Banjo* won the prestigious Amy Spingarn Prize and a year later *Bootblack Lover* was awarded the same honor.

Ten years later Richardson collaborated with Kelly Miller's daughter May to write *Negro History in Thirteen Plays*. May Miller Sullivan later became a nationally recognized author and poet.

The Honorable Oscar DePriest Residence

419 U Street, NW

The 400 block of U Street, NW, is the only remaining block of McGill-designed homes in LeDroit Park. These modest Italian villa-style duplex houses are interesting for their symmetrical facades, low-pitched, overhanging roofs, and absence of ornamentation. As the first black congressman since Reconstruction and the first elected from a Northern state, Oscar DePriest (1871-1951) lived in the white brick house on the corner during his three terms in the House of Representatives in the 1930s. Born in Alabama, DePriest's family moved to Kansas in 1878 to avoid the violence and lynchings of that period. At 17 he left home for Chicago where he became a successful real estate agent, Republican Party organizer, and politician. Oscar DePriest was the first black alderman elected to the Chicago City Council in 1915.

He won the Illinois Third Congressional District seat in 1928, becoming the first black elected to Congress in the 20th century. DePriest's legislative record was mixed. While his efforts to integrate the House of Representatives restaurant were futile (only black members could be served), he succeeded in sponsoring legislation desegregating the Civilian Conservation Corps in 1933. Opposed to much of President Roosevelt's New Deal economic program, DePriest was defeated by a black Democratic candidate, Arthur W. Mitchell, in the 1934 elections.

Reminiscent of the furor created in 1901 when President Theodore Roosevelt invited Booker T. Washington to luncheon at the White House, Mrs. DePriest found herself in a similar situation in 1928. The reaction to Mrs. Herbert Hoover's invitation to a White House tea for congressional wives was swift and furious, particularly from the Southern press and congressmen. The Texas legislature even voted to condemn the invitation. The First Lady "compromised" by holding a "special" tea for Mrs. DePriest and selected guests who had previously been informed that she would be there.

John H. Smyth Residence

414 U Street, NW

Educated in Philadelphia, Smythe became the first black student to be admitted to the Philadelphia Academy of Fine Arts. After the Civil War, he traveled to London to study for an acting career, but returned to Washington where he entered the Howard University Law School, becoming one of three students to graduate in the first class of 1871.

For Smyth's efforts on behalf of the successful Republican Party during the stalemated 1876 election, Rutherford B. Hayes appointed Smyth U.S. minister and consul to Liberia in 1878. He served until 1885 when he resumed his law practice in Washington.

Dr. Garnet C. Wilkinson Residence

406 U Street, NW

The illustrious Washington career of Dr. Garnet C. Wilkinson (1874-1969) is unsurpassed in dedication and accomplishment in the field of public education. Wilkinson's service as first assistant superintendent in charge of colored schools for almost thirty years was so distinguished that he postponed his retirement three times at the Board of Education's request. He finally retired at the age of 72, three years before the landmark Supreme Court desegregation decision of 1954.

Born in South Carolina, Wilkinson attended this city's public schools (Birney Elementary and M Street High School), Oberlin College (1902), and Howard Law School. Before directing Washington's black schools, he taught Latin and mathematics at M Street and was principal of Armstrong and of Dunbar High School when it opened in 1916.

Octavius Augustus Williams Residence

338 U Street, NW

Soon after Octavius Williams moved into his home at 338 U Street, a bullet was fired through the window leaving a hole that remained in the wall for years as a reminder to his children and grandchildren of times past. A barber in the U.S Capitol Building, Williams was probably the first black to move into exclusively white LeDroit Park about 1893.

Site of Alice Moore and Paul Laurence Dunbar Residence

321 U Street, NW

Paul Laurence Dunbar (1872-1906) was the first black poet to achieve international acclaim. His great supporter and one of America's leading literary critics, William Dean Howells, paid Dunbar high tribute, claiming that he was the first writer not only to feel black life esthetically but also to express it lyrically.

Dunbar's father, a plasterer, died when he was young; his uneducated mother, however, read to her children at night and taught Paul to read as a toddler. He was the only black student in his Dayton, Ohio high school, where he was a friend of the Wright brothers. Stating that "all the boys were very kind to me," he joined the literary club and edited the school newspaper.

After graduation he worked as an elevator operator to support his literary efforts, publishing his first book of poetry in 1892. His second volume, *Majors and Minors*, received a rave review from Howells in *Harper's Weekly*. The critic wrote the introduction to a subsequent volume, *Lyrics of Lowly Life* (1896), considered Dunbar's finest work.

During this same period a poem published in a Boston magazine attracted Dunbar's attention. After meeting the author, beautiful Alice Moore of New Orleans, the two were married in 1898. Dunbar had moved to Washington only months earlier, residing with Dean Kelly Miller on the Howard University campus and working as an assistant to Daniel Murray, a highly respected black member of the Library of Congress staff.

For nearly five years the Dunbars were in great demand by Washington's black society. Their LeDroit Park home, the cultural and intellectual hub of the black community, was described by one visitor:

> *Well-filled bookshelves, upon which were author presentation copies, lined the poet's study, and engravings and etchings of good pictures hung upon the walls.*

Invitations to dine with the popular Dunbars were coveted. Dunbar headed the prestigious Bachelor-Benedict Club and the young couple summered at Highland Park and Arundel-on-the-Bay, exclusive black resorts on the Chesapeake Bay.

Dunbar's intense writing efforts and strenuous schedule of lectures at black colleges caused the poet's health to deteriorate. After separating from his wife in 1904, Dunbar returned to Dayton where he died in 1906 at the age of only 34.

John and Julia West Hamilton Residence

320 U Street, NW

Julia West Hamilton (1866-1958) and her husband, John, lived in this LeDroit Park house. Washington's longtime leader in charitable and civic affairs, Mrs. Hamilton's accomplishments over sixty years are legendary: president of the Phillis Wheatley YWCA for 28 years; first woman president of the board of trustees of the Metropolitan AME Church; treasurer of the predominantly white Women's Relief Corps Auxiliary of the Grand Army of the Republic; and various offices with the National Association of Colored Women and the National Council of Negro Women. John Hamilton's professional career spanned thirty-one years in the registrar's office of the U.S. Treasury Department.

Julia West married John A. Hamilton, a missionary and social worker, after her parents moved to Washington in the early 1880s. One of their children, Colonel West A. Hamilton, who later earned the rank of brigadier general, was a member of the District of Columbia Board of Education and also lived in LeDroit Park at 413 T Street, NW. West and his brother Percy operated the Hamilton Printing Company at 1353 U Street and published one of Washington's black newspapers, the *Sentinel.*

Site of Christian Fleetwood Residence

319 U Street, NW

Christian A. Fleetwood (1840-1914) and twelve comrades were the first blacks to be awarded the Medal of Honor by the U.S. Congress. In 1863 Fleetwood enlisted in the 4th Regiment, U.S. Colored Volunteer Infantry. A year later he earned his award for heroism at the battle of Chaffin's Farm near Richmond, Virginia. Even with the support of every officer in his unit, however, his application for a commission in the army was turned down.

Fleetwood was among a few young blacks to receive a basic education at a small school in his native Baltimore. He often recalled his good fortune in knowing a local doctor who "had me come after nightfall to his residence and, after locking and barring the doors, took me into the back part of the house, and so, night after night, prepared me to enter what is now called Lincoln University, in Pennsylvania."

Fleetwood earned his living as a clerk at Freedmen's Savings and Trust Company on Lafayette Square and later at the War Department for 30 years. His popularity and civic reputation were the product of his active military life; he was instrumental in organizing black militia and National Guard units in the District. Moreover, he was the first instructor of the Colored Washington High School Cadet Corps, as it was then called. In 1897 he was succeeded by Captain Arthur Brooks. These two officers developed the tradition of military service among Washington's young black teenagers that led to their participation in great numbers during World War I.

Just as the Dunbars had their suppers, Mrs. Fleetwood invited like-minded friends to her weekly Thursday literary gatherings which she called "Evenings at Home." Known not only for her hospitality but also for her compassion, Sara Fleetwood entered the first nursing school class at Freedmen's Hospital at the age of 55 and became the first black superintendent of nurses at the hospital in 1901.

Major Fleetwood was also a fine musician and choirmaster, presenting popular musical programs in Washington's churches. As a widower he resided with his daughter at 1419 Swann Street from 1908 until his death six years later.

Lucy Diggs Slowe Hall

1919 3rd Street, NW

Slowe Hall, designed by black architect Hilyard Robinson, was constructed during World War II to ease the housing crunch caused by the enormous influx of government workers to Washington. Like its counterpart, the Meridian Hill Hotel for white women on upper 16th Street, Slowe Hall was for "colored" female war workers and the nearby George Washington Carver Hall was for single "colored" men (2nd and Elm Streets). In the postwar years, Slowe Hall was operated as a hotel that catered to foreign dignitaries. According to a real estate handbook, Slowe Hall offered "facilities for Foreign Diplomats who, being of a complexion hue, cannot secure accommodations in the down-town hotels."

Purchased by Howard University in 1948 for off-campus student housing, the dormitory was named in honor of Lucy Diggs Slowe (1885-1937), the first dean of women at the University. Lucy Slowe was a leader of social change and educational innovation. While majoring in English at Howard (1908), she was one of the founders of Alpha Kappa Alpha, the first Greek letter sorority organized for black women. Later she was the principal of Shaw Junior High School (1919), the first junior high school in Washington for black students. In 1935 she was, with Mary McLeod Bethune, a founder of the National Council of Negro Women. Along with these professional achievements, Lucy Slowe was renowned for her rich contralto voice and for her championship tennis skills.

The architect of LeDroit Park, James McGill, died in his home on this site in 1908. The residence was later razed for the construction of Slowe Hall.

Senator Edward Brooke Residence

1938 3rd Street, NW

Edward Brooke III was the first African American elected by popular vote to the U.S. Senate. He was born in 1919 to Edward and Helen Brooke who lived in this rowhouse. The elder Brooke was a lawyer for the Veterans Administration for fifty years.

As a youngster in LeDroit Park, Brooke spent his summers selling ice cream and hot dogs at nearby Griffith Stadium. He later recalled his childhood in this tight-knit neighborhood:

> *We lived in a Negro community that had everything within its limited society. I didn't know we were not part of the total society.*

After attending Shaw Junior High School and Dunbar High School, Brooke's family moved to 1262 Hamlin Street in Brookland when Brooke was a student at Howard University.

Edward Brooke was awarded the Bronze Star for his military service during World War II. With his dark hair and lightskinned appearance, he was able to infiltrate enemy lines to work with Italian partisans. After the war Brooke returned to Boston University Law School with his Italian war bride.

In 1962 the 43-year-old Brooke was elected attorney general of Massachusetts, becoming the first black to win statewide office there. His moderate to liberal Republican politics were popular in the state. In 1966 Brooke successfully ran for the U.S. Senate seat vacated by Leverett Saltonstall. During his two terms he led the fight against President Nixon's controversial Supreme Court nominations of Judge Clement Haynesworth, Jr., and Judge G. Harrold Carswell. Brooke was the first senator to call for President Nixon's resignation during the Watergate scandal. Brooke was defeated in 1978 by Paul Tsongas.

CHAPTER 8

Howard University and Georgia Avenue

Howard University Campus

The need for educational facilities for black refugees and freedmen after the Civil War was crucial. The Missionary Society of the First Congregational Church of Washington proposed establishment of an institution of higher learning. In March 1867, President Andrew Johnson signed legislation creating Howard University which opened in 1869 offering a normal or teacher education curriculum. Located on 150 acres overlooking Georgia Avenue, the University was named for General Oliver Otis Howard, a proponent of the university and Commissioner of the Freedmen's Bureau.

Howard is open to all students of any color, although it has traditionally had an overwhelmingly black student body. As the oldest black college in America, it is considered the most prestigious.

Founders' Library

With the adjoining state-of-the-art student library, Founders' Library (1929-1937) is the centerpiece of the university campus. Named in honor of the seventeen men who founded Howard University, the library occupies the site of "Old Main," the first building constructed on campus in 1867. The neo-Georgian building was designed by Albert I. Cassell, who established the Department of

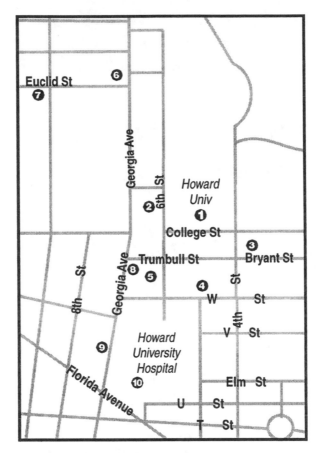

Howard University and Georgia Avenue
1. Howard University Campus
2. Site of Andrew Hilyer Residence
3. Site of John Mercer Langston Residence
4. Freedmen's Hospital
5. Site of Will Marion Cook Residence
6. Merriweather Home for Children
7. Benjamin Banneker Senior High School
8. La Savage Beauty Clinic
9. Temple of Freedom Under God, Church of God
10. Site of Griffith Stadium

Architecture, in 1921 and developed the university's 20-year building plan that envisioned the unified campus of buildings, walkways and open spaces.

The library also houses the Moorland-Spingarn Research Center, one of the world's largest collections of materials relating to the history and culture of black people in Africa, Latin America, the Caribbean and the United States. In 1873 the noted New York abolitionist Lewis Tappan gave the university his valuable collection of more than 1,600 items focusing on slavery—pamphlets, clippings and manuscripts. Through the efforts of Dean Kelly Miller, a dedicated proponent of establishing a Negro-Americana museum at Howard, Dr. Jesse E. Moorland (1863-1940) donated his remarkable private library of books on blacks in America and Africa. A Howard alumnus, Moorland left his Congregational church pastorate to become secretary and coordinator of colored activities for the national YMCA. In 1946 Howard purchased the outstanding collection of books by black authors in twenty languages which the president of the NAACP, Arthur B. Spingarn, had assembled. Howard president Mordecai W. Johnson proclaimed the Spingarn library "the most comprehensive and interesting group of books by Negroes ever collected in the world." These collections form the core of the vast holdings in the Moorland-Spingarn Research Center.

Andrew Rankin Memorial Chapel

The center of the university's religious life, Rankin Chapel stands just inside the university's main gates. The chapel was built in 1895 with funds donated by the widow of university president Jeremiah E. Rankin's brother. Mrs. Eleanor Roosevelt, President John F. Kennedy and Dr. Martin Luther King, Jr., have all addressed audiences from the chapel's pulpit. In 1930 the ground floor of Rankin Chapel served as the first home of the Howard University Gallery of Art.

Ira Aldridge Theater

Home of the Howard Players, the Ira Aldridge Theater is named for famed 19th century black American Shakespearean actor Ira Aldridge (1807?-1867). Aldridge was educated at the African Free School in New York City and in 1824 emigrated to Europe to make his way as an actor. His stage debut a year later at the Royal Coburg, London, brought him great acclaim. He traveled the British provinces, where his work earned the commendation of Edmund Kean, one of the outstanding actors of that time. In 1833 Aldridge performed the role of Othello at the Theatre Royal, Covent Garden, to enthusiastic reviews. His repertoire included Macbeth, Shylock, Lear and Richard II. Aldridge's greatest critical success, however, occurred on the Continent; a Viennese critic wrote that he was "without doubt the greatest actor that has ever been seen in Europe." Aldridge never returned to this country and died while on tour in Poland in 1867.

The James V. Herring Gallery of Art and the fine arts department occupy the building behind the theater.

Cramton Auditorium

One of the most beautiful concert halls in Washington at the time of its opening in 1961, Cramton Auditorium is named in honor of Congressman C.C. Cramton who was a loyal supporter of the university in the U.S. House of Representatives. The hall seats 1,500 people. Both the Aldridge Theater and Cramton Auditorium were designed by Washington's well-known black architect, Hilyard Robinson (1899-1986).

The *Freedmen's Column* (1989), a sculpture by internationally-known African American sculptor Richard Hunt, is located in the plaza in front of the Auditorium.

Howard Hall

The only remaining original university structure, Howard Hall was built in 1869 as the on-campus residence of General O.O. Howard, founder of the university. The Second Empire Style red brick home is now crowded between newer buildings, but during the 19th century it dominated the hilltop overlooking the city of Washington. A handsome piazza and terraced landscaping to Georgia Avenue surrounded the 16-room mansion. When General Howard, the last surviving Union Civil War general, died in 1909, the university purchased the residence. It served as the Conservatory of Music for many years; today it houses administrative offices. Howard Hall was designated a National Historic Landmark in 1974.

Charles Drew Building

(Howard University's Men's Dormitory)

This dormitory was named in 1960 for Washington native, Dr. Charles Drew, the world-renown physician who developed the method of preserving blood through the use of blood plasma.

A gifted surgeon and scientist, inspiring teacher and speaker, Drew grew up in modest circumstances in Foggy Bottom. After graduating from Dunbar High School, Drew was an outstanding student and athlete at Amherst College before becoming a professor and head of surgery at Howard University Medical School in the 1930s. Drew's research in blood groupings demonstrated that plasma—the liquid part of blood—could be stored much longer than whole blood. The blood banks which he developed were used to aid the wounded British soldiers at Dunkirk in 1940. A year later he headed the American Red Cross Blood Bank in New York City that collected blood for the U.S. armed forces in Europe. In 1942 Drew became head of the Department of Surgery at Howard and chief surgeon at Freedmen's Hospital.

Dr. Drew died in 1950 at the age of 45 in an automobile accident.

Miner Teachers College Building

Originally called the Miner Normal School, Miner Teachers College produced most of the black elementary school teachers employed by the Washington public school system from the early 1870s through World War II. Attending Miner, according to one graduate, was "a privilege...it was a place of intellectual stimulation. It left a mark on everybody who came through."

This unique black educational institution was founded in 1851 by Myrtilla Miner, a frail, middle-aged white teacher from upstate New York. From an impoverished family, Miner experienced difficulties completing her own education. After teaching in numerous schools, she went to Mississippi where she became committed to teaching young slaves. However, since education for slaves was nonexistent in the South before the Civil War, she moved to Washington, and established the Colored Girls School against the advice of Frederick Douglass who described her plan as "reckless, almost to the point of madness." The school prepared young women, drawn from the "best black families in the city," to teach and "to enlighten and raise the intellectual level of their people."

With privately solicited funds, including a $1,000 contribution from the proceeds of Harriet Beecher Stowe's recently published book, *Uncle Tom's Cabin*,

Myrtilla Miner purchased property in the block bounded by 19th and 20th Streets and N and O Streets, NW. Local opposition to her endeavor was fierce. Threats of personal violence and attempts to vandalize the school buildings simply fueled her missionary zeal and uncompromising attitude. She remarked to a friend that she lived in the schoolhouse alone, "unprotected except by God, [with] the rowdies occasionally stoning the house at evening and nightly retiring in expectation that the house would be fired before morning."

Because Miner spent an inordinate amount of time traveling to raise funds for the school, her fragile health deteriorated rapidly, forcing her to close the school on the eve of the Civil War in 1860. The institution had offered, according to historian Constance Green, "a better education than that available to most white children" in the city. "It is a hard thing that I have done," Myrtilla Miner wrote before she died at the age of 49. "I often feel I have not the strength necessary to perform well the part assigned; but if I can prepare the way for some nobler spirit, my duty will be done."

Although the school was inactive, Congress voted to incorporate and reopen it in 1863. During the postwar period the school was located at the Sumner School and then in its own building at 17th and Church Streets, NW, in 1872. Under the strong leadership of Dr. Lucy Moten from 1883 to 1920, Miner Normal School thrived and admission was highly competitive.

In the 1930s Congress reorganized the city's two teacher training institutions—Wilson for white students and Miner for blacks—into four-year colleges. Both were eventually merged with other institutions to become the University for the District of Columbia (UDC).

Site of Andrew Hilyer Residence

2352 6th Street, NW

Now part of the Howard University campus, 2352 6th Street, NW, was the residence of Union League founder Andrew Hilyer who believed that black survival depended on the ability of American blacks to gain economic security. In 1892 he founded the League to promote economic cooperation among the city's black citizens and to help eradicate adverse conditions and obstacles confronting blacks in business. Urging blacks to patronize establishments that hired black employees, the League published a directory of these businesses in 1892, 1894 and 1901.

Site of John Mercer Langston Residence

Hillside Cottage
4th and Bryant Street, NW

John Mercer Langston (1829-1897) became dean of Howard University Law School two years after the institution was founded in 1867. He remained at the law school until his appointment as counsel general and resident minister to Haiti in 1885. His role in Howard's formative years was substantial.

Langston was the third son of a freed woman and her former white master; both died when he was four years old. An heir to a portion of his father's estate, Langston received the finest schooling available, where he became the fifth black graduate at Oberlin College in 1849. Three years later he became the first black theological graduate in America, and after studying law in the offices of an antislavery advocate he is thought to be the first black attorney west of the Appalachian Mountains. This extraordinary young man was also the first black to be elected to public office when he became township clerk in Brownhelm, Ohio, in 1855.

During the Civil War, Langston recruited three regiments of black soldiers for the Union Army in Ohio and Massachusetts. He served as an inspector general for the Freedmen's Bureau after the war before being selected by the Howard University Board of Trustees to head the newly created law department. Classes for the two-year law program were held from five to nine in the evening so that students could maintain their daytime jobs. The University experienced a stormy and difficult period in 1872 when the Freedmen's Bureau closed. Charges of conflict of interest and mismanagement centered on General O.O. Howard, the University's third president and the head of the Freedmen's Bureau. With the University on the verge of financial collapse in 1873, Langston was appointed "vice-president and acting president." The Board of Trustees drew up a slate of five nominations for the presidency; the names of three black candidates including Frederick Douglass and Langston were submitted. The subsequent appointment of a white president was a bitter blow to Langston who denounced the selection in the New York *Evening Post* ten days later.

Howard University would not be led by a black president until the appointment of Mordecai W. Johnson in 1926.

After his service in Haiti, Langston won a hard-fought campaign for a seat in the U.S. House of Representatives from Petersburg, Virginia. Although praised as "the most scholarly Negro" in the U.S. Congress, Langston was defeated for reelection. The poet, Langston Hughes, his namesake, was his great-nephew. He died in 1897 in Washington, D.C. and is buried in Woodlawn Cemetery in Southeast Washington.

Freedmen's Hospital

520 W Street, NW

For more than 108 years Freedmen's Hospital served the black community of the nation's capital. Beginning in 1862 as a collection of tents and barracks in an open field at 12th and R Streets, NW, Freedmen's was remembered almost a century later as "a medical Harlem—attracting the very best."

As black contraband and refugees streamed into Washington, D.C., during the Civil War, health problems in an already unsanitary city increased. Medical aid, funded by the Freedmen's Bureau, was organized at a contraband camp in the Shaw neighborhood. The hospital administered to nearly 23,000 patients during its first year. The purpose of the hospital, according to the chief surgeon's 1874 report, was to provide "for the care and support of a large number of Aged, Blind, and Idiotic and permanently disabled freed men who were dependent for their existence upon the bounty of the Government."

A remarkable physician, Dr. Alexander T. Augusta, the first black superintendent at Freedmen's, guided the hospital through its early years. From its beginning Freedmen's staff was integrated; generally the hospital was administered by a black superintendent with white department heads. Skilled surgeon Dr. Daniel Hale Williams (1858-1931), founder of Chicago's Provident Hospital, the first racially integrated hospital in America, led Freedmen's with great energy from 1894 to 1898. Dr. Dan, as he was known to all, performed the first sucessful heart surgery in 1893. After Williams surgically repaired a stab wound in the heart of a patient, a Chicago newspaper headlined the achievement: "Sewed up the Human Heart." Williams' reorganization of Freedmen's included establishing a nursing school, instituting sterilization of medical equipment, and creating the hospital's first ambulance, a horse-drawn covered wagon.

After moving in 1908 into the half-million dollar building on W Street with its long, open wards, the hospital prospered under the 35-year directorship of Dr. William A. Warfield, Jr., and its prestige grew from its association with the world-famous Dr. Charles Drew (1905-1950), one of the pioneers in the development of blood plasma.

Ultimately, during the last years of segregation and into the 1960s, the outdated hospital—black Washington's primary medical facility—deteriorated dramatically from the burdens of overcrowding. Soon after Senator Hubert Humphrey called Freedmen's "a national disgrace," the Department of Health, Education and Welfare took over the administration of the hospital, making it the only federally-operated community hospital in the nation. In 1975, on the 108th anniversary of its founding, Freedmen's became the Howard University Hospital, located on Georgia Avenue in an enormous new building complex on the site of the old Griffith Stadium. Today the original building is used for administrative offices by Howard University.

Site of Will Marion Cook Residence

2232 6th Street, NW

An accomplished violinist, composer and musical director, Will Marion Cook (1869-1944) grew up in the home of his father John H. Cook, a graduate of Howard University's first law class (1871), dean of the law school, and one of the first black lawyers to practice in Washington. A violin prodigy Will Cook studied classical music at Oberlin College and at the National Conservatory of Music in New York where he was a classmate of the great singer, composer and arranger of Negro spirituals, Harry Burleigh.

In 1898 Cook collaborated on the musical hit *Clorindy, The Origin of the Cake-Walk* with Washington poet Paul Laurence Dunbar, who wrote the lyrics. The syncopated music of the folk opera was a forerunner of modern jazz. A 14-year-old chorine in the show, Washingtonian Abbie Mitchell, later married Cook and went on to Broadway stardom as a singer in black musical productions. Their son Mercer became a Howard University professor.

In 1902 Cook's musical *In Dahomey* opened in London and played for nearly a year. Its run included a command performance for King Edward VII. *In Abyssinia* opened at New York's Majestic Theater in 1903 and later at Convention Hall in Washington. These two productions and Cook's *Bandana Land* made stars of the comic acting team of Bert Williams and George Walker whose strutting cakewalk became the rage of New York society.

In 1905 Cook organized one of the first jazz bands in the country called The Memphis Students. Seven years later he conducted the 125-piece Clef Club orchestra at Carnegie Hall. Washingtonians James Reese Europe and Ford Dabney were members of that famous band. Alain Locke declared that remarkable recital the "formal coming-out party" for black music in America.

James Weldon Johnson called Cook "the most original genius among all Negro musicians" when he died in 1944. University expansion has engulfed the site of his former childhood home.

Georgia Avenue

Originally known as the 7th Street Pike when it opened as a toll road in 1829 and later as Brightwood Avenue (1890s), Georgia Avenue has always been one of Washington's main thoroughfares to Baltimore and points north.

The 2700 block of Georgia Avenue was the neighborhood village center. Here, shops such as Stein's Market, Garrett's Deli, Spearman's Barbershop, the Guild, and the University Grill catered to residents and students alike. At 2714 Georgia Avenue students gathered on the front porch of the Victorian family home of Harry Robinson, dean of the School of Architecture. Robinson's father was born in 1908 on what is now the 50-yard line of the Howard football stadium.

Across the street ice cream sodas were dished up at Doc Jones' drugstore in the Howard Manor. Still operating today at another location, the famous Cardozo Sisters Hairdressers turned out well-coiffed Washington women in the same building. Three granddaughters of educator Francis Cardozo, Sr. operated this venerable beauty salon for decades. Today Georgia Avenue, with its "eternal aroma of fried food and barbecue sauce," has changed according to one longtime resident. "What we used to call greasy spoons are now the fast food restaurants." And the smells of the block-long Wonder Bread bakery that linked this section of Georgia Avenue to the past are gone as the bakery closed in the 1990s.

The Merriweather Home for Children

733 Euclid Street, NW

This stately brick duplex was the site of the Congressionally-chartered Merriweather Home for Children, the only institution for the foster care of black children in the city. When contraband refugees were transferred from the city compound to Arlington Heights in 1862, nearly fifty abandoned children were found in the empty camp. A group of local women lobbied Congress to create the National Association for the Relief of Destitute Colored Women and Children. A building constructed in Georgetown with funds from the Freedmen's Bureau was used until the Euclid Street homes were purchased in the 1890s and named for Mrs. Mary Merriweather, a former president of the Board of Directors.

Mrs. Elizabeth Keckley, dressmaker and intimate of Mary Todd Lincoln, spent her last impoverished years as a resident of the "Home for Destitute Women and Children." In 1868 Mrs. Keckley had published a memoir, *Behind the Scenes*, about her life in the White House. The book caused a furor, particularly among

Republican Party officials who, fearing damage to the Party's reputation, attempted unsuccessfully to suppress it. Mrs. Keckley lost her seamstress patronage and was forced to enter the Home.

Benjamin Banneker High School

830 Euclid Street, NW

Founded in 1981, Banneker High School is the District's model school for academically gifted students. Approximately 300 applicants who must be honor roll students and have reading and math scores above grade level, compete on a city-wide basis for the 100 ninth-grade slots. These students must take a rigorous academic "prescribed curriculum" designed to include extra credits in basic courses. All 9th graders must take Latin and then three years of a modern foreign language and complete nearly 300 hours of community service.

In 1997 First Lady Hillary Rodham Clinton joined TV personality Derek McGinty as commencement speaker for the school's graduation. Every student in the class had been accepted to college. "Banneker is a powerful example of what can happen when a school sets high expectations and an entire community pulls together to help students be successful," Mrs. Clinton declared.

Banneker is named in honor of the talented black mathematician and astronomer who ably assisted Andrew Ellicott in the original survey of the District of Columbia.

Around the corner and across from Howard University at 2500 Georgia Avenue is the Banneker Recreation Center, the city's premier black outdoor recreation facility during the era of segregation. Built in 1934 Banneker had one of the few swimming pools in the city for black residents and a varied program that included track and field as well as music and dance activities and a mother's center.

Banneker, one of seven recreation facilities desegregated—declared "open"—in 1953, continues as an active center for the black community.

La Savage Beauty Clinic

2228 Georgia Avenue, NW

In 1938 a young North Carolina woman arrived in Washington "with two twins and two cans of milk." Quickly realizing that she wasn't suited to a routine government job, Grace Savage enrolled in the Madame C. J. Walker College of Beauty Culture at 1306 U Street, NW.

The Walker College was one of many such beauty schools across the country that taught the Walker System of hair care. So successful was the business originated by Madame Walker that a diploma from her college was a "passport to prosperity."

Born Sarah Breedlove Walker in 1867, Walker was widowed at the age of 20 and was forced to take in laundry to support her infant daughter. Walker claimed that the hair-growing formula that earned her a fortune was revealed to her in a dream. In 1905 she invented a hot iron that removed the tight curls in black women's hair; overnight her system of conditioning and straightening was a sensation. Her products were produced at the Walker Manufacturing Company in Indianapolis and were distributed through a network of franchised beauty salons. Within a few years Walker had a payroll of more then $200,000. When she moved to Harlem in 1914, Madame Walker was one of America's wealthiest women.

Grace Savage completed the Walker College night course and began a 40-year beauty career that "brimmed with flamboyance, flair, and a maverick's eye for the sure-shot gimmick and crowd-pleasing whoop-de-doo." The shrewd Savage opened her famous pink and black La Savage Beauty Clinic here after working for several years out of her home. Emblazoned with a sign "A Pretty Girl Is Like a Melody," her matching pink Cadillac convertible loaded with stunning Howard University coeds, was a mainstay of the annual Howard University homecoming parade. Madame La Savage, as she insisted on being called, became a wealthy woman known for her chic clothes, expensive jewelry, silver fox furs, and trademark silver hair streak.

When home permanents and the trendy Afro hair style damaged her business, La Savage turned her attention to promoting a line of cosmetics and perfumes. At the time of her death at 62 in 1981, a friend recalled that La Savage was "a lady on the go, still doin', still planning. Death wasn't on her mind."

Temple of Freedom Under God, Church of God

2030 Georgia Avenue, NW

His 1968 obituary described Elder Lightfoot Solomon Michaux (1885-1968) as a "religious leader, gospel song popularizer, showman, real estate developer, and friend of presidents." Thirty-five years earlier the Washington *Post* had asked editorially: Just who is Elder Michaux? The paper suggested that one ought simply to ask his radio fans, for the extraordinary radio evangelist "is the best-known

First Congregational Church was founded after the Civil War. The original building at 10th and G Streets, NW, was razed in 1959. (Harris & Ewing; Washingtoniana Division, D.C. Public Library)

The Washington *Bee* offices at 1109 1 Street, NW, were the home of Calvin Chase's weekly newspaper. This photo was part of the U.S. exhibition at the 1900 Paris *Exposition Universal*. (Courtesy Library of Congress)

The St. Charles Hotel at 3rd and Pennsylvania, NW, was equipped with basement cells for the housing of slaves. Later renamed the Capital Hotel, it was razed in 1929. (Washingtoniana Division, D.C. Public Library)

Benjamin Banneker assisted in the survey of the territory that became the nation's capital. (Moorland-Spingarn Research Center, Howard University)

Anacostia's Uniontown neighborhood, D.C.'s earliest suburb, was developed in 1854. (Copyright *Washington Post*; reprinted by permission of D.C. Public Library)

Cedar Hill was the beloved home of Frederick Douglass who became the first black resident of Anacostia in 1877. (Copyright *Washington Post*; reprinted by permission of D.C. Public Library)

Anacostia Neighborhood Museum, part of the Smithsonian Institution, was originally housed in the old Carver movie theater. (Copyright *Washington Post*; reprinted by permission of D.C. Public Library)

Woodlawn Cemetery, created in 1895, is the last surviving large black cemetery in Washington, D.C. (Copyright *Washington Post*; reprinted by permission of D.C. Public Library)

Marian Anderson sang in concert on Easter 1939 at the Lincoln Memorial; she had been refused permission to sing at the D.A.R. Constitution Hall. (Copyright Scurlock Studio, Washington, D.C.)

Charles H. Houston was called "one of the top ten advocates to appear before this court in my 35 years" by Supreme Court Justice William O. Douglas. (Courtesy Library of Congress)

James Wormley's elegant hotel was patronized by politicians and diplomats during the years after the Civil War. (Washingtoniana Division, D.C. Public Library)

The Freedmen's Savings Bank, founded during the Civil War as a banking institution for black soldiers and freedmen, was located across the street from the White House. (Moorland-Spingarn Research Center, Howard University)

The commercial corridor of 7th Street, NW, was devastated by the 1968 riots and fires. (Copyright *Washington Post*; reprinted by permission of D.C. Public Library)

Paul Laurence Dunbar (1872–1906) was America's first nationally-acclaimed black poet. He and his wife were among LeDroit Park's socially active young couples. (Courtesy Library of Congress)

Christian A. Fleetwood received the Medal of Honor awarded by Congress for valor during the Civil War. He and his wife were longtime residents of LeDroit Park. (Moorland-Spingarn Research Center, Howard University)

A horse-drawn wagon, acquired in the late 19th century, was the first ambulance of Freedmen's Hospital. (Moorland-Spingarn Research Center, Howard University)

Hillside Cottage was the home of John Mercer Langston, first dean of Howard University law school and later the university's "acting president." (Courtesy Library of Congress)

The Old Main Building (1867) was the first structure built at Howard University. Razed in 1940, it was replaced by the Founders' Library. (Courtesy Library of Congress)

Elder Lightfoot Michaux baptized over 150 converts in a canvas pool at Griffith Stadium's home plate in 1941 before a throng of 25,000. (Copyright *Washington Post*; reprinted by permission of D.C. Public Library)

Black professional baseball teams shared Griffith Stadium (7th Street and Florida Avenue, NW) during the late 1930s and 1940s. Here Pittsburgh's Homestead Grays play the New York Black Yankees. (Copyright Scurlock Studio, Washington, D.C.)

Thanksgiving Day football games in Griffith Stadium between Howard and Lincoln Universities often drew crowds of nearly 25,000. (Moorland-Spingarn Research Center, Howard University)

Resurrection City camped on the Mall when the Reverend Ralph Abernathy led the Poor People's Campaign to demand jobs and programs to eradicate poverty in May 1968. (Copyright *Washington Post*; reprinted by permission of D.C. Public Library)

The Howard Theater (1910) was a mecca to black musical and comedy genius and the oldest legitimate theater for blacks in D.C. (Courtesy Library of Congress)

HOWARD THEATRE WASHINGTON, D.C. THE MOST BEAUTIFUL

Blanche Kelso Bruce, one of Washington's leading citizens, was the first black to serve a full term in the U.S. Senate. (Courtesy Library of Congress)

Terra cotta bas relief sculpture enhanced the facade of Langston Terrace (1938), a federal housing project designed by Hilyard Robinson. (Copyright *Washington Post*; reprinted by permission of D.C. Public Library)

The original Dunbar High School (1916) was one of the premier black high schools in the country during the first half of the century. (Courtesy Library of Congress)

First Lady Eleanor Roosevelt and Alonzo Aden, co-owner of the Barnett-Aden Gallery, admired a painting by Candido Portinari in 1944. (Moorland-Spingarn Research Center, Howard University)

Dr. Anna J. Cooper's residence at 2nd and T Streets, NW, was also the home of the Frelinghuysen University during the 1920s, 30s and 40s. (Copyright Scurlock Studio, Washington D.C.)

Mrs. Mary Church Terrell and the Reverend W.H. Jernagin purchased tickets at a mid-town theater in 1953 after litigating the desegregation of Washington's theaters and restaurants. (Moorland-Spingarn Research Center, Howard University)

Archibald and Francis Grimké, major figures in the Washington black community's struggle for equal rights for over fifty years, entered Lincoln University (Pennsylvania) in 1866. (Moorland Spingarn Research Center, Howard University)

The corner of 14th and U Streets, NW, was the focal point of Washington's 1968 rioting following the assassination of Martin Luther King, Jr. (1969 photo Copyright *Washington Post*; reprinted by permission of D.C. Public Library)

Duke Ellington, one of America's greatest composers and jazz musicians, was raised at 1212 T Street, NW, in the Shaw neighborhood. (Moorland-Spingarn Research Center, Howard University)

Prominent Washington citizens and President Lescot of Haiti (second from left) attend Lincoln-Douglass dinner at MuSoLit Club, 1327 R Street, NW. (Copyright Scurlock Studio, Washington, D.C.)

Bishop "Sweet Daddy" Grace resided at 11 Logan Circle. Known for his flamboyant appearance, Grace founded the United House of Prayer for All People Church. (Copyright *Washington Post*; reprinted by permission of D.C. Public Library)

Protesters picket "Gone with the Wind" in front of manager Rufus Byars at U Street's Lincoln Theater in 1939. (Copyright Scurlock Studio, Washington, D.C.)

St. Augustine's, Washington's oldest black Catholic congregation, was originally located on a site occupied by the *Washington Post* building today. (Courtesy Library of Congress)

colored man in the United States today ... better known than hundreds of his race who are making their marks as college presidents, scientists, bankers and so on down the list...."

As a young man, Michaux (pronounced *mishaw*) was a fish peddler in his native Virginia. He received his "calling," he said, while delivering a load of fish to Camp Lee, much as the biblical Apostle Peter had.

Shortly after founding the home church, The Temple of Freedom Under God, Church of God, in a Georgia Avenue storefront in 1928 (later temples were established in Philadelphia, Harlem, Baltimore, and Newport News), Michaux originated his popular "Happy Am I" radio program on station WJSV in Alexandria, Virginia. Those call letters stood for Willingly Jesus Suffered Victory (over the grave).

One of Washington's most colorful citizens, Michaux became a national institution when CBS picked up his Saturday morning broadcast, opening with the familiar lines "God furnishes the spirit, Elder Michaux and his church, the enthusiasm, and the Columbia Broadcasting System, the service ... Well, Glory!"

An equally committed evangelist, Michaux's wife Mary organized "Purity Clubs" for the Temple's young women, urging them to "Be a Peach Out of Reach."

With a voice of "pure velvet," the "Colored Billy Sunday" mixed religion with a strong social conscience. His community-based programs exhibited a deep concern for the poor and helpless of Washington. In 1933 the church took over the operation of a foundering lunchroom run by the MacFaddon Foundation, a chain that served nutritious or natural food. Renamed the Happy News Cafe, the restaurant became a symbol of hope during the Depression, offering lunches for a penny a plate. Street beggars, sent by local citizens to the Cafe, were put to work selling the *Happy News* newspaper in exchange for two meal tickets. Although sustaining significant financial losses, the Cafe served 250,000 meals in 1934. Other temple projects included the repair of a dilapidated building on the southwest corner of 7th and T Streets to house nearly forty families, victims of eviction.

A devoted supporter of President Roosevelt and his New Deal program for economic recovery, Michaux called him "the Lord's chosen instrument." In a symbolic gesture, Elder Michaux nominated Eleanor Roosevelt for the vice-presidency at the 1940 Democratic Convention. Michaux is given major credit for reopening the Industrial Bank at 11th and U Streets after Roosevelt's 1933 bank moratorium. The evangelist negotiated an agreement whereby depositors were paid 35 percent of their deposits.

Michaux's world-famous Cross Choir was a pioneer in the gospel song movement. While singing, the 156 white-robed choir members moved in formation to create three different crosses, the WJVS radio call letters, and a crown.

But the high-powered showmanship of Elder Michaux was most evident in his gigantic baptisms and religious pageants. Prior to moving these elaborate baptisms to Griffith Stadium in 1938, Michaux hired excursion boats to take hundreds of baptismal candidates down the Potomac River. At Griffith Stadium enormous canvas tanks were installed with water provided by the D.C. Fire Department or, on at least one occasion, with water imported from the River Jordan! In 1948 the first mass baptism ever televised featured the immersion of 100 converts before the great Cross Choir.

Other staged extravaganzas at the stadium—with klieg lights, floating microphones, and the hosannas of thousands of spectators—included conversions, mass marriages, and healing ceremonies. Those healed often dashed the baseball bases on a "homerun for Jesus." During the "Ascension of Christ" tableau, a figure emerged from a 40- by 50-foot cloud attached to the left field lighting tower and descended as the so-called "dead" rose in the center field bleachers while the chorus sang "There'll Be Shouting on the Hills of Glory."

The present modern church building was built in 1958 at a cost of $335,000, the most expensive black church at that time. Ten years after the church's completion Elder Lightfoot Solomon Michaux died at the age of 83.

Site of Griffith Stadium

(Howard University Hospital)
2041 Georgia Avenue, NW

Griffith Stadium, a Washington institution for half a century, was located on the site of the Howard University Hospital complex. Player, manager, president, general manager and owner of the city's baseball team, Washington businessman Clark Griffith built the stadium that bore his name in 1914. When the Washington Senators beat the mighty New York Giants in 1924 and won the World Series, the black *Daily American* ran a jubilant headline: "Long Live King Baseball, The Only Monarch Who Recognizes No Color Line." Although blacks could not play in baseball's major leagues, the stadium grandstand was one of the few integrated public places in the District of Columbia.

Local black baseball teams—the Washington Elite Giants, the LeDroit Tigers and the Washington Pilots—and teams from the National Negro League competed in the stadium during the 1920s and 1930s. After 1937 the black Homestead Grays played at Griffith when the Washington Senators were out of town and in Pittsburgh when the Pirates were on the road. Frequently the Negro League teams were a greater draw than the Senators. One summer day in 1942, for instance, the Senators pulled 3,000 fans for a day game with the Boston Red Sox and the Grays drew 28,000 for their night game.

Two of the most anticipated social events each year took place at the stadium. On Thanksgiving Day the annual Lincoln-Howard (Lincoln University in Pennsylvania) football game drew crowds of nearly 25,000. And at the close of the school year in late May, the Colored Washington High School Cadet Corps' Annual Drill Competition between Armstrong and Dunbar High Schools (and later Cardozo) brought out thousands of citizens.

Griffith Stadium was the original home of the city's beloved football team, the Washington Redskins. Owner George Preston Marshall transferred his team from Boston to the nation's capital in 1937, opening before 30,000 enthusiastic new fans with "Slingin'" Sammy Baugh at quarterback. The Redskins remained an all-white football team until 1963 when they moved into the new Robert F. Kennedy Memorial Stadium, owned and operated by the U.S. Department of the Interior. Only an integrated professional football team would be permitted to use this federally-owned facility. That year the Redskins' first-round draft pick, Syracuse All-American Ernie Davis, was traded to the Cleveland Browns for Bobby Mitchell, one of the great wide receivers in football. Mitchell, still with the Redskins organization, became the first black Redskin and a member of the Football Hall of Fame and Washington's Hall of Stars.

CHAPTER 9

Shaw East: A Walking Tour

Bounded by North Capitol Street on the east, 15th Street on the west and M Street on the south, the Shaw neighborhood includes the elegant Victorian homes of the Logan Circle and Strivers' Section Historic Districts; old-timers call the neighborhood "14th and U" (after its major intersection). It gradually acquired its name, Shaw, from the local junior high school, named in honor of Colonel Robert Gould Shaw, who was mortally wounded leading a black regiment during the Civil War.

Shaw was open farmland until shortly before the Civil War, although there was some commercial activity on 7th Street. The two- and three-story brick and frame rowhouses reflect its working- and middle-class origins. The Shaw neighborhood contains the city's most influential black churches and "You" Street, as it was often spelled, was the business and retail hub of the city's black community and the center of its night life, both legal and illicit. Seventh Street with its bars, poolrooms, flophouses, and storefront "shouting" churches teemed with newly arrived rural Southerners. The end of segregation in the early 1950s precipitated Shaw's steep and steady decline. Blacks went downtown for shopping and entertainment, and the neighborhood's more affluent residents moved north or to the suburbs.

Efforts to renew this neighborhood began before 1968, but gained dramatic momentum after the devastating riots ignited by the assassination of Dr. Martin Luther King, Jr. The young pastor of New Bethel Baptist Church, the Reverend Walter E. Fauntroy, founded an umbrella group of fifteen local citizen organizations, called the Model Inner City Community Organization (MICCO). According to Fauntroy, MICCO's goal was non-violent land reform. To ensure minimal displacement of poor residents, MICCO would oversee the construction of new public housing and the rehabilitation of existing buildings. Feeling that past urban renewal had resulted in Negro removal, MICCO did not want Shaw cleared for

BLACK WASHINGTON

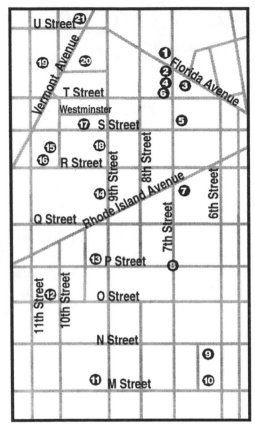

Shaw East
1. 7th Street
2. Site of "Red Summer" of 1919 Riots
3. Howard Theater
4. Site of Waxie Maxie's
5. S.H. Dudley Theater
6. Southern Aid Society/ Dunbar Theater Building
7. Asbury Dwellings/Old Shaw Junior High School
8. 7th Street between Rhode Island Avenue and M Streets, NW
9. First Rising Mount Zion Baptist Church
10. United House of Prayer for All People
11. Blanche Kelso Bruce Residence
12. Joseph's Club
13. Shiloh Baptist Church
14. Phillis Wheatley YWCA
15. Edward Cooper Residence
16. Lincoln Temple United Church of Christ
17. Daniel Murray Residence
18. New Bethel Baptist Church
19. The Evans-Tibbs Residence
20. Grimké Elementary School
21. Black Fashion Museum

new housing. A symbol of years of neglect and decay, the key to Shaw's revival was a new junior high school to replace the deteriorating Shaw Junior High at 9th and Rhode Island Avenue. The recent completion of the new District of Columbia government office building at 14th and U Streets and the opening of Metro's Green Line are further evidence of the neighborhood's revitalization.

7th Street, NW

Seventh Street, from the Mall to the Maryland line, was, from the very early years of young Washington town, an important route connecting the products of Tidewater Virginia and the docks in southwest Washington to the northern Maryland farms. A wasteland until after the Civil War, the 7th Street Pike was a natural for commercial development. Originally populated with foreign-born whites, by the early 20th century blacks settled along the pike and in several of the area's infamous alleys. Among the most populous and notorious of these alleys was Goat Alley, between 4th, 5th, and New York Avenue. By 1900 only one white family remained among the 400 dwellers in the alley.

Seventh Street was as vital and bustling as its neighbor, U Street, but in a seamier, louder way. Ninth Street divided the genteel and prosperous to the west and the poorer residents to the east. Seventh Street of the 1920s was where the action was, especially for the southern rural immigrants who flocked to the north for jobs during World War I and during the Depression. Noise and music from the traffic, poolrooms, storefront churches, barbershops, liquor stores, flophouses, and lunch counters mingled together, punctuated by the enormous audiences crowding into the matinees and evening performances at the Howard Theater around the corner on T Street. After the curtain fell on Howard stage shows, the beat went on well into the night at the Dreamland, Cafe De Luxe, Club Harlem, Old Rose Social Club and Off-Beat at 7th and T Streets. At the Southern Dining Room (1616 7th Street), Mrs. Hettie Gross served down-home Southern cooking on a workingman's budget. The Salvation Army was well located on the P Street corner.

Pool halls were second only to barbershops as important community gathering places. Ranging from poorly lit holes-in-the-wall to swanky emporiums, pool halls were of "more significance than the newspaper, since events and matters of interest are discussed here that never reach the press." Certain billiard parlors had more status than others and here, Howard University sociologist William H. Jones observed, "men gained their social standing through the force of their personalities, mental superiority or skill." The Silver Slipper (No. 1721), the Tierney (No. 1317), the Ideal (No. 1235), the Subway (No. 1817), and the Southern Aid

BLACK WASHINGTON

Building Billiard Parlor at T Street were just a few pool halls along 7th Street. Everyone came to the poolroom next door to the Howard Theater; Duke Ellington reminisced, "Frank Holliday's was a great place," filled with high school kids, hustlers, and gamblers.

The Washington Pool Checker Association at 1810 7th Street is a link with the past on contemporary 7th Street. Its clubhouse, a former photography studio before the riots of 1968, is a home away from home for checker players. "You can come in," according to William (Dog) Green, the club's septuagenarian president, "stay as long as you want, fix some food, wash your clothes, spend the night." The players are ranked—Mr. Green is top master—and no cheating is allowed. "By and large you find that your checker player is a pretty decent guy anyhow," according to Dog Green.

Seventh Street greatly influenced two of the great talents of the Harlem Renaissance period: Jean Toomer and Langston Hughes. Each lived in Washington for a short period in the early 1920s before moving to New York.

Jean Toomer was the grandson of P.B.S. Pinchback, the first black elected governor of a state (Louisiana). In 1893 Pinchback moved to Washington, D.C. where he practiced law, served as a U.S. Marshall, and entertained lavishly as a member of black elite society. Toomer published his novel *Cane* in 1923 while living at 1341 U Street with his grandfather Pinchback. Called by a critic "the most impressive product of the Negro Renaissance," *Cane* was a mixture of sketches and poems, several of which were set among the lowlife of 7th Street.

The nephew of Howard University's former acting president and dean of the law school John Mercer Langston, Langston Hughes joined his mother in Washington in 1924. While waiting for a scholarship to Lincoln University in Pennsylvania, Hughes worked for Carter Woodson's *Journal of Negro History* for several months and as a busboy at the Wardman Park Hotel on Connecticut Avenue. (Although *Crisis* magazine published his eloquent "The Negro Speaks of Rivers" in 1921, he was actually discovered four years later by Vachel Lindsay who called him the "busboy poet.") Despite living in middle-class black Washington, Hughes spent his free time on 7th Street, absorbing its sights, sounds and dialects. He was openly critical of Southern genteel traditions and the conventional lifestyles of Washington's black middle class, ridiculing what he called their "cultured, colored society." Two of his works describe aspects of 7th Street culture. One, *The Weary Blues*, integrated the rhythms of jazz and swing from its cabarets into literature. The other, *Fine Clothes for the Jew* (1927), derived its title from the profusion of pawn shops on the street.

The "Red Summer" of 1919 Riots

7th and U Streets, NW

Washington was one of 25 cities throughout the nation that experienced fierce racial rioting during the infamous Summer of 1919. Black soldiers returned home to what they hoped was a New America after fighting during World War I "to keep the world safe for democracy." They were greeted, instead, with hostility and continuing discrimination. Across the country an atmosphere of racial tension grew; there were seventy lynchings in the year after the War and several victims were soldiers in uniform.

In Washington, rigid Jim Crow regulations and the extension of segregation as official policy during the Wilson Administration depressed Washington's black community. Tensions increased as white servicemen roamed the city. A wave of street crimes and attacks on women by blacks received prominent attention in the city's newspaper creating a climate of fear and rumor. Any incident involving blacks and whites was sensationalized. "Negroes Attack Girl ... White Men Vainly Pursue," bannered a *Post* headline. The related story added that sailors and marines had begun to hunt for suspects in Southwest Washington.

When street fighting broke out, one newspaper announced "a mobilization of every available serviceman stationed in or near Washington" for the purpose of a clean-up. However, the response was also black mobilization. Citizens manned barricades; war veterans lined New Jersey Avenue and U Street; and alley dweller and merchant alike armed themselves to defend their neighborhoods. White mobs entering black areas were met with armed resistance, including several clashes at 7th and T Streets.

Black resistance, the occupation of federal troops, and a heavy rainstorm brought a halt to five days of street violence which left 30 dead and scores injured. To NAACP founder W.E.B. DuBois, the bold resistance of blacks in this urban riot signaled an end to submissiveness. In ringing terms, he declared:

> *We are cowards and jackasses if now that that war is over, we do not marshall every ounce of our brain and brawn to fight a sterner, longer, more unbending battle against the forces of hell in our own land.*

> *We return.*
> *We return from fighting.*
> *We return fighting.*
> *Make way for democracy!*

Howard Theater

624 T Street, NW

The Howard Theater, the first legitimate theater for blacks in the nation, ranked just behind Harlem's Apollo Theater as a shrine to black musical and comedy genius. The corner of 7th and T Streets had it all—from Shakespeare to "Shuffle Along," from big bands to be-bop, from rhythm and blues to rock.

One older resident remembered, "Speaking about Paris gowns, they could not be compared to those that were seen at the Howard Theater on New Year's night."

Now the tacky and deteriorating condition of the Howard's T Street facade makes it difficult to imagine how grand the Italian Renaissance (with touches of Spanish baroque and Beaux-Arts) building was 40 years ago.

Washington's black society was out in force when the Howard opened on August 22, 1910. An elegant arcade lined with statues and palm trees led to the lobby. The Washington *Bee* proclaimed the following morning that the Howard was "First class in every appointment, a theater for the people." Washington's Abbie Mitchell, who later won fame on Broadway introducing "Summertime" in Gershwin's *Porgy and Bess*, was a featured performer that evening. The following year Washington's James Reese Europe brought his 60-piece Clef Club orchestra from New York to play the Howard. Reese's band was the first black band to perform on a major Broadway theater stage.

The 1200-seat baroque auditorium with a balcony and eight boxes was equally rich in its decoration, and behind the stage the theater provided dressing rooms for 100 performers.

For nearly 20 years the theater booked road shows, vaudeville acts, circuses, and musicals. In 1929 after the stock market crash, the Howard closed its doors, leasing its space to Elder Lightfoot Solomon Michaux for evangelical revivals.

In 1931 the property was sold to the Stiefel brothers who imported Shepard Allen from Philadelphia to manage the theater. Shep Allen became "D.C.'s Dean of Show Biz," booking only the best black entertainment. The triumphant return of Duke Ellington to his hometown marked the gala reopening of the Howard on September 29, 1931. Armstrong High School student Billy Eckstein, who later headlined the Howard, caught every new show that came to the theater, but especially remembered the Duke. He was the "biggest inspiration we had ... the epitome of what we wanted to be. He gave us some dignity. When the Duke came, that was it—the Howard was our Broadway." Pianist Billy Taylor, another Washington native, recalled that the tux-clad Ellington band members were the only other people he had ever seen dressed like that except in *Life* magazine." In

1934 crowds waiting to see the Mills brothers were so enormous that the police had to convert T Street to a one-way street.

Washington-born Pearl Bailey received her show business break as a member of the high-stepping Howardettes chorus line. In 1942 she was a featured vocalist with the Sunset Regal Orchestra. As a child, Bailey had been enchanted by Ethel Waters' performance at the Howard: "This was who I wanted to be, what I wanted to do." Other artists such as Eckstein, Ella Fitzgerald, and Bill Kenny of the Ink Spots received their start at the Howard's weekly amateur nights. Shep Allen booked athletic heroes—Joe Louis, Jackie Robinson, and Sugar Ray Robinson—as stand-up comics and song-and-dance men.

Whites not only played the Howard—the big bands of Woody Herman, Stan Kenton, Artie Shaw and Louis Prima— but also often made up nearly a quarter of the audience. Even in rigidly segregated Washington, whites "would sit next to you in a minute to see all those great acts," recalled singer Mary Jefferson, who grew up behind the theater.

The Howard usually played four shows a day—at 2, 5, 7:30 and 10 p.m. with a midnight performance on Saturdays. Sometimes movies that occasionally ran between shows were dropped to cram in additional performances. The Lionel Hampton band, for example, played as many as eight times in one day. The great vocalists of the 1940s appeared during the war years with equally famous bands—Sarah Vaughn with Billy Eckstein, Dinah Washington with Lionel Hampton, and Lena Horne with Noble Sisle's orchestra. Al Hibbler headlined with the Duke in 1950. Fans sat mesmerized watching the dance artistry of John Bubbles, Bojangles Robinson and Sammy Davis, Jr., and the Will Masten Trio. They came in droves to catch the humor of Moms Mabley, Redd Foxx, and Pigmeat Markham, or the sartorial shenanigans of Peg Leg Bates, who changed the color of his wooden leg with each new outfit. Charlie Parker and other guests made the Howard the "Met of Jazz"; and Little Bits and Yo-Yo, Butterbeans and Susie, Chuck and Chuckles, and Spic and Span, black entertainers who never became popular in the white-dominated music world, played to full houses.

The Howard was the oldest of a string of black theaters, known as the "chitlin' circuit," that included the Apollo in Harlem, Baltimore's Royal, and the Uptown and Regal in Philadelphia and Chicago. Times and music changed in the mid-1950s. A new sound and beat now drew kids to see James Brown, Johnny Mathis, the Marvelettes, Patti La Belle and the Bluebelles, Martha and the Vandellas, and Gladys Knight and the Pips. "We arrived early so we usually got front-row seats for the live performances," remembered one of those youngsters. "That enabled us to catch the neckties and other memorabilia tossed by great artists like Smokey Robinson and the Miracles and Diana Ross and the Supremes."

The Supremes performed their first theater date at the Howard in October 1962. A teenager who grew up on rock 'n roll in the '60s talked of hanging out at Cecelia's Lounge across the street to catch a glimpse of the stars. "Somebody always yelled 'Get out of here!' because they didn't allow kids in. But I did see Marvin Gaye, Martha Reeves and one of the Temps in there one day."

Desegregation (black audiences and performers could now attend and play the downtown theaters), television, the deterioration of the neighborhood and the rise in crime, and spiraling costs of live performances brought about the Howard's demise. The theater was never touched by fire during the 1968 riots, but rather by time. The doors closed in 1970. Briefly reopened by a group of investors five years later, the theater's run lasted only two weeks. Today the boarded-up theater stands forlornly, a symbol of times gone by.

Site of Waxie Maxie's

1836 7th Street, NW

Waxie Maxie's, one of the great 7th Street landmarks, was burned to the ground during the 1968 riots. During the longest "jam session" in D.C. history, the Quality Music Shop opened with great fanfare in 1938. The police were needed to control the crowd that turned out for the celebration that ran continuously from 3 p.m. on Friday to 3 a.m. Saturday. Waxie Maxie was host for three live storefront radio broadcasts featuring personal appearances by Sarah Vaughn, Margaret Whiting, and drummer Buddy Rich. Washington's record king was Max Silverman, a successful jukebox entrepreneur, who opened Quality as an outlet for the used records from his business. Silverman's chain grew to nearly 25 record stores in the Washington area.

During the war years, Ahmet Ertegun, the young son of the Turkish ambassador, frequented Maxie's 7th Street flagship store, listening to and learning the music of rhythm and blues. When his parents left Washington, Ertegun stayed, practically "living at my store," according to Silverman. In 1947 Ertegun founded Atlantic Records, recording his own composition (under the pseudonym Nugeter), "Don't You Know I Love You." Sung by a local group, the Clovers, the record's success put the Atlantic label on the charts. For years Atlantic was synonymous with the best black artists including Erroll Garner, Mabel Mercer, Leadbelly, and Al Hibbler.

The riots of 1968 ravaged 7th Street. Many small businesses, such as Rich's Shoe store, relocated. Manhattan Auto, formerly at 7th and R Streets, left for the suburbs and the Crazy Baby Barber Shop never returned. "The riots took a neighborhood that was not the best," said the former head of the city's urban renewal agency, "and really made it a lot worse."

On the eleventh day of his presidency, Richard Nixon astonished Washington by touring gutted 7th Street. Standing at 7th and T Streets, the president raised high hopes by announcing a multi-million dollar rebuilding plan. However, very little of the pledged help ever materialized.

Some businesses did return after the riots. Irving Abraham was the first to completely rebuild his Log Cabin Liquor Store (1748 7th) in the riot corridor. Interestingly, the number of black-owned liquor stores in Shaw more than doubled—from 12 to 27—in the months following the riots. Previously, liquor store owners had refused to sell their businesses to blacks. But after April 1968 many white owners wanted out.

S.H. Dudley

1818 7th Street, NW

In 1911 Sherman H. Dudley, known as S.H. from an early age because he resented whites addressing blacks by their first names, formed Dudley Theatrical Enterprize at this address. With several other African Americans, Dudley purchased and leased three theaters in Virginia and one in Washington, creating his own vaudeville circuit. His young agent was actor Leigh Whipper, brother of Ionia Whipper, who lived nearby on Florida Avenue.

S.H. Dudley was one of America's most popular performers and comedians. Beginning in "medicine shows" where he sang and danced to attract an audience for patent medicine salesmen, Dudley then worked the minstrel circuit, working finally with the great Negro minstrel Billy Kersands, the star of Rusco and Hollands Georgia Minstrels. In the 1890s Sherman attained national fame when he created an act with a mule known as Dudley and His Mule.

At the turn of the century several talented black showmen began writing black shows that were serious efforts to depict authentic black life. Breaking the pattern of the minstrel caricature and the stereotypical image of the Negro, S.H. Dudley's *Smart Set* (1896) followed the examples of *Creole Show* by Sam T. Jack in 1890 and Bob Cole's *A Trip to Coontown*. Washingtonians Will Marion Cook and Paul Laurence Dunbar collaborated on *Clorindy, The Origin of the Cakewalk* during this period. After World War I, Dudley produced black shows including his own more up-to-date *Smart Set*, booking them into black theaters.

S.H. Dudley, entertainer, pioneer in black theater ownership, and a creator of shows that altered the image and substance of black musicals, died in 1940.

Southern Aid Society—Dunbar Theater Building

1901-1903 7th Street, NW

This early multi-use building was built just after World War I and served the needs of the black community in segregated Washington. Having just finished the elegant Whitelaw Hotel on 13th Street, black architect Isaiah Hatton designed this building in 1919. A movie theater occupied the ground floor, a pool hall was located in the basement, and among several office spaces on the upper floors were the headquarters of the Southern Aid Society, the oldest black life insurance company in the nation.

Asbury Dwellings

Old Shaw Junior High School
7th and Rhode Island Avenue, NW

This splendid brick and limestone Romanesque building is the former Shaw Junior High School named for Colonel Robert Gould Shaw, the white commander of the first black regiment in the Union Army during the Civil War.

Originally built in 1902 as Technical High School for white students (later named McKinley Technical), the school building had fallen into disrepair by 1928. In spite of the school's condition, the school board decided to transfer it to the black system, renaming it Shaw. Although a report on the District's schools after World War II noted that "no amount of rehabilitation could correct its faults," the school continued to be used.

Often called "Shameful Shaw," civil rights organizations called for a student boycott to protest the decrepit and overcrowded conditions in 1965. A year later, MICCO, the Model Inner City Community Organization, submitted urban renewal proposals for the neighborhood that included a new junior high school as the plan's cornerstone. After great community and governmental debate over its location—at one time the school was slated to occupy the John F. Kennedy playground near 7th and O Streets—the present $13 million community school was built in 1977. Spread over 7.5 acres, the new Shaw has open-space classrooms and contains an Olympic-size swimming pool.

At that time the community and Asbury United Methodist Church sponsored a $6.4 million rehabilitation project to convert the old Shaw school building to housing for elderly and handicapped citizens. The largest adaptive reuse of a

District school building to date, Asbury Dwellings contains about 150 units with kitchens.

Across the street is the Watha T. Daniel Public Library built in 1975 and named in honor of the first chairman of the D.C. Model Cities Commission.

7th Street between Rhode Island Avenue and M Street, NW

Although much of the outside financial help and support promised in the years following the 1968 riots failed to materialize, the neighborhood seized the initiative to provide new housing for the poor and displaced in Shaw. "Our shame is not the rage that ravaged the street," noted one community developer, "but the fact that the vacant lots and boarded-up buildings are still there."

The Lincoln Westmoreland Apartment building (1730 7th Street) was a unique joint development project undertaken by the black Lincoln Temple United Church of Christ and the white Westmoreland Congregational Church located in Bethesda, Maryland. Begun in 1971, the ten-story apartment building was the vanguard of Shaw renewal.

Other church-sponsored housing complexes followed the Lincoln-Westmoreland experiment. Built in 1973, the Gibson Plaza high-rise apartment building (1301 7th Street) for low-to-moderate income families was the joint venture of the nearby First Rising Mount Zion Baptist Church and MICCO, the community development organization. Sponsored by the Immaculate Conception Church, the 263-unit housing project at 7th and N Street (1330 7th Street) was the largest residential development in the District in the early 1970s. Financed by the Bible Way Church of Our Lord Jesus Christ World Wide and completed in 1975, the Golden Rule complex (901 New Jersey Avenue) added 85 townhouses and 40 garden apartments to the neighborhood.

Closed after the 1968 riots, the O Street Market at 7th Street has been restored. When "Boss" Shepherd, a member of the Board of Public Works, ordered the closing of the Northern Liberties Market at 5th and K Street, NW, in the 1870s for health code violations, the displaced dealers were allocated space at 7th and O. Built in 1888, the O Street Market is one of Washington's three remaining 19th century market buildings.

The nearby $1.5 million Giant Food Store is part of the O Street Market urban renewal project. The return of a major food chain establishment symbolized the neighborhood's continued revitalization.

Across the street is the John F. Kennedy Adventure Playground, a community park project undertaken after the 1968 riots.

First Rising Mount Zion Baptist Church

1240 6th Street, NW

In Washington's earliest years this was the site of the poorhouse and its burying grounds. The fanciful Victorian-style First Rising Mount Zion Baptist Church building dates from the 1880s. Beginning in a storefront at 1215 8th Street with sixty-five members, today First Rising Baptist church has over 1,000 parishioners. The congregation was led for many years by the Reverend Ernest Gibson, who, before his retirement, served as the executive director of the Council of Churches in the District of Columbia.

United House of Prayer for All People

601 M Street, NW

Dominated by the Spanish-style church topped with a golden dome, the complex of buildings on M Street between 6th and 7th Streets is the national headquarters of the United House of Prayer for All People. From a singing and shouting Harlem congregation in the 1920s, Charles M. "Sweet Daddy" Grace had built a 3-million-member religious empire spread over fourteen states by 1960.

Believed to be a Portuguese immigrant, Grace arrived in Harlem from North Carolina and purchased Father Divine's 54-room mansion, Main Heaven, which he promptly painted in his trademark colors—red, white, and blue. Nothing about "Sweet Daddy" Grace was understated. His long fingernails, painted in the three colors, and flowing mane of hair added to his flamboyant appearance. His fortune, estimated in the millions, provided a colorful lifestyle that included a fleet of cars and an 85-room Los Angeles mansion.

Bishop Grace always said that he never knew what his message from the pulpit would be because he "preached by appointment with God." While presses ran, printing his church magazine, pressmen prayed so that the poor and infirm could wrap themselves in the magazine pages for warmth and healing. His baptisms were legendary. Not to be outdone by Elder Michaux, who imported water from the River Jordan, Grace baptized 208 converts in the middle of M Street with water provided by special D.C. fire company equipment before a crowd of 15,000.

In his later years Bishop Grace spent as much time in court as in the pulpit. A would-be wife, claiming Bishop Grace had married her in the 1920s, sued him in 1957. At one point during the sensational trial, the judge ordered Grace to cease accepting money pressed on him by fans and citizens in the court corridors. The bishop and the Internal Revenue Service were continually at odds. In 1956 the IRS estimated Grace's earnings at $4,081,511; Grace had reported a net income of $408. The government settled his tax case for $1.9 million. At the time of his death in 1961, court records revealed that Grace had enormous real estate holdings including a Central Park West apartment building in New York City.

Following Bishop Grace's death (he was buried in a glass coffin and delivered his own pre-recorded eulogy), a power struggle between church factions ensued. Bishop Walter "Sweet Daddy" McCullough, who had begun his association with the House of Prayer as Grace's chauffeur, led the successful faction. Under McCullough's stewardship the church construction program has included the McCullough Seminary day care centers, retirement homes for the elderly, parsonages, and McCullough Plaza. Members of the House of Prayer, also known in the neighborhood as "God's White House," strictly adhere to the church's teachings of tithing, the prohibition of tobacco and alcohol, and marriage only within the church.

Blanche Kelso Bruce Residence

909 M Street, NW

This row of Victorian houses at the northern edge of downtown development stands as a lone survivor of a once-elegant neighborhood. The beautiful Second Empire-style home in the middle of the block was the Washington residence of Blanche Kelso Bruce (1841-1898), the first black to serve a full term in the U.S. Senate (from 1875 to 1881). The 33-year-old Bruce succeeded the nation's first black senator, Hiram R. Revels, who completed the unfinished term of Mississippi Senator Jefferson Davis.

Born a slave in Virginia, Bruce was tutored by his master. When war broke out he escaped to Missouri and then Kansas, founding the first elementary school for blacks in that state. After completing a two-year course of study at Ohio's Oberlin College, Bruce became a successful planter in Mississippi where he was active in Republican Party politics. As a delegate to the 1880 Republican Convention, Bruce actually received eight votes for the vice-presidential nomination.

On his U.S. Senate swearing-in day in 1876, Bruce's fellow white Mississippi senator refused to escort him, as was customary, to the well of the Senate to take the oath of office. New York Senator Roscoe Conkling stepped into the aisle and walked with him. To honor his lifelong friend, B.K. Bruce named his only son Roscoe Conkling Bruce.

In the U.S. Senate, Bruce was an outspoken advocate of civil rights legislation for Asians and American Indians. Upon completion of his Senate term, Bruce became registrar of the U.S. Treasury Department under President Garfield. His was the first signature by a black to appear on U.S. currency.

After Bruce's marriage to schoolteacher Josephine Wilson, the Bruces became one of the most popular couples in Washington. In 1883 the German-American *Sentinel* newspaper reported a patronizing view of black-white relations in Washington. "The colored people ... enjoy all the social and political rights that laws can give them, without protest and without annoyance.... But the color line is rigidly drawn in what is known as society.... In official circles Mr. Bruce is received in courtesy and as a political equal, but there the line is drawn."

Called "one of the most remarkable [careers] in history" by the New York *Times*, Bruce served as Recorder of Deeds for the District of Columbia, a presidential appointment, and on the boards of trustees for the D.C. public school system and Howard University. B.K. Bruce's death at the age of 58 was termed a "calamity to the whole Negro race" by the Washington *Post*. To the 3,000 persons—congressmen, Republican Party officials, scholars, clergy, and businessmen—who attended his funeral at Metropolitan AME Church, Bruce was truly a most successful public figure. His home is a National Historic Landmark.

Joseph's Club

1425 11th Street, NW

In 1971 Richard "Slim" Joseph, a retired trucker, founded the Indians Athletic Baseball Club. Part of the twelve-team Continental League, the home-grown Indians continue a popular inner-city tradition—sandlot baseball. "You have guys working two jobs," according to the team manager, "but still they come out and practice two times a week, then play sometimes three games in a row on the weekend."

The team's clubhouse, "Joseph's Club," a makeshift storefront, opened over 30 years ago as a working-class social center.

Shiloh Baptist Church

1500 9th Street, NW

Prior to their attack on Fredericksburg, Virginia, in 1862, the commander of the Union forces offered free transportation and protection to all black residents who wanted to evacuate the city before the hostilities. Among those who fled Fredericksburg were 300 black members of the Shiloh Baptist Church.

Upon their arrival in Washington, twenty-one members worshipped in various homes including the back bedroom of Henry Peyton's Georgetown residence. After purchasing a horse stable in the 1600 block of L Street, NW, the congregation organized one of the first black Sunday schools in the District. A council of white Baptist ministers from local churches recognized Shiloh Baptist and ordained one of the original founders, William J. Walter, as pastor of the church.

The congregation purchased the present church building in 1924; the following year a disgruntled member of the previous church set fire to the sanctuary and organ. Services were held at the Howard Theater during the months of repairs.

The 800-seat auditorium is brimming on Sunday; those who come late are forced to listen to the service and Shiloh's ten choirs from the basement. In 1982 the church dedicated its enormous $5.5 million Family-Life Center. A nonprofit multi-use facility designed by architect and Howard University professor Robert Nash, the center has saunas, restaurants, bowling alleys, and racquetball courts. The Family Life Center represents Shiloh's belief that inner-city residents need the same recreational facilities to combat the stresses of daily life that the suburbs offer.

Phillis Wheatley YWCA

901 Rhode Island Avenue, NW

In the spring of 1905 members of the Book Lovers Club, under the leadership of Mrs. Rosetta Lawson, met at the Berean Baptist Church (now the Star of Bethlehem Church) at 11th and V Streets, NW, to consider the establishment of a Young Women's Christian Association chapter to provide urgently needed shelter for young black women seeking work in Washington. The Colored YWCA became the oldest YW group in the metropolitan area.

From its original headquarters in the Miner Institution Building (not to be confused with the Miner School Building) in Southwest, the Y moved to a larger ten-room townhouse in LeDroit Park (429 T Street, NW) before acquiring this building with funds from the War Work Council.

Resisting efforts in the early 1920s by the national Y organization to retain the designation "Colored" in their title, the membership instead changed the name to the Phillis Wheatley YWCA.

Phillis Wheatley was indeed a symbol of black achievement. Brought to Boston in 1761 on the slave ship *Senegal*, Wheatley was purchased by well-to-do Bostonians, Susannah and John Wheatley. She was taught to read and write and in 1773 she published the first book of poetry by a black woman, *Poems on Various Subjects, Religious and Moral.* This volume certainly challenged the prevailing notions that blacks lacked the intellectual and moral characteristics to be equal to whites. Her influence was, no doubt, an element in many New Englanders becoming abolitionist activists, who often used her poems in their literature and speeches. Phillis Wheatley received her freedom from the Wheatleys in 1773, five years before their death. She lost her inheritance from them during an unhappy marriage to a free black man. In 1784 she died destitute in her early 30s within hours of the death of her only surviving child.

During World War I, the Phillis Wheatley Y provided travelers' aid to black southern Americans migrating to urban jobs in Washington and the North. And again during World War II, the Y was the location for the USO for black soldiers who were denied entrance at the white USO center.

The building is currently vacant and its future is uncertain.

Edward Elder Cooper Residence

1706 10th Street, NW

Described as "the best all-around newspaperman the colored race has yet produced," Edward E. Cooper (1862-1908) gained a reputation as the father of illustrated African American journalism. Beginning his career with the *Indianapolis World* and then the *Indianapolis Freeman* (1888), the first pictorial newspaper published by a black journalist, Cooper moved to Washington in 1893. Here he founded *The Colored American*, a classy 16-page weekly which was the major competition for Calvin Chase's *Washington Bee*. However, the paper consistently lost money and ceased publication in 1904. Four years later Edward Elder Cooper died at his 10th Street home, an impoverished and broken man.

Lincoln Temple United Church of Christ

1701 11th Street, NW

Church Sunday schools frequently provided the only schooling that many black children received during the first half of the 19th century. Independent of white supervision and controlled by blacks, "sabbath schools" became extremely popular.

In 1863 the Freedman's Bureau established the Wisewell Barracks Sabbath School at 7th and O Streets for the children of Civil War refugees in the nearby contraband camps; the school was often protected by soldiers because many whites were opposed to educating black children. The American Missionary Association bought the site at the corner of 9th and R Streets to build a two-story frame school, known as the Lincoln Mission, for "the use and education of the colored children of Washington"; active community outreach and night school programs continued for ten years. In 1880 ten black members of the First Congregational Church formed a religious club in the mission building which within a year became Lincoln Memorial Church. Under the pastorate of the Reverend Sterling N. Brown, father of Washington's famous poet, Lincoln took its present name in 1901 when it merged with the Park Temple Congregational Church.

In 1911 Lincoln Temple celebrated the 100th anniversary of the birth of Harriet Beecher Stowe. Stowe's grandson delivered the principal oration and the grandson of Frederick Douglass, a well-known music teacher, presented a violin recital. Lincoln Temple member Mary Church Terrell authored a pamphlet commemorating the work of Mrs. Stowe.

Daniel Murray Residence

934 S Street, NW

Daniel Murray (1852- 1925), a prominent employee of the Library of Congress for more than fifty-two years, was a national authority on books by and about blacks.

During the Civil War, Baltimore native Murray joined his brother who supervised the U.S. Senate restaurant in Washington. He began his career at the Library of Congress in 1871, advancing to Assistant Librarian ten years later. In 1899 Murray was asked to organize the Negro literature exhibit for the American pavilion at the 1900 Paris Exposition. This project led him to devote the rest of his life to researching a listing of every book and pamphlet written by persons of African ancestry; by about 1910 he had cataloged over 12,000 titles by black authors. Murray personally collected nearly 1500 volumes which he donated to the Library. This material became the Library's "Colored Author Collection."

In 1910 he also began an even more ambitious project—to compile a six-volume encyclopedia that would survey black progress and achievements from "antiquity to the 20th century." Murray was concerned that most sources of black history were written by whites. "What would have been the nature of history for Greek posterity ... if it had been written exclusively by Romans?" Because he had difficulty finding a publisher, Murray attempted to sign up subscribers. Upon his death in 1925 his book-length manuscript and his more than 250,000 index cards were left to the State Historical Society in Madison, Wisconsin.

New Bethel Baptist Church

9th and S Streets, NW

The Reverend Walter E. Fauntroy has pastored the New Bethel Baptist Church since his graduation from Yale Divinity School in 1959. A native Washingtonian and Dunbar High School Alumnus, Fauntroy was the District's first elected representative (nonvoting) in the U.S. Congress in 100 years. A civil rights activist in the 1960s, Fauntroy was appointed director of the Washington Bureau of the Southern Christian Leadership Conference by Dr. Martin Luther King, Jr. In 1963 he was the D.C. coordinator for the historic March on Washington for Jobs and Freedom and directed the Selma-to-Montgomery march two years later.

New Bethel was organized by seven members from the Salem Baptist Church in 1902. Its first home was on 15th Street between Euclid and Fuller Streets, then it moved to a church building at 9th and S Streets, NW. That deteriorating structure was demolished in 1977, making way for New Bethel. This contemporary church represents to the congregation and the neighborhood the fulfillment of a dream—a new church in a new community.

The Evans-Tibbs Residence

1910 Vermont Street, NW

The small house at the corner of Vermont Avenue and 10th Street was the home of Lillian Evans Tibbs (1890-1967), the first internationally acclaimed black professional opera singer, who performed under the name Madame Evanti. This cream-colored rowhouse, built in 1894, was purchased by the Evans family ten years later when nearby U Street was becoming the commercial and cultural center of black Washington. Designated a historic landmark in 1985, the house retains the neoclassical columns and moldings added in an extensive 1933 interior remodeling.

Lillian Tibbs began singing at the age of four and was well-known for her vocal and piano concerts during her teens. Following in the footsteps of her father, Charles Wilson Evans, longtime principal of Armstrong Technical High School, she taught kindergarten in the public schools after earning her degree in music from Howard University. Lillian Evans married Professor Roy W. Tibbs, her vocal instructor. Evans continued her studies in Europe, and in 1925 made her professional operatic debut in Nice, France, singing Delides' *Lakme*. At that time she took her stage name, Madame Evanti, a contraction of her two surnames, at the suggestion, it is said, of her friend, novelist Jessie Fauset.

Her career took her to the opera stages of Europe, Africa and the Caribbean. But in 1932, she was not allowed to enter Germany because of her race. She returned home and suffered further disappointment when she was refused an audition at the Metropolitan Opera in New York City for the same reason. She made her Washington concert debut in 1933 and performed at the White House two years later.

After a goodwill trip to South America with Maestro Toscanini and the NBC Orchestra, Madame Evanti helped found the Negro National Opera Company. In 1943, she sang the role of Violetta in *La Traviata* at Washington's Watergate Theater.

After her death in 1967 her Harvard-educated grandson, Thurlow Tibbs, Jr., lived in the home as the director of the Evans-Tibbs Collection, one of the most important private collections of African American art ever assembled. Begun with paintings left to him by Mme. Evanti, the entire collection of hundreds of works included paintings by black master Henry O. Tanner and Harlem Renaissance artist Aaron Douglas. Recent works by nationally-known Betye Saar, Washington painter Lois Mailou Jones, and photographs by Harlem's James Van Der Zee and Washingtonian Addison Scurlock were represented in the Collection as well as extensive archival material. It is said that Tibbs sold his boyhood coin collection to finance his first major purchase, a portrait of Henry O. Tanner's wife.

During the 1970s and 80s, Tibbs curated a series of exhibitions at his home with scholarly catalogs; the openings with music played on his grandmother's grand piano were splendid affairs with the Howard University crowd mixing with Washington art lovers.

In 1996, a year before his death, Thurlow Tibbs donated over 30 major paintings and photographs estimated to be worth over $1 million to the Corcoran Gallery of Art, making it a major center for the study of African American art.

Grimké Elementary School

1923 Vermont Avenue, NW

Now the administrative offices for the Department of Corrections and D.C. Fire Department, Grimké Elementary School bears the name of an illustrious family. Brothers Archibald and Francis and their aunts, Sarah and Angeline, were all major figures in the struggle for freedom and equal rights in this country. The extraordinary story of the Grimké brothers began in antebellum Charleston, South Carolina. Both were the publicly acknowledged sons of wealthy planter and sometime lawyer Henry Grimké and his slave, Nancy Weston. Grimké left instructions in his will that his slave sons should be freed at the time of his death. However, Francis was enslaved by his white half-brother, Montague, for a short time. During the last year of the war, both brothers were legally freed and received a secondary education at a school run by the wife of Charleston's mayor. She was so impressed by their abilities that in 1866 she arranged for their admission to Pennsylvania's Lincoln University.

Two years later, their remarkable academic achievements came to the attention of Henry Grimké's sisters, the famous antislavery advocates, Sarah Moore and Angeline Weld. Angeline corresponded with the young men and learned that they were indeed her nephews. At their Lincoln University commencement, in a moving and courageous gesture, Angeline Grimké Weld publicly acknowledged the brothers as her relatives. With their meager finances, both sisters supported the further education of the brothers.

Graduated from Princeton Theological Seminary in 1878, Francis, as pastor of one of the black community's most powerful churches, became a tireless fighter against racial injustice in the nation's capital. (See 15th Street Presbyterian Church.)

Archibald's career spanned the era from slavery to the Great Depression. The second black to graduate from Harvard Law School, Grimké practiced law in Boston, served as consul to the Dominican Republic (1894-1898), and was active in Republican Party politics. He broke with the party after President Theodore Roosevelt's unwarranted dismissal of black soldiers during the infamous Brownsville, Texas, incident of 1906. (See Former Home of Senator Foraker.) The radicalized Grimké became a follower of W.E.B. DuBois and a member of the original Committee of Forty (1909), forerunner of the National Association for the Advancement of Colored People.

In 1905 Archibald Grimké, a widower, moved to Washington with his daughter Angeline, who became a well-known poet and respected teacher at Dunbar High School. Grimké served as president of the American Negro Academy (1903-1916), contributing numerous pamphlets and articles addressing racial questions of the time. As head of the Washington branch of the NAACP, Grimké was a vigorous opponent of President Woodrow Wilson's racial policies. In recognition of his efforts on behalf of black rights, he received the coveted Spingarn medal in 1919. After his retirement at 75 in 1925, Archibald Grimké died at home on February 25, 1930.

Black Fashion Museum

2007 Vermont Avenue, NW

In 1988 Harlem's Black Fashion Museum opened a mobile mini-museum in Washington, D.C., circulating exhibits to schools, churches and civic organizations. Joyce Alexander Bailey, the Executive Director, located the museum permanently at the Vermont Avenue site in 1994.

Founded in 1979 by Ms. Bailey's mother, Lois K. Alexander, the Black Fashion Museum was created to dispel the persistent view that black designers were only recently working during the past twenty years. In its inaugural exhibition, "Contributions of Blacks to Fashion: 1865-1965," Mrs. Alexander highlighted the work of former slave and Washingtonian, Elizabeth Keckley, who designed the inaugural gown of Mary Todd Lincoln while working at the White House.

Besides spotlighting the achievements of blacks in the fashion industry, the museum has created a permanent collection that includes clothing sewn by anonymous slaves, the works of Anne Lowe who designed the dress of Jacqueline Bouvier for her wedding to Senator John F. Kennedy, a dress made by Rosa Parks, the "Mother of the Civil Rights Movement," costumes from Broadway musicals such as "Eubie," "The Wiz," and "Bubbling Brown Sugar," and clothes by well-known contemporary designers Geoffrey Holder and the late Patrick Kelly.

When the New York museum on 126th Street closed in 1996, the Vermont Avenue brownstone became the Black Fashion Museum headquarters. It is open by appointment.

CHAPTER 10

Shaw West: A Walking Tour

14th and U Streets, NW

With the exception of 1600 Pennsylvania Avenue, 14th and U Streets may be the most well-known address in Washington. While U Street was "the black Connecticut Avenue" and 7th Street was the "soul" street bustling with Southern rural immigrants, 14th Street was one of the main streets of black America, comparable to 125th Street in Harlem and 103rd Street in Watts. However, by the late 1950s and 1960s this intersection was synonymous with crime and drug dealing.

Fourteenth Street, north of U Street, was a 20-block-long shopping strip. Beyda's Women's Wear, Maxsi's Men's and Boy's, Murray's Fine Shoes, and Mitchell's Sports Shop were among the stores that catered to a black clientele until the disastrous riots of 1968 that nearly wiped out the length of 14th Street. Lower 14th Street, from U Street south to M Street, had its share of landmark establishments. Among them was the studio of Washington's premier black photographer, Daniel Freeman, who guaranteed a true likeness for $5 and up. He opened his studio downtown in 1885, and moved to 1516 14th Street at the turn of the century. The Union League directory described him as a "natural born artist" and even noted that his photographic scenery "is from his own brush." In 1895 Freeman designed and installed the Washington exhibit in the Negro Building at the Atlanta Exposition.

Originally a shoe store, Richard Ware's business at 1832 14th Street evolved into the city's first black-owned department store. Ware's Department Store became a thriving business after its opening in 1915.

Billiard parlors such as the Penny Saving Club at No. 1917 and the Combine at No. 1731 thrived during the 1920s. Dr. T.A. (Pastor Theresa) David, founder of the 1,000-seat Free Evangelistic Church at the corner of 14th and T, held forth

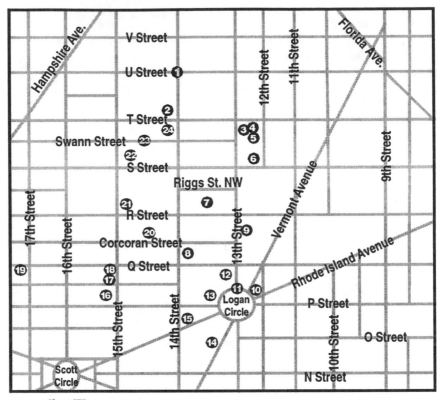

Shaw West

1. 14th and U Streets, NW
2. T Street Post Office
3. Whitelaw Hotel
4. Edward "Duke" Ellington Residence
5. Anthony Bowen YMCA
6. The Thurgood Marshall Center for Service and Heritage
7. MuSoLit Club
8. John Wesley African Methodist Episcopal Zion Church
9. Site of Camp Barker
10. Smith-Mason Gallery
11. Logan Circle
12. 11 Logan Circle
13. 8 Logan Circle
14. Mary McLeod Bethune Council House National Historic Site
15. The Association for the Study of Afro-American Life and History
16. St. Luke's Episcopal Church
17. Alma W. Thomas Residence
18. Patterson Residence
19. Site of Syphax Family Residence
20. 1400 block of Corcoran Street
21. 15th Street Presbyterian Church
22. Georgia Douglas Johnson Residence
23. 1400 block of Swann Street
24. Francis L. Cardozo Residence

to the faithful. Teenagers flocked to the popular Board and McGuire's drugstore for sodas at 1912½ 14th Street.

Fancy automobile showrooms gave these blocks of 14th Street their identity. However, no black businessman owned a dealership until Richard J. Wood purchased an Oldsmobile franchise in 1969.

The red brick building at 1901 14th Street (now home to Arena's Living Stage) began as a grand billiard parlor and bowling alley in 1907. It was converted to a Chevrolet showroom during the heyday of Automobile Row. In 1937 the building was the exhibition hall for the National Memorial to the Progress of the Negro Race in America. In 1940 it became a restaurant and, shortly thereafter, the legendary Club Bali, one of the city's premier jazz clubs. Louis Armstrong, Billie Holiday, and Charlie Ventura played the Bali, which advertised "The Best Food and Entertainment" in town.

By the 1950s 14th Street was a Southern rural workingman's street. Clubs such as the Dixie Bell and chicken wing carry-outs flourished. During the civil rights struggles of the 1960s, Martin Luther King, Jr., established his Washington headquarters for the Poor People's Campaign in a deteriorating building just south of the corner of 14th and T.

Shortly after 7 p.m. on Thursday, April 4, 1968, the rage and anger of the ghetto erupted with the news of Dr. King's assassination in Memphis. Notorious for tension and trouble, this inner-city intersection became the rallying point. Looting of the Brookland Hardware store and other local businesses was followed after midnight by rampaging fires. Just past noon the next day the Washington police chief received an ominous message: "It's starting up again, and it looks bad." That night Washington burned on 14th Street, 7th Street, and on H Street, NE, from 3rd Street to Bladensburg Road. After three days of serious rioting and twelve days of occupation by federal troops, the city and the Shaw neighborhood counted its staggering losses. Twelve citizens had died, nearly 1,200 were injured, and property losses ran into the tens of millions. Prior to the rioting, businesses on 14th Street grossed between $75 and $100 million. By 1970 the corridor had lost nearly ninety commercial establishments; business receipts totaled less than $4 million.

The following decade was bleak. Promises of funds from the city and the federal government to rebuild the area never materialized. However, in 1986 the large District Office Building opened at the corner of 14th and U, an optimistic step toward the revitalization of the community.

Today small theater companies are sprouting along 14th Street and the area is quickly gaining the reputation as Washington's fringe theater district. Joining the

Source, Studio, and Woolly Mammoth Theaters, Arena Stage's Living Theater purchased 1901 14th Street in 1984.

T Street Post Office

1409 T Street, NW

The "Tea Street" postal station was a unique response to segregation. Denied window assignments at the main post office next to Union Station, black postal workers confronted the local postal union. The resolution was the establishment of the T Street Post Office, staffed entirely by blacks. Opened in September 1940, the station became one of the most successful in the District of Columbia, compiling the largest volume of postal savings in the city by 1951.

Whitelaw Hotel

1839 13th Street, NW

Completed in 1913, the Whitelaw Hotel was the city's only first-class hotel and apartment building for black visitors and residents. Though some still hold to the legend that the hotel was named for the "white laws" that segregated all places of public accommodation in the nation's capital, the hotel was actually named after its builder, successful black entrepreneur John Whitelaw Lewis. Founder of the Industrial Bank in 1913, Lewis was an ardent advocate of African Americans becoming economically self-sufficient. Designed by black architect Isaiah T. Hatton, the exterior is in the Italianate style, while the interior features Beaux-Arts designs and treatments typical of that era.

It was known as the "Embassy" to its out-of-town visitors, including boxer Joe Louis, scientist George Washington Carver and entertainers performing at the Howard Theater such as Cab Calloway, Louis Armstrong, and Earl "Fatha" Hines. The stately gray brick hotel was also the scene of elegant dances and debutante balls with "... ladies in their beautiful sequined and beaded gowns and the men in their formal wear ..." The Non Pareils, a social club, held their annual dances at the Whitelaw for many years.

During the Depression the Whitelaw became an apartment hotel for low-income families. By the late 1960s the hotel was an abandoned building frequented only by vagrants and junkies, reflecting the community's deterioration. In 1977 the building was closed by city inspectors for more than 350 code violations. The hotel was recently restored as an apartment building, providing 35 one-to-three bedroom units for middle and low income residents and it is a major element in the rejuvenation of the Shaw neighborhood.

Edward "Duke" Ellington Residence

1212 T Street, NW

While U Street was the vibrant core of commercial activity, T Street was the main residential street for Shaw's respectable and hard-working middle class. Physicians, businessmen, government clerks and professionals lived in the stately T Street rowhouses. The street's most famous citizen, one of America's greatest composers, Duke Ellington, grew up at No. 1212.

Even as a teenager, Edward Kennedy Ellington was known for his impeccable dress, fastidious manners, and sophisticated demeanor. Thus, his nickname "Duke." His father, an imposing figure with an aristocratic bearing, worked as a butler and caterer before becoming a blueprint technician at the Navy Department. "Uncle Ed," as he was called by everyone in the neighborhood, had the "speech of a Southern planter and the ability to strut even when sitting down."

Although the Duke was born in 1899 at the home of his grandparents at 1217 22nd Street, NW, he grew up in Shaw, taking piano lessons at the insistence of his mother who wanted to keep him off the streets. He spent his summer afternoons selling ice cream at nearby Griffith Stadium; Duke's passion for baseball rivaled that for the piano. In high school, Ellington won an NAACP poster contest and a scholarship to Pratt Institute in New York city to study art. However, he left Armstrong High School before graduation to study piano with his T Street neighbor Henry Grant, the music teacher at M Street High School.

While working as a soda jerk after school, Ellington composed his first piece, "Soda Fountain Rag," and sat in with local bands playing the Poodle Dog Cafe near U Street and Florida Avenue. His first gig with his own band, "Duke's Serenaders," was at True Reformers Hall, a popular dance spot during World War I. Married at 20, the brief union produced his only child, Mercer, who became an accomplished trumpeter and the road manager for his father's band.

By 1920 Ellington's "Washingtonians" was one of the leading society bands in the city. However, their future was in Harlem. The band, with Arthur Whetzel on trumpet, drummer Sonny Greer, Otto Hardwicke on saxophone, and Barney Rigard on clarinet, left for the big time in 1923. The Duke hit paydirt five years later when his almost full-size swing band, with the additions of Joe "Tricky Sam" Nanton, Bubber Miley and the great Harry Carney, won a permanent job at the Cotton Club. From that point the "man who made the Twentieth Century swing" belonged to the world; he returned triumphantly to his native Washington to reopen the Howard Theater in 1931.

Great musicians—Cootie Williams, Johnny Hodges on alto sax, and singer Ivie Anderson—were added to the growing band in the 1930s, and Ellington wrote special music for their talents and instruments. The Duke was a prolific and masterful arranger as well as a composer of more than 6,000 works, including a series of sacred pieces and such American classics as "Satin Doll," "Solitude," "Mood Indigo," "Do Nothin' til You Hear from Me," and "Don't Get Around Much Anymore." He collaborated with arranger Billy Strayhorn on "Take the A Train" and "Perdido." Known to write anywhere—in taxis and buses—Ellington composed "Black and Tan Fantasy" without a piano.

In a legendary 1943 concert Ellington was the first nonclassical musician to perform at Carnegie Hall. However, the post-World War II years saw his popularity decline. But he hit his stride again when the Ellington Band wowed the Newport Jazz Festival in 1956. A new generation of Americans had discovered the Duke and his music. During his late years, Ellington traveled the world as an ambassador of good will, sharing his incomparable music.

Duke Ellington died at the age of 75 in 1974. His proud hometown renamed the Calvert Street Bridge to honor its son as "composer, performer, playwright, and international statesman of good-will." The Duke Ellington School of the Arts keeps his spirit and memory alive, educating the most artistically gifted of this city's young people.

Anthony Bowen YMCA

1816 12th Street, NW

In 1853 former slave Anthony Bowen founded the first YMCA in the world for "colored men and boys" only two years after the nation's first Y was established in Boston. Born in Prince George's County, Maryland, in 1809, Bowen was a prominent educator, religious leader, and clerk at the U.S. Patent Office. In 1845 Bowen organized the Wesley Zion Sunday School in southwest Washington and eleven years later opened a mission church on E Street, SW, which became St. Paul's AME Church, site of one of the earliest day schools for black children in the city. Constructed in the early 1870s on land donated by Bowen, a public elementary school for black pupils was named in his honor.

Before it finally located permanently on 12th Street, Washington's Colored YMCA had several homes—1609 11th Street, NW, in 1892 and later at the True Reformers Hall on U Street, NW. Construction of the new Y on 12th Street united

Washington's black community in an unprecedented fund-raising effort. To match $25,000 contributions from both John D. Rockefeller and Julius Rosenwald (the head of Sears Roebuck and Company), local residents raised more than $27,000 toward the building's $100,000 cost with President Willliam Howard Taft attending a fund-raiser at the Howard Theater for the final $15,000. On Thanksgiving Day in 1908 President Theodore Roosevelt in his cornerstone-laying address called the Y "a monument to the advancement of the city of Washington." Upon its completion in 1912, Rockefeller noted that he felt "proud to have been permitted to participate in the work," and congratulated the Y on "this notable success of the colored men in the nation's capital in demonstrating their capacity, as men, to accomplish large things."

An original Y brochure noted that every brick had been laid by a black worker. Designed by William Sidney Pittman, one of the nation's early black architects and the son-in-law of Booker T. Washington, the modern five-story headquarters had seventy-two rooms and a swimming pool often used by local churches for baptisms.

The Twelfth Street Branch, as it was called until it was renamed the Anthony Bowen YMCA in 1972, was instrumental in organizing a Community Chest Program (the precursor of the United Way Campaign) for the city and, later, in eliminating the program's discriminatory policies. The Y ran summer camps for black youth and helped the Traveler's Aid Committee maintain service at Union Station. Young men from the Y met trains hourly, directing travelers to "colored" hotels, boarding houses, restaurants, and places of "safe" entertainment.

The deteriorating Bowen Y, where Langston Hughes once stayed and Elgin Baylor played pick-up basketball, was declared unsafe by the Metropolitan Washington YMCA and closed in 1982. Outraged residents accused Y officials of neglecting Bowen and concentrating resources on the new state-of-the-art YMCA on Rhode Island Avenue. With the support of the city government and active community organizations, and its designation as a historic landmark in 1995, there is hope that the Anthony Bowen Y will be saved. It is scheduled to become the home of the Thurgood Marshall Center for Service and Heritage after renovations.

Thurgood Marshall Center for Service and Heritage

1816 12th Street, NW

The Anthony Bowen YMCA had a proud and long tradition of providing shelter and activities to black visitors and residents of the District. It served as a sports facility and community Center and provided dormitory rooms for nearby Howard University students and tourists. After the current capital campaign for the restoration of the Bowen Y is completed, this building will be the home of the Thurgood Marshall Center for Service and Heritage and will once again become the center for activities in the Shaw neighborhood.

Thurgood Marshall was born in Baltimore, Maryland, in 1908 and after graduating from Pennsylvania's Lincoln University, he entered Howard University Law School. After working for the Baltimore branch of the National Association for the Advancement of Colored People, Marshall became director of the NAACP's newly-created Legal Defense and Education Fund in 1940. His spectacular career fighting to end racial separation culminated in 1954 when he won the momentous *Brown v. Board of Education* Supreme Court case, ending the legal basis for racial segregation in America.

He was nominated to the Second Circuit Court of Appeals by President John F. Kennedy in 1961, appointed U.S. Solicitor General by President Lyndon B. Johnson in 1964 and elevated to the U.S. Supreme Court in 1967, becoming the Court's first black Justice. He served on the Court until his retirement in 1991; he died in 1993 at the age of 84.

MuSoLit Club

1327 R Street, NW

Founded in 1905 with Francis L. Cardozo, Sr., as its first president, the MuSoLit Club was a *mu*sical, *so*cial, and *li*terary society that met in this handsome rowhouse. For men only, the MuSoLit was also exclusively Republican; its annual Lincoln-Douglass birthday celebration in February was the social highlight of the year. In fact, its programs, featuring distinguished speakers, were far more political than cultural.

At the time, social clubs were legion in the city, according to Sterling Brown writing in the 1942 *WPA Guide to Washington, D.C.* Among the most prestigious were the Oldest Inhabitants Association (Colored), which fostered civic pride

146

among its membership of longtime residents, and the Columbian Education Association, a social service organization. Purely social groups such as the Bluebirds, Back Biters, Earls, Buggy Riders, Boobs, Hellions, Guardsmen, and the Bachelor-Benedicts, who presented young debutante women to society, were popular among the community's middle class. What Good Are We, founded in 1914 for Howard University students and graduates by Dr. R. Frank Jones, director of Freedmen's Hospital, was renowned for its fancy dress balls, where members danced to the music of Duke Ellington's orchestra. The Cinderellas, Girlfriends, Circallettes, Dolls, Inc., Just Us, and the Pollyannas and Saps for the younger set, were among the numerous social clubs for women. The elite Jack and Jill for the youth of the most well-to-do, and Links, Inc., a social and service club, were chapters of national organizations.

John Wesley African Methodist Episcopal Zion Church

1615 14th Street, NW

In 1860 there were 11 black churches with a membership of 3,800 in the city of Washington. Of the six Methodist, four Baptist and one Presbyterian churches, the largest was the Asbury Methodist at the corner of 11th and K Streets, NW. One of the central religious, cultural, and charitable institutions in the 19th century, the church provided schools and maintained cemeteries for the black community.

In order to form a more independent religious group, John Brent, John Ingram, and seven other blacks broke away from Asbury Methodist Episcopal in 1847 because of its "white-only" ministry. Known as the Little Society of Nine, they established John Wesley AME Zion, which moved to its present location at 14th and Corcoran Streets in 1913.

Under the leadership of its pastor, Stephen Gill Spottswood, President of the D.C. branch of the NAACP, Wesley became an important center for civil rights activities. Committees were formed at the church after World War II to work for the desegregation of the District's restaurants. The Committee on School Desegregation held its early meetings here that led to the landmark 1954 *Brown vs. Board of Education* Supreme Court decision.

A disastrous fire in 1979 almost destroyed the church building. Containing 12,000 pieces of stained glass, the Victory Skylight is the centerpiece of a five-year restoration. The skylight's designer described the wingspan of the angels in the skylight as a "unity symbol that is used throughout Africa."

Site of Camp Barker

Block of 12th and 13th Streets,
Q and R Streets, NW

During the first months of the Civil War, slaves, fleeing the fighting in the South, straggled into the nation's capital. Approximately four hundred found refuge in a group of townhouses known as Duff Green's Row on Capitol Hill (now the site of the Library of Congress) and in the homes of compassionate local residents. In March 1862 Washingtonians and humane Northerners organized the Freedmen's Relief Bureau to furnish these refugees with "clothing, temporary homes, and employment and, as far as possible, to teach them to read and write, and bring them under moral influences." As their numbers increased, the military governor for Washington established a "contraband department" with headquarters at an army barracks outside the city at 12th and O Streets to provide a more efficient system of processing the new arrivals. Slaves used by the confederacy in the war effort and captured by Union forces were considered "contraband of war" and officially free. When Duff Green's Row was converted to a military prison, the occupants were moved to Camp Barker, a tent enclave near the headquarters. This arrangement was adequate even after the number of refugees leaped from the original 400 in April 1862 to more than 4,200 in October. By the spring of 1863, more than 10,000 persons seeking asylum were living in Washington. Additional villages were established in Arlington, Virginia. However, rather than pick up stakes again to move to outlaying villages, many of the refugees refused to leave Washington, even though they had to occupy squalid slums in the downtown "Murder Bay" area and the city's overcrowded alleys.

Smith-Mason Gallery

1207 Rhode Island Avenue, NW

The four-story Victorian rowhouse around the corner from Logan Circle was home to Helen and James Mason and their unique contemporary art gallery, opened to the public in 1967. A longtime art teacher in the D.C. public schools, Helen Mason and her retired real estate executive husband were dedicated to encouraging black artists and exhibiting their work after the Barnett-Aden Gallery closed. "There was nowhere," according to Mrs. Mason, "for black artists to show except in private homes or churches or on the White House fence." In addition, the Masons exhibited the art of Africa on the third floor and conducted weekend art classes for students on the top floor.

Logan Circle

Logan Circle was saved by neglect, according to architectural critic Wolf von Eckhardt. Built during the last twenty years of the 19th century, the Victorian neighborhood is virtually unchanged. No other circle in Washington has trees that are higher than the buildings. Characterizing the multiple architectural styles as "Charles Addams Whim," von Eckhardt noted that the circle had "all the reasonableness of a Lewis Carroll limerick—internally coherent if a bit mad by normal standards."

Originally appearing on L'Enfant's plan as a triangle and one of his special places, Iowa Circle, as it was then called, did not develop until the heyday of "Boss" Alexander Shepherd's civic improvements in the 1870s. During the Civil War years the circle was an area of unkempt fields on the edge of the city where contraband and freedmen crowded into hastily erected wooden shacks. Sixty percent of the residences in this eight block area were built between 1874 and 1887, making it the most complete Victorian facade left in the city.

The neighborhood was originally white, prosperous, and solidly middle class. At the turn of the century the more wealthy Logan Circle residents moved out, many building larger mansions on Massachusetts Avenue west of Dupont Circle. Although Logan Circle lost its chic, it retained its respectability as middle-class black families moved into the neighborhood. The Circle became, together with LeDroit Park, an intellectual and social center of residential black Washington. Among its most famous residents was the boxer Jack Johnson who lived for a time just off the Circle at 13th and R Streets.

It was not until 1930 that Congress renamed Iowa Circle in honor of Civil War General John Logan. A U.S. senator from Illinois, the general is credited with originating the legislation establishing the Memorial Day holiday.

The Logan Circle area declined after World War II when the more well-to-do black residents moved either to the neighborhoods of upper 16th Street or to the suburbs. The huge mansions on the circle became boarding houses, frequently owned by absentee landlords. Whether through neglect or luck or both, the circle has somehow survived physically and has not suffered the grim fate of nearby Thomas and Scott Circles. In the early 1970s its 132 Victorian dwellings were declared a Historic District.

11 Logan Circle

In the 1950s Bishop "Sweet Daddy" Grace, founder of the United House of Prayer for All People at 6th and M Streets, lived in luxury in a 17-room mansion at 11 Logan Circle, a sharp contrast to the surrounding deterioration of his low-rent neighborhood. Grace's flamboyance is still evident in the peeling red, white and blue trim on the house's porch pillars that matched his long, striped fingernails! For years pictures of "Sweet Daddy" faded in the windows of No. 11 where he died in 1960 at the age of 78.

8 Logan Circle

Among Washington's most respected citizens, Belford V. and Judge Marjorie M. Lawson, lived at 8 Logan Circle from 1938 to 1958. Often in the forefront of landmark civil rights decisions, Belford Lawson was the lead attorney in the 1938 *New Negro Alliance v. Sanitary Grocery* case that upheld the right of blacks to use the secondary boycott. And in 1950 the University of Michigan graduate and first black varsity football player at that school was a member of the legal team that won the *Henderson v. Southern Railway Company* case, abolishing segregation in railroad dining cars.

Marjorie Lawson's career was as distinguished as that of her husband. Having served as U.S. representative to the United Nations Economic and Social Council and vice-president of the National Council of Negro Women, Mrs. Lawson was appointed District of Columbia juvenile court judge by President Kennedy.

Belford Lawson's college classmate, the forceful and colorful congressman from Harlem, Adam Clayton Powell, Jr., rented the third floor of their house during his tenure in the House of Representatives. Powell—politician, minister, and militant activist—succeeded his father in 1939 as the pastor of the influential and third oldest Baptist congregation in America, Harlem's Abyssinian Baptist Church. In 1923 the senior Powell, a graduate of Yale University Divinity School, supervised the building of the 2,000-seat Gothic and Tudor church on West 138th Street where five years later his son delivered his first sermon, "If You'd Walk a Mile for a Camel, Why Not Walk Down the Aisle for God?"

Adam Clayton Powell, Jr., was energetic, ambitious, and an effective community leader. He led fights for black jobs in local businesses, utility companies, and on the city's buses. When the Harlem Congressional District was created, Powell, the city's first black councilman, knew that it was a lifetime seat. He entered his name in all party primaries and was elected with no opposition in 1944.

His effective legislative work on the Education and Labor Committee (becoming chairman during the Kennedy presidency) was often overshadowed by his unconventional lifestyle and his running battles with the Internal Revenue Service. Charged with misuse of expense account funds and flaunting a court judgment in New York State, the House Democratic caucus ousted him from his committee chairmanship. In 1961 the House of Representatives removed Powell from his congressional seat. With the support of his Harlem constituency he not only won a special election, but was also reelected in the next regular election. The House seated him as a freshman congressman and levied a $25,000 fine. Resorting to the courts, Powell won the day and his seat. The Supreme Court ruled that because Powell had fulfilled the requirements of age and residency, Congress acted illegally in denying him the seat to which he had been duly elected.

Mary McLeod Bethune Council House National Historic Site

1318 Vermont Avenue, NW

The handsome four-story rowhouse at 1318 Vermont was the last residence of Mary McLeod Bethune, educator, civil rights activist, advisor to presidents, and advocate for women's equality. She was the most celebrated African American figure of President Roosevelt's New Deal era. In 1943 Mrs. Bethune purchased this house where she lived, worked and entertained national and international leaders, including Eleanor Roosevelt, Ralph Bunche and President V.S. Tubman of Liberia. Although this splendid Second Empire Victorian townhouse retains the original marble fireplaces, chandeliers, and heavy wood paneling of its day, most of Mrs. Bethune's memorabilia and furnishings are in her Florida residence.

Council House served as the headquarters of the National Council of Negro Women, founded by Mrs. Bethune in 1935. The museum, opened in 1979, mounts exhibitions and houses the National Archives for Black Women's History, the nation's largest collection of manuscripts relating to black women. The museum was designated a National Historic Site in 1982 and is now owned by the National Park Service.

The Association for the Study of Afro-American Life and History

1401 14th Street, NW

The Association for the Study of Afro-American Life and History was the life work of historian Carter G. Woodson (1895-1950). Prior to 1971 it had been headquartered at 1538 9th Street, NW, Woodson's residence.

Tireless in his efforts to keep the world informed about the role of blacks in American history, Woodson devoted his life to his conviction that an accurate historical record must be available so that the achievements of the race would not be forgotten or claimed by others. History, as Woodson often pointed out, had been written by whites and the "lost" black history had to be found.

In 1915 Carter Woodson founded the Association for the Study of Negro Life and History to encourage young scholars to undertake historical research, often paying for their training at the best graduate schools. A year later, he founded the *Journal of Negro History* and, in 1937, *The Negro History Bulletin* for young readers. Woodson also established his own company, the Associated Publishers, to publish the work of black authors. His concept of Negro History Week to showcase the accomplishments of black Americans became a reality in 1926. As part of the 1976 Bicentennial observance, the celebration was expanded to the month of February—Black History Month.

Born to former slaves in Virginia, Woodson worked in the coal mines of West Virginia during his teen years. After finishing high school at the age of 21, he attended Kentucky's Berea College and earned a master's degree at the University of Chicago. He continued his studies at the Sorbonne in Paris and completed his Ph.D. degree at Harvard University at the age of 37, becoming the second trained black historian in the U.S. (The first was W.E.B. DuBois.) Woodson culminated his academic career as the dean of the School of Liberal Arts at Howard University.

An obsessively private person, Woodson remained a bachelor, devoting his energies to his work. In 1950 Carter Woodson died in his living quarters on the second floor above the association offices. The Carter G. Woodson Junior High School in Anacostia is named in his honor.

St. Luke's Episcopal Church

1514 15th Street, NW

The first independent black Episcopal church in Washington, St. Luke's was established in the tradition of "breaking away" from white congregations. The church traces its roots in antebellum Washington to St. John's Episcopal Church on Lafayette Square and later to St. Mary's Episcopal Church in Foggy Bottom.

St. Luke's was the creation of the fiery orator and proponent of black solidarity, the Reverend Alexander Crummell. A native of New York, Crummell was an 1853 graduate of Queen's College at Cambridge University in England. Before returning to this country in 1873, he was a minister and teacher for several years in Liberia. After organizing the small mission church of St. Mary's on 23rd Street, NW, Crummell moved with approximately thirty-five parishioners to establish the completely independent St. Luke's in 1879.

At a 1930 church celebration an elderly church member recalled how impressed he was to meet Crummell, "a stately black man ... of royal descent. His mother and her people had been free for several generations. His father, who was the son of the King of Timanee in Africa, had been trapped by slavers, sold into slavery and brought to America."

Crummell left St. Luke's in 1895 to found and later to become the first president of the American Negro Academy. Described by the Union League directory as the "most ambitious intellectual organization of the race," the academy had a limited membership of fifty authors, scholars, and artists. Francis Grimké, Kelly Miller, and Paul Laurence Dunbar joined W.E.B. DuBois as founding members; Anna J. Cooper was the only female member. Dedicated to "the promotion of literature, science, and art, the fostering of higher education, and the publication of scholarly work...," the Academy was a 19th century think tank addressing the critical issues of the day and rising to "the defense of the Negro" against any "vicious assault."

Picturesque St. Luke's is one of the oldest remaining church buildings specifically constructed for a black congregation in the District. During his studies in England, Crummell is said to have been so impressed by William Shakespeare's parish church in Stratford that he recommended its country-Gothic style to Calvin T.S. Brent, Washington's first black architect. Built of local bluestone quarried near the Potomac River, the church was nearly complete when the first service was held on Thanksgiving Day in 1879.

Alma W. Thomas Residence

1530 15th Street, NW

The modest rowhouse with green trim was for almost seventy years the home of educator and nationally-acclaimed artist Alma W. Thomas. In 1907 the Thomas family moved from Columbus, Georgia, to Washington to live with relatives so that their three daughters could continue their education in the District's fine public schools. Thomas, a graduate of Armstrong Technical High School and Miner Teachers College, enrolled in the home economics department at Howard University in 1922. She was encouraged to switch concentrations and become the university's first art major by a young instructor, James V. Herring, founder of the Department of Fine Arts. Upon her graduation in 1924, Thomas was probably the first black woman fine arts graduate in the United States.

Alma Thomas taught art for thirty-five years at Shaw Junior High School. It was not until her retirement at the age of 60 that she was able to devote her full energies to her own art. When Howard University offered Thomas a major exhibition in 1966 she was barely able to complete the paintings because her arthritis was so severe that she had to soak her hands in hot water to hold a paintbrush.

Her artistic career was crowned with two great achievements. The first, a 1972 retrospective exhibition at the Corcoran Gallery of Art along with a mayoral proclamation declaring its opening date "Alma W. Thomas Day" in the District of Columbia; a year later, Thomas was the first black woman artist honored with a solo exhibition at the Whitney Museum of American Art in New York City. Her work is owned by the National Museum of American Art and the Hirshhorn Museum and Sculpture Garden.

The 1875 rowhouse, designated a Historic Landmark in 1986, was both her home and studio—she painted in the kitchen. The inspiration for her luminous and colorful abstract paintings was, as she never tired of telling her visitors, the sunlight that filtered through the enormous holly tree in her front yard and poured into her front window. After heart surgery in 1978, Alma Thomas died at the age of 86 at Howard University Hospital.

Patterson Residence

1532 15th Street, NW

During the late 19th century the rowhouse next to the Thomas family was the home of a mason, Henry I. Patterson. Mary Jane Patterson, one of the family's six children, is generally considered to be the first black woman to earn a college degree in America. After graduating from Oberlin College in 1862, Miss Patterson became the second principal of the Preparatory High School for Negro Youth, later M Street/Dunbar.

Site of the Syphax Family Residence

1501 17th Street, NW

Now demolished, the residence of the Syphax family, among Washington's most socially prominent citizens, was located at the corner of 17th and P Streets, NW. A free man, grandfather William came to Alexandria, Virginia, from Canada around 1800 and purchased the freedom of his wife and three daughters. His only son, Charles, was the slave of George Washington Parke Custis, the grandson of Martha Washington. As chief dining room butler in the Custis family mansion, now called Arlington House in Arlington Cemetery, Charles grew up with the Custis family's only child, Mary, who later married Robert E. Lee. Charles Syphax fell in love with Maria Carter, the daughter of Custis and one of his house slaves who served Martha Washington. Custis was delighted with the match and the two were married in a glittering wedding in the mansion in 1821.

Charles and Maria Syphax and their first children, Elinor and William, were freed and with their subsequent eight offspring lived on their own 15-acre spread on the Custis estate. Son William (1825-1891) was an employee of the Department of the Interior for over forty years, and was the first president of the Board of Trustees of the Colored Schools of Washington (1868-1871). A vigorous opponent of segregation, he fought for equal education for Washington's black students throughout his life. A public school was named in his honor shortly after his death in 1891.

1400 Block of Corcoran Street, NW

Several prominent Washingtonians lived in the 1400 block of Corcoran Street, although their homes no longer survive. James E. Miller, who operated a music studio and directed a well-known local band, lived at No. 1407. The house at No. 1415 was the last residence of the Grimké brothers, Archibald and Francis. The Reverend Walter H. Brooks, pastor of the 19th Street Baptist Church, lived at No. 1425. His daughter, Antoinette, married an actor and lived in Paris where she operated a restaurant, patronized, it is said, by the Duke and Duchess of Windsor.

15th Street Presbyterian Church

15th and R Streets, NW

Few churches in the District of Columbia are as significant to the religious and educational life of black Washington as Fifteenth Street Presbyterian.

In 1841 the First Colored Presbyterian Church of Washington was organized in a frame schoolhouse on 15th Street between I and K Streets by John F. Cook, Sr. (c. 1810-1855), the first black Presbyterian minister in the city. Born a slave, Cook gained his freedom when his remarkable aunt, Alethia Browning Tanner, purchased from the proceeds of her vegetable garden near Lafayette Square not only her own freedom but also that of her sister and Cook's four siblings. In 1834 Cook became the master of Union Seminary, one of the few schools in the city for black students. He fled to Pennsylvania for a year after the Snow Riot of 1835 when a mob of white citizens burned his one-room schoolhouse.

After Cook's death in 1855, Union Seminary continued under the direction of his two sons, John, Jr. and George F.T. Cook, until it closed in 1867. The following year George F.T. Cook was appointed superintendent of the Colored Public Schools of Washington and Georgetown, a post he held until 1900, resigning when the black and white schools were placed under a single, white superintendent. Under his vision and leadership, the District's segregated public school system for blacks had a reputation as one of the finest school systems in the nation. John F. Cook, Jr., (1833-1910) pursued a career in government, serving as collector of taxes for the District of Columbia.

The public school system for black students was organized in the basement of the Fifteenth Street Presbyterian Church in 1870. With four students—Rosetta Cookley, John Nalle, Mary Nalle, and Caroline Parke—the Preparatory High School for Negro Youth became the first black high school in America. Beginning as hardly more than an advanced grammar school, the school developed through vigorous leadership and improved curriculum, and was the precursor of the famed M Street High School, later Dunbar High School.

In April 1863 Fifteenth Street Presbyterian Church hosted a grand celebration commemorating the first anniversary of the Emancipation Act for the District of Columbia. Arranged by Elizabeth Keckley, Mrs. Abraham Lincoln's dressmaker, and other women of the church, the program's highlight was a poem composed by I. Willis Menard, said to be the first black to hold a white-collar job in the federal government:

> Almighty God! We praise thy name
> For having heard us pray;
> For having freed us from our chains,
> One year ago today.

Preceded as pastor in the 1860s by the well-known antislavery lecturer and writer, the Reverend Henry Highland Garnet, Francis J. Grimké (1850-1937) led 15th Street Presbyterian for nearly sixty years. A leader and agitator against Washington's racial discrimination during his long tenure, Grimké continued the militant traditions of his fiery predecessor. (see Grimké Elementary School.)

Fresh from Princeton Theologial Seminary, the young Grimké took over the pastorate of Fifteenth Street in 1878 and in the same year married Charlotte Forten (1837-1914) of Philadelphia, granddaughter of black abolitionist James Forten. Under the auspices of the Freedmen's Bureau, Charlotte Forten taught the children of freed slaves and refugees in South Carolina after the Civil War.

In 1894 Mary Church Terrell, Mary Jane Patterson, and Charlotte Forten Grimké founded the Colored Women's League. Committed to the idea of a national organization for black women, the league offered racial uplift programs that included kindergarten teacher training.

In 1918 Fifteenth Street Presbyterian Church moved north, purchasing the building at the corner of 15th and R Streets from the Christian Science church. The present contemporary church was built in 1979.

Georgia Douglas Johnson Residence

1461 S Street, NW

Georgia and Henry Lincoln Johnson moved to Washington from Atlanta in 1908. Johnson, active in Republican Party politics, was rewarded for his support by President Taft with an appointment as recorder of deeds for the District of Columbia, a city government position traditionally reserved for blacks.

Late at night, after completing her fulltime job as a Commissioner of Conciliation at the Department of Labor and fulfilling her roles as wife and mother of two sons, Mrs. Johnson nurtured her literary career. Her first book of poetry, *The Heart of a Woman*, dealt with the yearnings of black women and others to be free. W.E.B. DuBois published two of her poems, including "The Dreams of the Dreamer," in *Crisis* magazine and wrote the introduction to her volume *Bronze*. Her friend Alain Locke introduced her collection *An Autumn Love Cycle*. Mrs. Johnson also wrote six plays and thirty-two song lyrics; one, "I Want to Die While You Love Me," was set to music by Harry T. Burleigh.

On Saturday night the S Street home became the social hub of the Washington Renaissance. In 1926 Professor Kelly Miller wrote in the journal *Opportunity* that "the Capital city furnished the best opportunity and facilities for the expression of the Negro's innate gaiety of soul. Washington is still the Negro's heaven and it will be many a moon before Harlem will be able to take away her sceptre." However overstated Miller's view may be, it is clear that the political and cultural ferment that took place in Harlem during the 1920s occurred not only in New York but also in cities such as Detroit, Chicago, and Washington. In the District of Columbia this cultural awakening can be traced to the halls and campus of Howard University during and after World War I. The Howard University Players, launched after the war, were envisioned by Professor Alain Locke and the head of the drama department as the nucleus of a national Negro theater company. At the same time, Locke, known as the "presiding genius" of the Renaissance, founded the Howard literary magazine *The Stylus*. One of its student contributors, Zora Neale Hurston, rose to national acclaim as a novelist during the 1920s.

As the philosopher of the Harlem Renaissance, Alain Locke also supplied its manifesto. In 1925 he compiled a special issue of *Survey Graphic* magazine devoted to Harlem. This hugely successful issue was edited further into a book, *The New Negro*. Almost half of the thirty-five contributors of essays and articles in the publication were born in Washington or had attended Howard University, or had lived or worked there. These young artists and writers gathered—to talk, debate, criticize, and to encourage the lonely artist in a segregated society—at the home of Mrs. Johnson. Between 1924 and 1926 Langston Hughes often dropped in to "eat Mrs. J's cake and drink her wine and talk poetry and books and plays."

The Howard crowd—Kelly Miller and his daughter May, Alain Locke and Carter Woodson—were joined by poet Angeline Grimké who taught at M Street High School, the young playwright Willis Richardson, novelist Jean Toomer, artist Richard Goodwin, Richard Bruce Nugent, Marita Bonner, and Albert Rice. When in town, James Weldon Johnson, W.E.B. DuBois, novelists Claude McKay, Countee Cullen and Jessie Fauset, and Fiske University president Charles Johnson, mixed with the locals. It was, as one guest noted, "a house full of ideas."

Mrs. Johnson kept tight control of her evenings—"if dull ones come, she weeds them out, gently, effectively...."

Georgia Douglas Johnson was widowed in the late 1920s and her evenings became less frequent during the Depression years.

1400 Block of Swann Street, NW

Several of black Washington's most distinguished citizens lived in the 1400 block of Swann. For a short time (1880-1881) the longtime pastor of 15th Street Presybterian Church, the Reverend Francis Grimké lived at No. 1419 before moving to Corcoran Street. Former LeDroit Park resident Major Christian Fleetwood lived on this block with his daughter from 1908 until his death in 1914.

One of Washington's most civic-minded citizens and a teacher at Dunbar High School for many years, John Wesley Cromwell, resided at No. 1439. Active in Republican party politics and Virginia's Reconstruction government, Cromwell arrived in the District in 1872, working at the Treasury Department while attending Howard University law school. Several years later he founded and published a weekly journal, *The People's Advocate*. Involved in the intellectual pursuits of Washington's black community, Cromwell was a charter member and secretary of the American Negro Academy.

Lindsay's, an after-hours club at 1752 Swann Street NW, was an illicit private club that catered to a mixed clientele. It operated for years before the neighbors realized its existence.

Francis L. Cardozo Residence

1463 Swann Street, NW

Swann Street was named Pierce Street during the 1880s when Francis Cardozo, Sr. (1837-1903) lived here. Following the Civil War, Cardozo was a major figure in South Carolina's Reconstruction politics, serving that state as treasurer and secretary of state. After the removal of federal protection in the South, Cardozo moved to Washington in 1877.

As the principal of several D.C. schools, including M Street High School, Cardozo organized the first business department in a Washington high school. In 1928 the Department became a separate school, Cardozo Business School, at the former M Street School building. In 1950 the school became a neighborhood school and moved to its present site at 13th and Clifton Streets, a building that had formerly housed the white Central High School for many years.

By 1896 Cardozo had moved to 2216 13th Street to live with his son, Francis, Jr., also a prominent D.C. educator. One Cardozo granddaughter, Eslanda, married the great singer and actor Paul Robeson, while three others operated a city institution, The Cardozo Sisters beauty salon on Georgia Avenue.

CHAPTER 11

U Street and Strivers' Section: A Walking Tour

U Street, NW

Often called Washington's "Black Broadway," U Street was the black community's leading commercial and business district by day and the center of nightlife and sporting activity after dark. "Sportin" Daniels, Lester Dishman, Black Jam, and Hip Joe were colorful characters during the days when "You" Street was pulsing with action and vitality.

Whether shopping during the week or strolling after church on Sunday, everyone dressed up on U Street. Elderly Mr. Robinson, who began operating his cleaning establishment at 1214 U in 1944, recalled the annual Easter parades: "After church the people would parade up and down the street in front of the theaters. They really dressed in those days!"

The street was the focal point of the celebrations, beauty pageants, and reunions that accompanied the Capital Classic football games. A highlight of the social season, the Classic pitted the top black college football teams on the East Coast. The first contest between North Carolina College (now North Carolina Central University) and Kentucky State drew 18,000 fans to nearby Griffith Stadium in 1942. Profits from the initial game were donated to a fund to fight Jim Crowism in taxicabs at Union Station; later the proceeds went to student scholarships. The brainstorm of former North Carolinian C.C. Coley, owner of the largest black juke box business in the District, the Classic dissolved soon after it was moved to RFK Stadium in the 1960s.

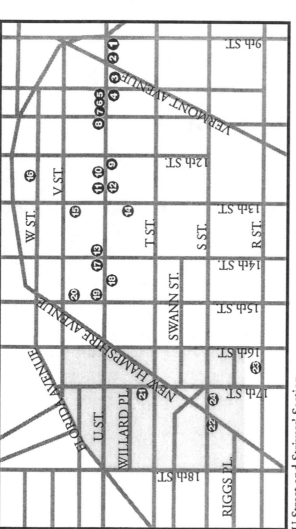

U Street and Strivers' Section
1. Site of Scurlock Photography Studio
2. Murray Brothers Printing Company
3. Future Site of African American Civil War Memorial
4. Prince Hall Masonic Temple
5. Site of Bennett's Barber Shop
6. Site of Valentine's Western Union
7. Bohemian Caverns
8. The Industrial Bank of Washington
9. True Reformers Hall
10. Ben's Chili Bowl
11. Lincoln Theater
12. Duke Ellington Mural
13. New Negro Alliance
14. Terrell Law School
15. Walker Memorial Baptist Church
16. Site of Mary Ann Shadd Cary Residence
17. Frank D. Reeves Center for Municipal Affairs
18. Site of Artist Sam Gilliam's Studio
19. Site of Dunbar Hotel
20. St. Augustine's Catholic Church
21. Strivers' Section
22. Corrigan-Curtis Residence
23. Charlotte Forten Residence
24. Benjamin O. Davis, Sr., Residence

Just as U Street's popularity arose from the restricted life of Washington's segregation when folks "didn't go downtown," it declined with desegregation after 1954. U Street simply couldn't compete with downtown Washington—and with television. But remnants of the glory days of U Street between 7th and 15th Streets still remain.

Site of Scurlock Photography Studio

900 U Street, NW

The 64-year career of photographer Addison N. Scurlock documented the personalities, institutions, events, and activities of black Washington. Noted black Americans traveled to Washington from across the country to have their portraits struck by the talented Scurlock. However, like photographer James Van Der Zee, his contemporary in Harlem, Scurlock only received national recognition later in life.

Born in North Carolina, the 17-year-old Scurlock moved to Washington in 1900 where he apprenticed with photographer Moses P. Rice in his Pennsylvania Avenue studio. After winning the Gold Medal for photography at the 1907 Jamestown Exposition, Scurlock opened his own studio at 9th and U in 1911.

Scurlock's photographs chronicled the world of the elite middle class in the capital's Secret City, as black residential Washington has been called. With affection, respect and superb technique, these pictures documented "how black society lived, how it dressed, how it worshipped, married and mourned." In fact, a mark of arriving socially was to have one's portrait hang in the window of Scurlock's shop. During the Depression the photographer created a newsreel on black life and activities that ran in the Lichtman chain of movie theaters. Scurlock died in 1964.

Now located on 18th Street, the family business continues under the direction of Scurlock's son Robert. Robert Scurlock paid tribute to his father, calling him "a member of a gone breed, a real painstaking artisan. He believed in art, not this snap-and-run technique some commercial photographers use today."

Murray Brothers Printing Company

922 U Street, NW

It is said that a small hand press received at Christmas inspired the three Murray youngsters—Raymond, Morris, and Norman—to establish a printing business.

Founded and opened in 1908 as the Murray Brothers Printing Company, it became Washington's largest black-owned and -operated printing business. The company published black Washington's most influential newspaper, the *Washington Afro-American and Tribune*, which had a circulation of 30,000 and sold for 7 cents a copy.

Murray's Palace Casino, the popular nightclub that occupied the second floor over the print shop, carried the family fortunes through the lean years of the Depression. Later, the Cortez Peters Secretarial School occupied the second floor.

Built entirely by black laborers, the building at 922 U Street was designed by prominent black architect, Isaiah T. Hatton.

Future Site of the African American Civil War Memorial

10th and U Streets, NW

"Their time has come," declared D.C. Council member Frank Smith at the ceremony announcing a memorial to commemorate the volunteer units known as the U.S. Colored Troops who fought in the Civil War. Over 178,000 black soldiers commanded by white officers fought in 449 battles in every theater of the war, losing approximately 37,000 men. However, the U.S. Colored Troops were excluded when over 200,000 Union soldiers paraded for two days down Pennsylvania Avenue in the Grand Review of 1865 at the war's end. Not one black unit was included.

African Americans were permitted to join the military in 1863; by war's end they constituted 10 percent of the Union Army. Because of concern that white residents of the Capital would be alarmed to see black men armed with weapons, the District of Columbia recruits were trained in relative secrecy on what is now Roosevelt Island in the middle of the Potomac River across from Georgetown.

The Memorial, to be located in the heart of the Shaw neighborhood which is named for Colonel Robert Gould Shaw, the white commander of the famed black 54th Massachusetts Regiment, will be the first national monument to honor the black soldiers of the Civil War. The names of these soldiers and their 7,000 white officers will be inscribed on a series of walls. Sculptor Ed Hamilton has been selected to design the centerpiece of the Memorial that will depict a line of Civil War infantry and sailors on one side of a semi-circular structure with the family figures left behind—those for whom they were fighting—included on the other side.

American University professor Ed Smith, an authority on African American history, declared that "Black soldiers had a real love of country, even when disliked by that country. They had a love of the land and a desire to prove their manhood and be compensated with winning their right to freedom."

Prince Hall Masonic Temple

1000 U Street, NW

The Grand Masonic Lodge of the District of Columbia was founded by ten free black men in 1825. Erected in 1922, this six-story marble and concrete neoclassical building housed a bowling alley, restaurant, ballroom, and offices. Prince Hall Temple was a popular locale for the community's social and business activities during segregation. It was also the headquarters of the first black Masonic order chartered below the Mason-Dixon line.

The local Lodge was named in honor of Prince Hall, the first Freemason of color. As a teenager in 1765, Hall worked his passage from his native Barbados to Boston where he became a property owner and gained the right to vote. After participating in the Battle of Bunker Hill during the Revolutionary War, Hall petitioned for membership in a white Masonic Lodge. In 1775, twelve years after his rejection on the basis of his race, Hall founded African Lodge No. 459, becoming its grand master in 1791.

An influential member of Boston society, Hall lobbied the Massachusetts State legislature for the abolition of slavery. And in 1796 he successfully pressured the city of Boston to provide public schools for black children.

Site of Bennett's Barber Shop

1007 U Street, NW

Next door to the popular Japanese Sweet Shop (1009 U Street), where a double scoop of ice cream cost a nickel, was Bennett's Barber Shop, a splendid hair care emporium with a staff sporting suits and ties. In the black community, barber shops and beauty salons were an important meeting place and center of leisure recreation. Here in the U Street establishments, men and women gathered to converse, banter, and discuss the issues of the day.

Offering "toilet articles for sale, shoes shined, clothes pressed while you wait," the Peerless, Hart's (1023 U), Farr's (1203 U), Aurora (1109 U), and the Elite Shaving Parlor (1204 U) were barber shops lining the commercial boulevard. At the corner of 12th and R Streets, Dr. George H. Cardozo operated a drugstore and manufactured "Queen Pomade," Washington's best-selling hair preparation.

During the mid-1920s, there were fourteen barber shops between 4th and 14th Streets on U Street. According to an area study, six had electric pianos and three had radios. The social intercourse that took place in barber shops "furnished a mass of social news, chiefly of a local nature. Reports on the poker games and other festivities of the previous night are given to attentive and interested listeners. Strangers and persons who have been away from the city are likely to make the barber shop the first place of visitation. Old acquaintances are renewed and new ideas are advanced," according to the study.

Site of Valentine's Western Union

1011 U Street, NW

After the Urban League conducted a study to prove that such an undertaking would be a good risk, the first black-staffed postal telegram office was opened in January 1941. Located in the heart of the black community, the office became the prosperous Valentine's Western Union a few years later, the first black-owned Western Union office in the United States. Dressed in their finest clothes, the five messengers delivered telegrams throughout the city. Valentine's success was due in part to the patronage of the neighborhood's blue collar and domestic workers who regularly sent money home to relatives in the South.

Bohemian Caverns

2001 11th Street, NW

In the boom days of the 1920s, 30s, and 40s, U Street was the entertainment capital of black Washington. Cabarets, jazz spots, supper clubs, dance halls, and cafes featured the best black artists of the day. The Bohemian Caverns was the doyenne of U Street on the 11th Street corner at 2001 U Street. Opened in 1926 in the basement of the Davis drugstore, Night Club Bohemia was patronized by black Washington's leading citizens. In those early years, evening dress was mandatory. As times changed so did the name of the club. Known as Crystal Caverns for years, it was billed as the Club Cavern—"The Rendezvous of Washington's Socially Elite"—in the late 1940s. Today, facing a questionable future, the fire-stained landmark bears witness to changed tastes in music and entertainment.

Nat King Cole and Art Tatum held forth at the upscale Club Bengasi (1425 U Street), a mecca for cafe society. Around the corner at 14th Street's Club Bali the swinging band sounds of Jimmy Lunceford's orchestra filled the air. The Casbah, Jimmy McPhail's, Rocky's, Cecelia's, the Capitol Pleasure Club, the Madre and Una Clubs, the Rendezvous, and the Dance Hall at 9th and V Streets where Louis' Armstrong appeared, jumped. At the Jungle Inn, across from the Green Parrot at 12th and U Streets, patrons jived to the music of Jelly Roll Morton over a 25¢ pitcher of beer. Washington's own Pearl Bailey got her first break there as a dancer, later performing at Republic Gardens and Murray's Palace Casino, where Cab, Duke, Charlie Barnett all played, according to owner Freeman Murray.

South of U Street at the corner of 9th and R, Louis Thomas managed Oriental Gardens, the oldest black cabaret in the city. Catering to a racially mixed crowd, the Gardens, where young Duke Ellington worked with the legendary Bricktop, featured female singers and dancers in a basement room and occupied a larger upstairs space in the Clef Club building. The classy Phoenix Inn at 13th and U also drew mixed audiences.

In 1947 a young unknown, Harry Belafonte, was the prime attraction at Lewis and Alex's recently opened restaurant at 1211 U Street. However, dissatisfied with his performance, the management cut short his stay!

By the 1960s and 70s the watering holes of black nightlife were spread around the city—Chez Brown was downtown, Billy Simpson's and Ed Murphy's Supper Clubs were popular on Georgia Avenue, and Manny's Lounge was across the river in Anacostia.

The Industrial Bank of Washington

2000 11th Street, NW

A mix of commerce and entertainment made the intersection of 11th and U Streets an ideal location for a bank. One of the liveliest corners in this neighborhood, Dr. George Davis' drugstore, one of the oldest black businesses in the city, was across the street at 1027 U Street, NW, and the Night Club Bohemia opened in its basement in 1926. During the silent movie era the Hiawatha Theater, with Professor George Battle playing piano, was located around the corner at 2008 11th Street. (Published since 1892, the black community's largest circulation newspaper, *The Afro-American*, left their longtime U Street address in the mid-1970s to relocate at 2008 11th Street.)

Known as "wage earner's bank," the Industrial Savings Bank was founded in 1913 by pioneer black financier, John Whitelaw Lewis. After arriving in Washington, Lewis soon organized his fellow hod carriers into a building and loan association. These laborers became the earliest customers of Industrial. After Lewis' death in 1925, the bank was directed by Texas-born Jesse Mitchell who was able to reorganize and reopen after the bank crisis and closing of 1932, changing the bank's name to the Industrial Bank of Washington.

Mitchell moved to the District in 1907, becoming a clerk in the Navy Department. After earning a law degree from Howard University and attending the Wharton School of Finance and Commerce, the enterprising Mitchell founded a realty and investment company in 1919. Later, with $200,000 in assets and five employees, he opened Industrial Bank upon the ashes of the Bank Holiday. Mitchell was forced to offer classes on the second floor of the bank to train his own employees. He could not hire experienced white staffers and white banks would not hire black employees in Washington. Thus, there were no black "experience qualified" bankers available.

Industrial Bank and other black banking institutions were critical to those in the black community seeking loans. Although blacks could make deposits in white banks, they were not eligible to borrow. In a few short years Industrial had 16,000 depositors, far ahead of leading black banks in other U.S. cities.

By the time of Mitchell's testimonial celebration at the Willard Hotel in 1952, the assets of Industrial had increased 30-fold. Mitchell's son, Benson Doyle, succeeded him as chief operating officer of the bank two years later.

True Reformers Hall

1200 U Street, NW

True Reformers Hall was built in 1903 by the United Order of True Reformers, a non-secret fraternal benevolent society that served as a bank and insurance company catering to blacks. Local historian Henry Whitehead declared, "The True Reformers led the way for U Street to become a main street for black Washington." The building has been a central location for black social and business activity in Shaw neighborhood for almost a century.

Desiring both a national presence in the capital and a building "to the credit of the Negro race," the Richmond-based society hired a black Lynchburg, Virginia construction firm and the dean of black architects, John A. Lankford, to construct their $60,000 headquarters. When 100,000 persons attended the dedication of the gray brick and limestone trimmed building, the Washington *Post* headline read: "Erected by Negroes, White Race Had No Hand in Any Part of Work." True

Reformers Hall was a source of immense pride within Washington's black community.

The hall was the first major commission for 28-year-old John A. Lankford after his arrival in Washington in 1902 with a Tuskegee Institute degree in mechanical engineering. His wife was the granddaughter of AME bishop Henry M. Turner, an outspoken advocate of African colonization of American blacks in the early 19th century. In 1907 Lankford was selected to plan the Negro Building at the Jamestown, Virginia Exposition. A year later, Lankford, whose large and up-to-date offices were located at 1448 Q Street, NW, became the principal architect for the African Methodist Episcopal Church, designing AME church buildings and parish houses all over the country.

"It can be said without any exaggeration," the Washinqton *Bee* enthused, "that it [Reformers Hall] is the best office, store, hall, and lodgeroom building that the Negro owns in the United States." Behind modern plate glass windows were a variety of retail, entertainment, and vocational establishments including the Colored Business Centre, Chapman's Tailoring and Designing School, and the Silver Slipper Club. Off the great hall, a young Duke Ellington who had just formed a band rented Room 10 to perform for a teenage crowd.

Dr. Amanda Gray, who received her Pharmaceutical Graduate degree in 1903, operated a drug store here with her pharmacist husband. She was energetically involved in the civic and cultural life of black Washington, devoting hours to the Treble Clef Club, the Book Lovers Club and the organization of the Phillis Wheatley YWCA. After her husband's death in 1917, Dr. Gray married prominent civic leader Andrew F. Hilyer, who died two years later. She continued her active community service until her death in 1957.

In addition, the hall's basement contained a drill room and armory for the First Separate Battalion, Washington's black national guard unit. During the last decades of the 19th century many of the city's leading black citizens were members of several local militia organizations, including the Washington Cadet Corps and the Capital City Guards. The 1889 reorganization of the entire District of Columbia National Guard decreased the company strength of those units formed by veterans of the Civil War and greatly demoralized the black community. In 1891 when General Albert Ordway ordered these companies to disband, furious public outcry brought about their reinstatement. The old black units were, however, consolidated into the segregated First Separate Battalion.

In 1916 the First Separate, commanded by Major James E. Walker, a teacher and supervisor in Washington's public schools for over a quarter of a century, finally received its chance to serve when it policed the Mexican border after repeated incidents there with Pancho Villa's revolutionaries. The following year the battalion was the first American unit mustered into federal service to defend the nation's capital—guarding its bridges and water supply—before the formal declaration of war. In response to this honor one observer wryly commented that "color, which was the basis of discrimination in time of peace, was considered *prima facie* evidence of unquestionable loyalty in time of war."

In 1917 True Reformers Hall was purchased by the Knights of Pythias as their temple. The huge second-floor auditorium, seating over 2,000 people, became a popular dance hall during the years after World War I.

In 1937 the great hall was converted to a gymnasium by the police department as the home of Metropolitan Police Boys Club #2, the only one in the city to admit black children. Before an audience of 2,000 neighborhood residents, First Lady Eleanor Roosevelt cut the dedication ribbon. Within three months 4,100 youngsters were enrolled in the many activities of the Boys Club program.

True Reformers Hall served as a recruiting station for the armed forces in World War II prior to its purchase by the Metropolitan (Duron) Paint Company.

Ben's Chili Bowl

1213 U Street, NW

Ben's Chili Bowl is a culinary landmark of black Washington. Operated by Ben and Virginia Ali since 1958, the restaurant is the home of the halfsmoke and "the Finest Hot Dogs and Chili Served with a Touch of Class." When in Washington, comedian Bill Cosby, who courted his wife Camille here, always stops in. "We used to sneak out because our parents didn't want us meeting," Cosby recalled, "but they used to know because of the onions on her breath!"

In 1986 the Alis opened a back dining room, called the Minnehaha after D.C.'s first silent moving picture theater located on this site. Later called the S.H. Dudley, after the famous comedian, the theater's facade is still visible behind the Chili Bowl sign.

During the 1920s and 30s several pool halls were located nearby. The Idle House Billiard Parlor, a classy, six-table, operation at 1110 U, operated a popular Annex at 1207 U. The prosperous Narrow Gauge Billiard Parlor at 1217 U was followed by Charlie Buck's Place, where "you had to be good" to play.

Lincoln Theater

1215 U Street, NW

Of three major movie palaces on U Street—the Republic, the Booker T and the Lincoln—only the latter remains today. The Booker T stood on the present site of the District Office building in the 1400 block. The stately Republic, demolished in 1976 along with the Booker T, was located a few doors east of the Republic Gardens at 1343 U Street.

Owned by the famous Crandall Theater Corporation, the Lincoln Theater was opened in February 1922 under black management. In 1927 the 1,600-seat theater was sold to the Lincoln-Howard Corporation, which operated both the Lincoln and Howard theaters. The Republic Theater, on the other hand, was part of the District Theater chain, established by well-known white businessman Abraham E. Lichtman. District's twenty-six theaters served black communities in D.C., Maryland, and Virginia. Although most of the operating staff for the theaters was black, the company had reorganized to include black stockholders at the time of Lichtman's death.

Most of Washington's movie theaters were segregated prior to the 1950s. Ralph Bunche recalled the time he was refused a ticket at the downtown Capital Theater. He then walked to the nearby Palace Theater and asked for a ticket in French; the cashier readily sold it to him thinking that he was part of the French legation in Washington.

Poet Sterling Brown recalled an incident in 1939 when he, Ralph Bunche, and other Howard University radicals boycotted the Lincoln Theater's blockbuster film, "Gone with the Wind." "All the maids got off Thursday and came to the movie and said we were crazy—that's how slavery was. We just told them to go back and wash some windows and we kept on picketing."

The Lincoln was a classy, first-run movie house. During the 1920s concert organist Louis N. Brown played the magnificent Manuel Mohler organ. First Lady Eleanor Roosevelt and Joe Louis, the heavyweight boxing champion of the world, drew enormous crowds to the Lincoln during a March of Dimes rally. A popular dance hall was located behind the theater. Entered through a tunnel from the street, the Lincoln Colonnade was the scene of many banquets and glittering formal balls featuring the music of the big bands of the day.

The Lincoln has recently been renovated as a community performing arts center.

Duke Ellington Mural

U Street-Cardozo Metro Station
13th and U Streets, NW

Washington's most active mural artist, G. Byron Peck, completed his most recent work, a tribute to local neighborhood great, Duke Ellington, in the summer of 1997. With support from Shaw businesses and Mobil Oil Corporation, Peck worked on the 24-by-32-foot mural with a team of D.C. student painters hired under the city's summer jobs program.

Other works by artist Peck with African American themes are a tribute to Frederick Douglass overlooking a parking lot at Massachusetts Avenue and 12th Street NW and a mural called "The Black Family Reunion" at the corner of 14th and Florida Avenue NW.

New Negro Alliance

Hamburger Grill
U Street, NW

In 1933 not far from the Lincoln Theater, the white owner of the Hamburger Grill, whose patronage was exclusively black, fired his black employees and replaced them with white workers. A group of young neighborhood activists picketed; the owner closed the restaurant the next day and three days later rehired the fired workers. From this success the New Negro Alliance, using slogans such as "Don't Buy Where You Can't Work," became one of the nation's first grass-roots protest organizations to employ economic weapons in the struggle for social change and civil rights.

Blacks were, according to Howard's Kelly Miller, "the surplus man, the last to be hired and the first to be fired." The job situation was even more critical during the Depression and the migration to urban areas of rural Negroes seeking employment.

After their Hamburger Grill success, 21-year-old John Aubrey Davis, who grew up in the nearby Strivers' Section, and his young friends quickly targeted other white businesses. They intended that this new alliance be more aggressive and confrontational than previous conservative efforts by the NAACP or Alain Locke's more intellectually- and culturally-based New Negro movement of the 1920s. Early members of the Alliance were college students and young professionals and included recent college graduate M. Franklin Thorne, who would soon become manager of Langston Terrace, Washington's first federal housing project; William H. Hastie, dean of Howard's Law School; James Nabritt (later President of Howard University); Dutton Ferguson and Charlie Houston.

The next target was the Washington *Star* which had no black newspaper boys. After three weeks of negotiations and the threat of a boycott, the *Star* changed its hiring policies. The Alliance picketed Kaufman's Department store on 7th Street during its busy Christmas season. From triumph to triumph the activists brought economic pressure on U Street businesses, including High's Ice Cream stores (Shaw Junior High School students gave up ice cream!) and the national A & P Food chain. A new A & P had opened on the corner of 9th and S Streets with an all white staff. Within weeks, A & P had hired a black manager and other employees and the boycott was called off.

Refusing to hire blacks or to integrate its lunch counters, the 40-store People's Drug chain endured almost two years of picket lines at the 14th and U and 7th and M Street stores. Although sales dropped dramatically as a result of the black boycott, People's ultimately sustained their discriminatory hiring practices and segregated food counters. At the same time the Sanitary Grocery Company (later Safeway) obtained an injunction against the actions of the Alliance. However, in a landmark 1938 decision, the Supreme Court affirmed the legal right of blacks to bring consumer pressure against commercial establishments that refused to employ black workers. Argued by the Alliance's Belford V. Lawson and Thurman L. Dodson, *New Negro Alliance v. Sanitary Grocery* was won by black lawyers, trained in a black university, for a black-run organization.

The *Sanitary* decision proved the power of the boycott and the picket line and paved the way for the struggles of the sit-ins and civil rights movement twenty years later.

Terrell Law School

1922 13th Street, NW

Located in a former fraternity house around the corner from U Street, Terrell Law School was opened in 1931 after Howard University discontinued its night law classes. Terrell, named after the city's first black judge, offered a full evening law curriculum. In 1936, 96 of the 167 black students studying law in Washington were enrolled at Terrell. After graduating approximately 600 students, Terrell closed in 1950 due to lack of funds and loss of students to the city's other recently desegregated law schools.

Walker Memorial Baptist Church

2020 13th Street, NW

A significant meeting in Washington's civil rights history was held in the old Walker Memorial Church building at 2020 13th Street. In 1910 the local organizing committee for the Sixth World's Sunday School Convention refused to seat delegates from black churches. At a mass meeting Washington's black ministers, including the Reverend Francis Grimké, gathered here to protest their exclusion. Their resolution stated in part:

> *The thirteen colored delegates of the District of Columbia ... were elected ... in precisely the same manner as the delegates of the white Sunday School Association of the District of Columbia.... We wish all the delegates from Europe, Asia, Africa, the Americas and the islands of the seas to know that in our hearts we welcome them; but because of unchristian prejudice, ... we cannot show our hospitality.*

The congregation, which celebrated its 100th anniversary in 1990, moved into this contemporary church building in 1981.

Site of Mary Ann Shadd Cary Residence

1421 W Street, NW

Mary Ann Shadd (1823-1893) was an outspoken champion of the rights of fugitive slaves and free blacks. After passage of the Fugitive Slave Law in 1850, Shadd, her brother and other family members, emigrated to Ontario, Canada, where they believed there were greater opportunities. She edited an aggressive and respected journal, *The Provincial Freeman*, and taught school for the American Missionary Association. During the Civil War she recruited black volunteers for the Union forces in Indiana.

Mrs. Cary moved to Washington after the war and wrote articles for Frederick Douglass' *New National Era* and John Wesley Cromwell's *The People's Advocate*. In 1869 Mary Shadd Cary entered Howard University Law School, earning her degree in 1883, becoming the nation's first black woman lawyer. She practiced law for many years and worked for the National Women's Suffrage Association. Her home was designated a National Historic Landmark in 1976.

Frank D. Reeves Center for Municipal Affairs

14th and U Streets, NW

The $38-million District Office Building, completed in 1986, is expected to trigger the revitalization of the 14th Street corridor. The gleaming glass and stone eight-story building houses more than 1,000 city workers. The building, which includes street-level shops and a day care center, is named the Frank D. Reeves Center for Municipal Affairs, after the city's first black Democratic Party committeeman, who died in 1973.

Site of Artist Sam Gilliam's Studio

1428 U Street, NW

Sam Gilliam, one of Washington's most recognized and successful artists, creates his large, colorful paintings on the top floor of this building. After earning a graduate degree at the University of Louisville in Kentucky, Gilliam moved to Washington in the early 1960s. A younger member of the city's most significant art movement, the Washington Color School, Gilliam began his career teaching art in the D.C. public schools. After his highly acclaimed one-person exhibition at the Phillips Collection in 1967, he was able to devote his total energies to his art. Gilliam's work, including the historically important, unstretched, draped canvases of the late 60s, has been exhibited at the Metropolitan Museum of Art and Museum of Modern Art in New York City, the Chicago Art Institute, and the Corcoran Gallery of Art and National Museum of American Art in Washington.

Site of Dunbar Hotel

Northeast Corner of 15th and U Streets, NW

The largest apartment building in the city was built on the corner of 15th and U Streets in 1897, well before the great Connecticut Avenue apartments of the 1920s and 30s. Commissioned by German immigrant Robert Portner, the Portner Flats were Washington's first to include a swimming pool and tennis court.

In 1946 the building was sold and reopened as the Dunbar Hotel, named after former local resident and poet Paul Laurence Dunbar. By 1950 the Dunbar had become the leading black hotel in the city and, some said, the largest black-owned hotel in the nation. Famous sports figures and entertainment stars, particularly those playing the Howard Theater, stayed at the Dunbar. The Hotel's Tropical Room and Club 2011, where the community's prestigious black fraternities often met, anchored the west end of the lively U Street nightclub strip.

The good times were short-lived. Prostitutes, gamblers, and drug dealers frequented the clubs; as a result, the hotel lost its liquor license in 1951. Renamed the New Dunbar to counter negative publicity, the 485-room hotel could not compete with the city's other hotels after integration in the mid-1950s. By the 1960s the Dunbar had deteriorated to the point where the city purchased it in 1970. Construction crews razed the hotel to build the Campbell Heights Apartments shortly thereafter.

St. Augustine's Catholic Church

1425 V Street, NW

Dominating the surrounding neighborhood at the corner of 15th and V Streets, the towering Gothic St. Augustine's is the oldest black Catholic congregation in the nation's capital. Its roots go back to a dedicated group of emancipated slaves who, in 1858, founded a chapel and school on 15th Street between L and M Streets. Those original parishioners would, according to one contemporary, "come home after work ... lay their pails and lunch buckets down, have their dinner, and then they would go right down (in the dark) to help dig the foundation."

Fund-raising efforts for the church received a boost on July 4, 1864, when President and Mrs. Abraham Lincoln hosted a "strawberry festival" on the White House lawn. St. Augustine's Church, named for the African Bishop of Hippo, was dedicated in 1876.

On Christmas Eve 1947 the last Mass was celebrated before the church's demolition to make way for the present Washington *Post* building. St. Augustine's moved up 15th Street to the Bishop's Gate site for several years before merging with St. Paul's in 1961. St. Paul's Catholic Church, located in the present church structure built in 1893, was a largely white congregation, whose only black worshipers were often the members' chauffeurs who sat on the simple pews in the back of the church. The parish was renamed St. Augustine's in 1983.

Strivers' Section

Neighborhood Between 15th and 18th Streets and R Street and Florida Avenue, NW

The integrated area between Dupont Circle and the Shaw neighborhood became predominately black from 1900 to 1920 and was known as the Strivers' Section, a "community of Negro aristocracy." Like LeDroit Park and Logan Circle, the homes in the Strivers' area were acquired from whites. The most important residences in the section are the rowhouses, built in 1902-04, lining the 1700 block of U Street. "That block along U Street," one resident observed, "meant we had arrived." One of the well-known residents was journalist Dutton Ferguson, an editor of *Opportunity* magazine and one of the founders of the New Negro Alliance.

The row of Second Empire townhouses around the corner at 2000-2008 17th Street was probably built for Frederick Douglass in 1876. Douglass' son Lewis lived at No. 2002 for thirty-one years (from 1877 to 1908) and Douglass heirs owned the properties until 1965. Lewis H. Douglass (1840-1908) was a printer with the U.S. Government and a partner with his father as publishers of the *New National Era* newspaper from 1869 to 1872. Later he dealt in real estate before becoming president of the newly-organized Industrial Building and Savings Company. His next door neighbor and colleague, James E. Storum, founder of the Capital Savings Bank, was closely associated with the Industrial Building and Savings, the first banking institution owned and operated by blacks in the District.

The house at 1700 V Street, NW, was the residence (1891) of black architect Calvin T.S. Brent, who designed St. Luke's Episcopal Church on 15th Street. And Todd Duncan, a young vocal instructor at Howard University, lived at the corner of 17th and T Streets. At the age of 33, Duncan sang the lead in George Gershwin's *Porgy and Bess* on Broadway.

Among those who lived in the Strivers' Section on R Street were Freedmen's Hospital's surgeon-in-chief Dr. William Warfield (No. 1522) and Elder Lightfoot Solomon Michaux (No. 1712). Judge Robert and Mary Church Terrell moved from their LeDroit Park home to 1615 S Street, where she lived until her death in 1954. Poet May Miller Sullivan, daughter of Dean Kelly Miller of Howard University, lived on the same block.

John W. Osbome, a Howard graduate and government worker, became the first black resident of the 1600 block of S Street in 1920. His white neighbors on the block included Frank Noyes of the Washington *Star* and Joseph Rizik, the owner of a chic Connecticut Avenue women's dress shop.

In the 1700 block of S Street were the Murray family, publishers of the Washington *Tribune*, and the William L. Houston family at 1744 S Street. Known as "Mr. Civil Rights," son Charles Houston was an expert in constitutional law and a lead litigator in many landmark Supreme Court cases that dealt with labor, housing and educational issues. Justice Thurgood Marshall hailed Houston's contributions in the final assault on segregated education in the United States, the monumental *Brown v. Board of Education* case. Supreme Court Justice William O. Douglas noted that Charlie Houston was "one of the top ten advocates to appear before this court in my thirty-five years."

In the early 1930s Dorothy Waring Howard opened Washington's first private pre-school for black children in this S Street block. The Garden of Children school, which later included grades one through three, was a popular school for middle-class black youngsters, including the children of Dr. Ralph Bunche. The fenced-in roof of the garage was the school's playground.

Perry W. Howard, who practiced law with the prestigious black firm of Cobb, Howard and Hayes in downtown Washington, lived at 1829 S Street. Always active in Republican politics, Howard was honored at the 1960 Republican Convention for being the oldest continuous delegate.

The Strivers' Section was declared a Historic District in 1980.

Corrigan-Curtis Residence

1727 S Street, NW

The occupants at this residence became the central players in the historic struggle against restrictive covenants during the middle years of the 20th century. In 1920 a majority of the white residents in the 1700 block drew up a document whereby each was bound not to sell or rent to African Americans. Interestingly, nine black families already lived at the end of the block in a row of more modest houses.

Almost immediately absentee owner Irene Corrigan, who had signed the covenant, sold her home to Dr. and Mrs. Arthur Curtis, prominent African Americans. A white attorney and neighbor filed for an injunction in the District's Supreme Court which "confirmed covenanters' right to restrict property owner-ship." After Corrigan and Curtis lost on appeal, they filed in 1926 in the United States Supreme Court, which, determined they had no jurisdiction, allowing the lower court's decision to stand. Covenants were legal. The effect of this case reverberated throughout the nation and such covenants quickly multiplied.

Coincidentally, Charles Houston was also living in this block by 1925. Over twenty years later the Supreme Court agreed to hear arguments in a cluster of covenant cases, one of which was a D.C. case, *Hurd v. Hodge*. Charlie Houston was the lead attorney in that suit. In 1948 the Court reversed their previous rulings, and declared that restrictive covenants were unenforceable in the Courts. Covenants could still be written, but the courts could not be used to enforce them.

Charlotte Forten Residence

1608 R Street, NW

The daughter of a wealthy Philadelphia family, Charlotte Forten was educated in Salem, Massachusetts. She became a radical abolitionist while teaching there and was included in a circle that included William Lloyd Garrison, John Greenleaf Whittier and Wendell Phillips. Forten often contributed essays and poems to Garrison's *Liberator*. Upon her return to Philadelphia, she took up the struggle for women's rights and suffrage.

In 1862 Forten answered General Sherman's call for teachers to come to Port Royal, SC, to educate over 10,000 abandoned slaves. She kept a journal of the challenges in providing a basic education to the freedmen of St. Helena Island.

Charlotte Forten married the Reverend Francis J. Grimké, pastor of 15th Street Presbyterian Church, in 1878. They lived in the R Street house while she pursued her work for social welfare and education for African Americans until her death in 1914.

Benjamin O. Davis, Sr. Residence

1721 S Street, NW

Benjamin O. Davis, Sr. (1877-1970), the first black to attain the rank of general in the U.S. armed forces, lived at 1721 S Street, NW. A product of the D.C. public schools where he was captain of his cadet corps unit at M Street High School, Davis dropped out of Howard University to organize and lead a group of volunteers who served in the U.S. Infantry during the Spanish-American War. His long military career was spent with black units until his elevation to brigadier general by President Franklin Roosevelt in 1940. Davis coordinated the war effort recruitment of black soldiers into the U.S. Army—increasing the ranks from

3,640 in 1939 to almost 100,000 two years later. In 1942 Davis joined General Dwight Eisenhower, serving as liaison between black soldiers and the British citizenry. In 1948 he moved to this house after his White House retirement ceremony. Following in his father's military footsteps, Benjamin O. Davis, Jr. became the first black general in the U.S. Air Force.

CHAPTER 12

16th Street, NW

In all but name, 16th Street was an avenue. The north-south axis of Washington, 16th Street was dominated by the massively imposing stone mansion of former Missouri Senator John Henderson and his wife, Mary. Located on Meridian Hill at the northwest corner of Florida Avenue, Boundary Castle was described as the Victorian answer to a medieval castle. Calling the White House a "modest beauty," the Hendersons envisioned Boundary Castle as a much more impressive home for the president. Mrs. Henderson, the "Empress of 16th Street" for over forty years, spearheaded 16th Street's short-lived name change to "Avenue of the Presidents" in 1902. She was far more successful in remaking the street the "Avenue of Embassies," encouraging many foreign countries to locate on 16th Street rather than on its rival Massachusetts Avenue. The Henderson's deteriorating castle home was razed in 1949 to make way for Beekman Place, a 213-unit townhouse development.

During the 20th century, upper 16th Street neighborhoods became racially integrated and desirable locations for Washington's professional black families.

Site of Foraker Residence

Northwest corner of 16th and P Streets, NW

The gracious city mansion of Ohio Senator Joseph B. Foraker, whose political career was ruined by the Brownsville Incident, was razed in 1960 to make way for the Sunday School Annex of the Foundry Methodist Church.

On the night of August 13, 1906, the 25th U.S. Infantry's all-black battalion, stationed on the Rio Grande border, was accused of perpetrating the infamous raid on Brownsville, Texas. Charged with shooting up the town and killing one person, the battalion's troops were ordered to confess by President Theodore

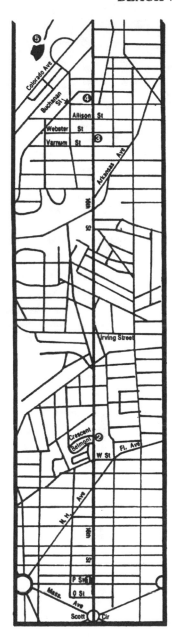

16th Street, NW
1. Site of Foraker Residence
2. Malcolm X Park (Meridian Hill)
3. Upper 16th Street:
   The Gold Coast
4. 19th Street Baptist Church
5. Carter Barron Amphitheater
6. Shepherd Park
7. North Portal Estates

Roosevelt. All swore their innocence; 167 members of the battalion were dishonorably discharged.

Believing the evidence thin and inconclusive, Senator Foraker championed the troops' cause, attacked the president for administering such severe punishment, and advocated a public trial for the black battalion. "They ask no favors because they are Negroes," Foraker stated, "but only justice because they are men." President Roosevelt's vendetta against Foraker's crusade included harassment by Secret Service agents, refusal of all the senator's federal appointment recommendations, and attempts to force Foraker's exclusion from Washington's social circles.

Senator Foraker was defeated for reelection in 1908. Sixty-eight years later, in 1976, President Gerald Ford exonerated the Brownsville battalion. The battalion's lone survivor, 87-year-old Dorsie Willis, received the pardon in person at the White House.

Malcolm X Park

(Meridian Hill Park)
16th Street between Florida Avenue and Euclid Street, NW

Until the 1880s the east side of the 16th Street hill developed haphazardly. During the Civil War a farmhouse was used as a hospital, and a Massachusetts Brigade and the New York 77th bivouacked on its grounds. The Wayland Seminary, founded by the Baptist church in 1865 for the education of black preachers and teachers, purchased the northeast corner of the park for its headquarters, a three-story brick building with mansard roof and tower which was completed in 1874. At the turn of the century the seminary moved its headquarters to Richmond, Virginia.

Although supported by Senator and Mrs. John Henderson who lived across the street, plans for a colossal presidential mansion and a memorial to Abraham Lincoln located in the park never materialized. Completion of the architecturally elaborate 12-acre Meridian Hill Park took decades. During the late 1960s the run-down park became the rallying place for civil rights groups and was unofficially designated Malcolm X Park in honor of the assassinated black nationalist leader.

Upper 16th Street: The Gold Coast

North of Shepherd Street, NW

Bordered by fine old mansions and World War II vintage homes built in large part by prosperous Jewish families, the northern portion of 16th Street is known locally as the Gold Coast. Crestwood, an exclusive neighborhood of spacious detached homes on the west side of 16th Street south of Carter Barron Amphitheater was built at the beginning of World War II. With its adjoining 1920s-period residences on the east side of 16th Street, upper 16th Street was one of the earliest integrated areas in the city after restrictive residential laws were declared unconstitutional by the courts in the 1950s. It gained its Gold Coast nickname when it became a fashionable address for Washington's black middle class.

19th Street Baptist Church

4606 16th Street, NW

After most of its parishioners had left its inner city neighborhood, 19th Street Baptist Church moved to the Gold Coast area in 1975. The congregation purchased the B'nai Israel Jewish Synagogue whose members had moved to the suburbs.

For 135 years a Baptist congregation had worshiped at 19th and I Streets, NW. "The Baptist Church of Washington, D.C.," as it was originally called, was founded by four ministers and six lay persons in 1802. Many of the black members of the interracial congregation were slaves and servants of the white parishioners as the church records indicate:

> *Lord's Day, May 9, 1819: Previous to the celebration of the Lord's Supper—two letters of dismission were presented—one from the United Baptist Church Hepziban in favor of Susan (Servant of President Monroe)....*

In the early 1830s the church moved to the present site of Ford's Theater on 10th Street, NW. In 1839 the black members organized the First Colored Baptist Church of the City of Washington and purchased property on 19th Street.

In 1872 the Reverend Walter Henderson Brooks began his legendary pastorate ten years after the present church was built and renamed the 19th Street Baptist Church. For sixty-three years the fiery temperance orator and chaplain to the Anti-Saloon League of D.C. led his congregation. Born a slave in Virginia and freed at the end of the Civil War, Dr. Brooks often recalled in his sermons the sale of his sister on a Richmond auction block. At the age of 15, Brooks entered Lincoln University (Pennsylvania), completing academic and divinity courses with fellow classmates Archibald and Francis Grimké. Always active in civic affairs, Brooks served as vice-president of the Bethel Literary and Historical Association under John W. Cromwell. After his death in 1945, his successor in the 19th Street pulpit, the Reverend Jerry Moore, Jr., carried on his tradition of community involvement, serving several terms as a city councilman in the 1960s and 70s.

Carter Barron Amphitheater

Rock Creek Park
16th Street and Colorado Avenue, NW

Washington's 1800-acre Rock Creek Park is one of the most beautiful natural city parks in the world. Until the 1950s the park's picnic areas, as well as the city's public golf courses, swimming pools, tennis courts and playgrounds were segregated. Through a system of picnic permits, blacks were confined to a single separate section in the park. Signs designating white and black areas were erected in the 1930s, but a stormy public outcry succeeded in bringing about their removal.

Carter Barron Amphitheater in Rock Creek Park was Washington's "under the stars" setting for black entertainment and music during the 1960s and 70s. Erected in 1950 to celebrate Washington's sesquicentennial, the amphitheater hosted Broadway musicals, ballet performances, singers and other performers. After the 1968 riots, audiences abandoned Carter Barron. Thereafter, the amphitheater became "the summertime palace of second-string soul" for black teenagers. In 1984 the Washington *Post* drama critic observed that "Carter Barron is now more celebrated as a parking lot."

Adjacent to the amphitheater is a 15-foot totem monument entitled *Family Tree of Hope*. Begun in May 1970 by sculptor Dennis Stroy, Jr., who worked at his own expense on weekends, the sculpture, carved from a red oak tree donated by the National Park Service, represents a black family that the artist knew while he lived in New York City.

Shepherd Park

East side of 16th Street, north of Alaska Avenue, NW

Shepherd Park, known for its "tree streets"—Holly, Hemlock, Juniper, Locust—was originally the 18th-century estate of Marylander Montgomery Blair. Later, "Boss" Alexander Roby Shepherd built his country home, Bleak House, on the present site of 7714 13th Street, NW. Vice-president of the Board of Public Works and governor of the District of Columbia, Shepherd generated those urban improvements—street paving, sewer system, tree plantings—that turned a muddy village into a modern capital. Extravagant expenditures and cost overruns not only caused Shepherd to flee to Mexico, but also resulted in the District's loss of its brief Home Rule status in the 1870s.

Called 16th Street Heights when it was developed after World War I, the neighborhood took its present name from the Shepherd Elementary School, built in 1936.

In 1958 Shepherd Park residents joined with those in Brightwood, Manor Park, and Takoma, D.C., to form Neighbors, Inc., a neighborhood association dedicated to maintaining the multiracial character of the neighborhood. These residents created the association in response to the heavy real estate blockbusting that occurred after the Supreme Court's 1948 decision declaring restrictive covenants unenforceable. Real estate agents often sold one property on a previously segregated block to a black family. Playing on fear, the agents pressured white homeowners to sell quickly at bargain basement prices. To combat panic tactics and to create "an intown, interesting, integrated community," Neighbors, Inc., offered social and recreational programs and a free housing information service to white and black sellers and buyers in a 250-block area.

One of the country's oldest associations for neighborhood stabilization, Neighbors, Inc., was a brave, innovative experiment in promoting an integrated and open community.

North Portal Estates

West side of 16th Street north of Holly Street, NW

Sometimes called the Nouveau Gold Coast or the Platinum Coast, North Portal Estates has been called "an urban neighborhood wrapped in suburban attire." Located at the northern tip of the District, the 214 detached homes built in the 1930s constituted one of the city's last housing developments. Black families began buying into the neighborhood in the late 1960s and early 70s as the original families left for the suburbs. With street names such as Tulip, Redwood, and Primrose, North Portal Estates, which borders on Rock Creek Park, is one of the city's most prestigious black upper middle class neighborhoods.

CHAPTER 13

Midtown and Lafayette Square

Metropolitan African Methodist Episcopal Church

1518 M Street, NW

Considered the national cathedral of the African Methodist Episcopal church movement, Metropolitan AME Church was completed in 1886. The church was built by black artisans and parishioners who cleaned and washed every brick from the razed Bethel Hall down the street.

Encircled by contemporary glass office buildings, the red brick Gothic church stands in the millenium as evidence that its loyal and tenacious congregation has hung on. After refusing purchase offers of nearly $4 million, a member noted recently that "You could not replace with money what this [church] represents to us." Originally surrounded by the homes of its members, Metropolitan AME is now the oldest continuously black-owned property in downtown Washington.

Founded by Richard Allen, the AME movement grew out of black dissatisfaction with early 19th century discriminatory practices in Methodist churches in Philadelphia, Baltimore, and Washington. Metropolitan is the product of a merger between two breakaway congregations—the Israel Bethel AME Church whose members left a white congregation in 1820 and the Union Bethel AME Church, organized by several black Georgetown groups in 1838.

Mrs. Alethia Tanner, aunt of the Reverend John F. Cook, founder of 15th Street Presbyterian Church, was the first female member of the church. After purchasing her own freedom for $1,400 in 1810, Mrs. Tanner then bought the freedom of Cook and numerous other family members.

With a seating capacity of 2,500, the church became the center for important local assemblies including the graduation ceremonies of Howard University and M Street High School. Here distinguished black political, religious, cultural and

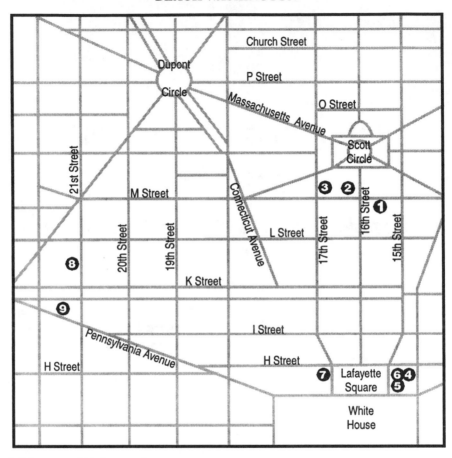

Midtown and Lafayette Square
1. Metropolitan African Methodist Episcopal Church
2. Site of The Bethel Literary and Historical Association
3. Sumner School Museum and Archives
4. Site of Wormley Hotel
5. Site of Freedmen's Savings Bank
6. Site of Belasco Theater
7. Decatur House
8. Stevens Elementary School
9. Site of Dr. John R. Francis Sanatorium

academic leaders such as John Mercer Langston, Mary Church Terrell, and Kelly Miller debated major racial issues of the day, from quality education to anti-lynching legislation. Chief Justice John Harlan and presidents McKinley, Taft and Theodore Roosevelt addressed literary society meetings at Metropolitan. In 1942 Mrs. Eleanor Roosevelt urged a capacity crowd to bring an end to racial schisms, underscoring the need for national unity in the war effort.

Plaques on various pews commemorate three remarkable church members: civic activist and president of the Phillis Wheatley YWCA, Julia West Hamilton; the first nationally recognized black poet, Paul Laurence Dunbar; and statesman Frederick Douglass. In 1895 Douglass, whose oratory had often thundered from the pulpit, was accorded a state funeral at Metropolitan AME. Supreme Court justices and members of Congress gathered with 2,500 mourners to hear Douglass eulogized by Elizabeth Cady Stanton, among others. Flags in Washington flew at half staff, and all colored public schools closed. Echoing the grief engulfing the black community, one participant lamented: "Howl, fir tree, for the Cedar of Lebanon is fallen."

During the bleak years of segregation at the turn-of-the century, Metropolitan AME was the scene of one of Washington's few integrated events. Conducting the United States Marine Band, world-famous Anglo-African composer Samuel Coleridge-Taylor presented the American premier of his Hiawatha trilogy to an overflow audience in 1903. The next day the Washington *Post* praised the chorus as "magnificent from start to finish.... Their precision and response to every move of the composer's baton was a lesson in choral singing ... they did justice to the splendid compositions."

A joyous 1912 celebration of the 50th anniversary of the Emancipation Proclamation in the District of Columbia preceded a somber and angry meeting a year later. After President Woodrow Wilson referred to segregation as "a benefit," thousands of outraged citizens poured into the church to protest the officializing of a Jim Crow policy in the federal government. "I have never seen the colored people of Washington," wrote Booker T. Washington, "so discouraged and so bitter as they are at the present time."

Site of the Bethel Literary and Historical Association

M Street between 16th and 17th Street, NW

Literary societies and lyceums such as the Lotus Club, the 19th Century Club, Monday Night Literary, and the Book Lovers Club (a women's reading circle) flourished during the 1880s and 90s. The American Negro Academy, founded in 1897 and often called the Cosmos Club of Washington's black community, was the most ambitious and intellectual of these organizations. However, the Bethel Literary and Historical Association, probably the best-known black society in the nation, was the forerunner of all these groups. Organized by AME bishop Daniel A. Payne in 1881, the original seventy-five member group met in Bethel Hall (now the site of Magruder School) before they moved the meetings to the nearby Metropolitan AME Church.

Overflow crowds heard provocative addresses on the welfare and future course of black America and enjoyed intense debate at the weekly meetings. In 1882 Frederick Douglass presented his treatise, "The Self-Made Man," a speech that he later delivered to meetings across the country.

Sumner School Museum and Archives

17th and M Street, NW

In 1981 a Washington *Post* architecture critic predicted that the 1600 block of M Street would become one of the most "visually interesting blocks in the city." Today, the immaculately restored Sumner School (1872) and its renovated younger neighbor Magruder School (1896), stand out on a street lined with 130 years of first-rate architecture.

A few years after the Civil War three desperately needed new public schools for black students—Sumner, Stevens, and Lincoln—were constructed. Adolph Cluss, a highly respected local architect specializing in school buildings, designed Sumner as a companion to his fine Franklin School (still standing on Franklin Square) for white students. Cluss' models and drawings for the modest but handsome Sumner were awarded the Medal for Progress ... in Education and School Architecture at the 1873 Exposition in Vienna, Austria.

The school's name honors U.S. Senator Charles Sumner, the outspoken advocate of integrated public education. Declaring that "the separate school is not equivalent," Sumner, with Congressman Thaddeus Stevens, introduced measures to ban segregation in education and public places. The defeat of this legislation in the early 1870s resulted in the dual school system that operated in the nation's capital until 1954.

Sumner's goal, from the moment in 1851 when the icy, emotionless senator was elected, was the abolition of slavery in the District of Columbia. After a particularly passionate speech in which he argued that it was illogical and immoral for persons to be held in bondage, Sumner was caned and beaten on the Senate floor by South Carolina Senator Preston Smith Brooks. Although it took Sumner several years to recover completely from his injuries, he never relented in his struggle to repeal all fugitive slave laws; to equalize the pay of black and white soldiers during the Civil War; and to establish a Freedmen's Bureau to act as a "bridge from slavery to freedom." Senator Sumner lived a few blocks west of the school on the northwest corner of H Street and Vermont Avenue, NW.

Hailed as "the single most important building in the development of free public instruction for blacks in the District of Columbia," Sumner School has served as a cornerstone in the evolution of educational opportunities for Washington's black community for more than a century. The building housed both a primary school and, for a few years, the first black public high school in the nation. The superintendent and board of trustees for the Colored Public Schools of Washington and Georgetown were also headquartered here in the tower offices.

The award-winning restoration of Sumner was completed in 1986 when it reopened as a museum and archives of the District public schools. The school's space is used for lectures, art exhibitions, and performances by community and non-profit organizations and learned societies.

Site of Wormley Hotel

Southwest corner of 15th and H Streets, NW

"Of all the black businesses of the 19th century," historian Letitia Brown observed, "James Wormley's Hotel was the most widely known." News of the skilled and successful hotelier's death in 1884 was announced on the front page of the Washington *Star*, describing Wormley as "one of the most remarkable colored men in the country."

Born in 1819 to a prominent free black family in the District, Wormley worked first as a hacker in his father's livery stable business on Pennsylvania Avenue. Lured to California by the Gold Rush, Wormley later served as a steward on transatlantic ships, Mississippi River steamboats, and, upon his return to Washington, he was employed at the exclusive Metropolitan Club. Just before the Civil War, Wormley established a prosperous catering and restaurant business. So widespread was his reputation in the culinary arts that Reverdy Johnson, the U.S. ambassador to the Court of St. James, convinced Wormley to leave his family and accompany him to London as his valet after the war.

Returning home with linen, crystal, and china which he had purchased, Wormley opened his fashionable hotel at 15th and H Streets, NW, in 1871. The stately five-story hotel quickly became a favorite of congressmen and foreign dignitaries who appreciated the establishment's European atmosphere and its meticulous attention to detail. The hotel's bar, first-class barbershop, and dining room, renowned for its superb food, made Wormley's a gathering place for the rich and powerful and a favorite of Vice-President Schuyler Colfax, generals Winfield Scott and George McClelland, and Assistant Secretary of State John Hay. During the initial weeks following the shooting of President Garfield, Wormley was called upon to prepare the meals for the fatally wounded president.

The hotel was the location of the so-called Wormley Conference of 1877. Although Wormley did not participate himself, politicans from both political parties conducted a series of clandestine meetings to resolve the stalemated Hayes-Tilden election. The resulting secret agreement provided for the end of Reconstruction and the removal of federal troops from the South in exchange for the election of Rutherford B. Hayes.

Indicative of his unique status in the nation's capital, Wormley was a charter member of the Washington Board of Trade and was selected by the U.S. Senate to be among those who accompanied the body of Vice-President Henry Wilson home to Massachusetts after his death in 1875. At the time of his friend Senator Charles Sumner's death, Wormley purchased the furnishings from the senator's home and placed them in the hotel's Summer Parlor.

After Wormley's death the Reverend Francis Grimké eulogized him as "a manly man, a man who respected himself and who demanded respect from others ... there was nothing cringing or obsequious about him in his contact with white people. He was a race man, in the sense that he was thoroughly interested in the welfare of the race."

The hotel continued under the management of Wormley's eldest son, James T., who had established a reputation as the proprietor of the city's first black-owned pharmacy in 1870. Renamed the Colonial by new owners in 1897, the hotel was razed nine years later, to make way for the present Union Trust Company building.

Site of Freedmen's Savings Bank

Northeast corner of Pennsylvania Avenue and Madison Place, NW

Freedmen's Savings Bank, organized in 1865, was a showcase of black economic achievement until massive mismanagement and fraud caused its collapse in 1874.

The bank stemmed from efforts during the Civil War to establish banking facilities on army posts to protect the paychecks of black soldiers and employees who were often the targets of swindlers. Chartered in New York by Congress in

1865 to teach freedmen thrift and honest enterprise, Freedmen's quickly established thirty-two branches throughout the South. Although General O.O. Howard was its president, the bank had no connection with the Freedmen's Bureau which he headed.

In 1868 the bank transferred its headquarters to a magnificent Second Empire-style building across the street from the White House in Washington. One of the city's most costly commercial buildings at that time, the thrift institution was criticized by some for its elaborate trappings. Built almost entirely by black artisans and laborers, the interior of the brownstone was lavishly furnished with black walnut woodwork and desks, marble countertops, and the latest burglar-proof safe.

Prior to 1870 the bank was conservatively managed by a white board of trustees. After the bank's move to Washington, notable blacks were added to the board. Nearly half of the bank's tellers and cashiers were black. Overjoyed with the existence of a bank to serve his people, Frederick Douglass in his autobiography described his early exhilaration:

> ... I often peeped into its spacious windows, and looked down the row of its gentlemanly and elegantly dressed colored clerks, with their pens behind their ears and button-hole bouquet in the coat-fronts, and felt my very eyes enriched. It was a sight I had never expected to see. I was amazed with the facility with which they counted the money. They threw off the thousands with the dexterity, if not the accuracy, of old experienced clerks.

The overextension of credit for real estate investments, neglectful New York trustees, racial opposition to the bank in the South, incompetent bank managers and cashiers, and the Panic of 1873, all contributed to Freedmen's collapse. In March 1874 Frederick Douglass was elected to the bank's presidency. Chosen for his prestige and integrity, Douglass knew very little about the banking business or the bank's precarious financial position. The eminent leader was at the helm when Freedmen's closed in June. Thousands of citizens lost their life savings; the Washington *Post* noted that when the bankruptcy was announced, "there was gloom among the colored population of the country."

Site of Belasco Theater

17 Madison Place, NW
(Court of Claims Building)

The old Lafayette Opera House, the "swankiest place in all of Washington" and scene of Helen Hayes' stage debut at age five, was renamed the Belasco when the Shubert Company owned and operated it after World War I. Black patrons were admitted only to the balcony during these early years of the century.

It was at the Belasco that black actor Charles Gilpin made his Washington debut in the highly acclaimed production, *The Emperor Jones*. Opening in New York on November 1, 1920, the play established the young playwright Eugene O'Neill as a giant American talent and made Gilpin a star. The first black to play a major role in an American tragedy, Gilpin was one of ten honorees selected by the Drama League for their contributions to the American theater that year. After the play's brilliant four-year run and tour, the actor and playwright had a falling out over Gilpin's interpretation of O'Neill's dialogue. For the 1925 revival the playwright cast a new actor, Paul Robeson, to play the demanding role of Brutus Jones, the Pullman car conductor cum emperor. Gilpin slipped into obscurity and died on a New Jersey chicken farm in 1930.

Decatur House

Northwest corner of Lafayette Square
Jackson Place and H Street, NW

Decatur House, one of the capital's most elegant residences, was the site of a notorious slave pen during the 1830s and 40s. Designed by Benjamin Latrobe for naval hero Commodore Stephen Decatur, the mansion became the property of former Alexandria tavernkeeper John Gadsby sixteen years after young Decatur's untimely death in 1820 on the dueling fields of Bladensburg, Maryland.

The proprietor of the well-known National Hotel at Pennsylvania Avenue and 6th Street, NW, Gadsby also dealt in the slave trade, keeping slaves destined for the rear courtyard auction block quartered in the attic and in the brick ell section of the house fronting on H Street. "At night," wrote one contemporary, "you could hear their howls and cries." It is thought that many of these slaves were shipped to Georgia's vast cotton plantations.

The slave activities of Gadsby, reputed to be among the richest of Washington's citizens, did not inhibit his entry into Washington's social circles. The socially elite were accustomed to the lavish parties given in this gracious home by the previous owners; Gadsby, the hotelier, continued that tradition of splendid entertainment. He did not, however, fool all of his guests. The French minister wrote that his host was "an old wretch who has made a fortune in the slave trade, which does not prevent Washington society from rushing to his house and I should make my government very unpopular if I refused to associate with this kind of people."

Stevens Elementary School

21st Street between K and L Streets, NW

Nestled among the modern office buildings, Stevens School, one of the oldest surviving black elementary schools in the District, remains a regal link to 19th century Washington.

The colored public school system, organized in 1862, was, in theory, to receive 10 percent of all tax revenues from black citizens. That amount was inadequate; therefore Congress passed additional legislation in 1866 to allocate a portion of total tax funds for the support of black education in the District. Stevens was built in 1868 at a cost of $26,000. Chairman William Syphax of the Colored Schools Board of Trustees suggested naming the school to honor Pennsylvania congressman Thaddeus Stevens. In 1976 Stevens became one of the most famous public schools in the United States when President Carter's daughter Amy enrolled here. In 1997 Stevens School was on the School Board's list for closure.

Site of Dr. John R. Francis Sanatorium

2112 Pennsylvania Avenue, NW

In a three-story Victorian townhouse, Dr. John R. Francis, a black physician and former assistant surgeon-in-chief at Freedmen's Hospital, offered the "treatment of a hospital, combined with the comforts of home" in his well-equipped sanatorium on Pennsylvania Avenue. "To look into its clean, well-kept rooms," according to one account, "makes one think, if he must be sick, this is the place to be." Patients were accommodated at the sanatorium without regard to race, making it a unique establishment in Washington at that time.

CHAPTER 14

Georgetown

Herring Hill, named for the main food staple fished from Rock Creek by that neighborhood's families, was a 15-block area in east Georgetown that was home to that town's black community. From the mid-1800s to the turn of the century, most of black Georgetown lived south of P Street between Rock Creek Park and 31st Street. A majority of these 1000 families worked as cooks, domestics, gardeners, and stable boys for the area's white residents.

By the 1920s Georgetown's many Victorian rowhouses and stately Federal houses were in poor condition. A former resident recalled that by 1940 Georgetown was a transitional neighborhood, "a crossroad between black and white families and 29th Street was the border." During the administration of President Franklin D. Roosevelt, New Dealers converged on Washington looking for affordable housing. Black home owners were offered high prices by real estate operators who quickly turned over the renovated rowhouses to the new white residents. Although most of Georgetown's original black families have moved to the suburbs or other areas of Washington, several of their churches endure, still energetically maintained by their scattered congregations.

The First Baptist Church of Georgetown

27th and Dumbarton Avenue, NW

Founded in 1862 by a former slave, the Reverend Sandy Alexander, First Baptist Church is the earliest known Baptist church in Georgetown. During its first twenty years the congregation worshipped in a makeshift frame building at 21st and O Streets, NW, known as the Ark. After the Reverend Alexander raised $300 in the North and borrowed an additional $300 to begin building, he presided at

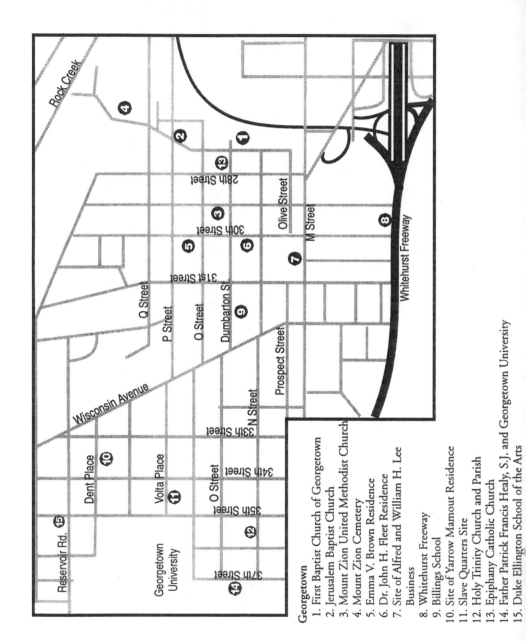

Georgetown
1. First Baptist Church of Georgetown
2. Jerusalem Baptist Church
3. Mount Zion United Methodist Church
4. Mount Zion Cemetery
5. Emma V. Brown Residence
6. Dr. John H. Fleet Residence
7. Site of Alfred and William H. Lee Business
8. Whitehurst Freeway
9. Billings School
10. Site of Yarrow Mamout Residence
11. Slave Quarters Site
12. Holy Trinity Church and Parish
13. Epiphany Catholic Church
14. Father Patrick Francis Healy, S.J. and Georgetown University
15. Duke Ellington School of the Arts

the cornerstone ceremony for the present brick church in 1882. The church paid off this debt during Alexander's nearly 40-year minstry.

A dissident group of parishioners left First Baptist in 1908 and founded Montgomery Memorial Baptist, named after First Baptist's extraordinary pastor. In 1909 they purchased the property at 2709 N Street where the church is now located.

Jerusalem Baptist Church

2600 P Street, NW

As the number of Baptists increased in Georgetown, First Baptist's Reverend Alexander helped found a sister church, Seventh Baptist, in 1870. The present red brick building with its two glorious stained glass windows facing P Street was completed in 1903 when the church was renamed Jerusalem Baptist.

Mount Zion United Methodist Church

1334 29th Street, NW

Mount Zion United Methodist Church is considered the oldest black congregation in the District of Columbia. Dissatisfied with their segregated status in the Montgomery Street Church (now the Dumbarton Avenue United Methodist Church) and constituting nearly half of the congregation, blacks organized the church in 1816. The congregation purchased a parcel of land from Georgetown foundry owner Henry Foxhall, and the small frame dwelling, pastored by a white minister from the parent church, was called "The Little Ark." The church adopted the name Mount Zion in 1846.

In 1823 the church established one of the earliest schools for black children and later became an active station on the Underground Railroad route to Canada and freedom. Fleeing slaves were hidden in a burial vault in the nearby Mount Zion Cemetery (2700 Q Street, NW).

Records indicate that the church's membership declined from 469 in the mid-1850s to 331 in the late 1860s. The fate of these members was often cryptically noted after their names. "Lost" referred to tragic and mysterious disappearances; "taken away" meant that they had been captured by patrollers or bounty hunters; and "gone away" indicated that they had been sent by the Railroad to Harper's Ferry on the road to Canada.

The site for the present church was purchased in 1875 from local black businessman Alfred Pope. Much of the construction work was performed by black workers and church members. The Gothic red-brick church building was dedicated in 1884.

The tiny community house around the corner at 2906 O Street was built in 1813, probably as a slave quarters. The church purchased it in 1920 for meetings and for the city's first black library. It is the last standing English-style brick cottage in the District and was lovingly restored by the church in 1982.

Mount Zion continues to be a vigorous family church, although many of its members no longer live in Georgetown.

Mount Zion Cemetery

2700 block of Q Street, NW

In 1879, "for the sum of one dollar in hand," Mount Zion Church, one of Washington's several black churches, leased a burial ground for 99 years at the east end of the Dumbarton Church cemetery (known as the Old Methodist Burying Ground.) The Female Union Band Society, a benevolent association of black women formed in 1842 to provide for the burial of free blacks, purchased land nearby. Both graveyards—adjacent but separate—have constituted the Mount Zion Cemetery for over a century.

Interments continued into the 1950s when the Board of Health closed the dilapidated cemetery. Much sought after by developers and speculators, community activists and organizations planning the 1976 U.S. Bicentennial celebration protested and went to court. In 1975 Judge Oliver Gasch of the U.S. District Court ordered the restoration of the adjoining cemeteries declaring the violation of their cemetery "involves the destruction of a monument of evolving free black culture in the District of Columbia." Each October a neighborhood festival raises funds for the care of the cemeteries.

The cemetery is located behind the row of townhouses on the north side of the 2700 block of Q Street, NW.

Emma V. Brown Residence

3044 P Street, NW

Emma V. Brown devoted her life to the education of Washington's black children. Educated at Oberlin College, Miss Brown studied with Myrtilla Miner (see Miner Teachers College Builing) and later became her assistant. In 1861 she opened a school for Georgetown's black children in her home. When the first publicly financed school for blacks was organized in the basement of the Ebenezer Methodist Church on Capitol Hill in 1864, Miss Brown became one of the two teachers.

In 1870 Emma Brown was appointed by the board of trustees of the Colored Public Schools to head the John F. Cook School on O Street, NW. A year later she became the principal of the Sumner School at 17th and M Street, NW.

Dr. John H. Fleet Residence

1208 30th Street, NW

One of three black physicians in the District of Columbia prior to 1864, Dr. Fleet purchased the modest rowhouse at 1208 30th Street for $800 in 1843. Educated at the Lancastrian School in Georgetown, where attorney Francis Scott Key was a teacher, Fleet studied medicine with a former assistant surgeon of the U.S. Army under the sponsorship of the American Colonization Society. When Fleet completed his course of study and refused to emigrate to Liberia, he was denounced by the Society. Dr. Fleet was described in a 19th century history of District schools, as "a refined and polished gentleman, and conceded to be the foremost colored man in culture, in intellectual force and general influence in the District...."

Dr. Fleet's career was spent in education and music rather than medicine. In 1843 he opened a school for black students which was burned "by an incendiary." His second school near N and 23rd Streets was very successful. A violinist and "one of the ablest colored musicians in the city," Fleet also taught music.

Fleet's daughter Genevieve attended Oberlin College and became the principal of Stevens Elemetary School in the early 1870s.

Site of Alfred and William H. Lee Business

2906 M Street, NW

Alfred Lee was among the city's most prosperous black merchants. Established in 1830, his Flour, Grain, Feed and Hay business quickly flourished, and prior to the Civil War the wealthy Lee purchased a mansion on H Street, NW, that had formerly housed the British legation. Worth over $300,000 at the time of his death in 1893, his business was operated well into the 20th century by his widow and son, William H. Lee.

Probably descended from the famous Lee family of Virginia, one of Lee's obituary notices wryly concluded that, "on the whole, the career of the 'Honorable' Alfred seems to have been far more serviceable to his country than that of the other branch of the family."

Whitehurst Freeway

Georgetown Waterfront, above K Street, NW

The Whitehurst Freeway (1949), as well as the Tidal Basin Bridge and seawall near the Jefferson Memorial, were two of the many engineering projects in the 42-year career of Archie A. Alexander. Graduated with honors from the University of Iowa where he was the first black varsity football player, Alexander founded his own general contracting firm before joining a college classmate in the partnership of Alexander and Repass. Always active in community affairs and civil rights, Alexander changed the "white" and "colored" restroom signs to read "skilled" and "unskilled" on his construction sites.

In 1954 Alexander was appointed governor of the Virgin Islands by President Dwight Eisenhower.

The Billings School

3100-3108 Dumbarton, NW

The Billings School was considered "one of the earliest and finest schools" where Georgetown's black children could receive a quality education. In 1800 Mary Billings, who was white, arrived in Georgetown with her husband from England. After her husband's death seven years later, Mrs. Billings opened her school. Because she taught both black and white students, her first attempt was short-lived. A mixed school was unacceptable to the local white community and her school closed.

Undaunted, she opened a second school, exclusively for black children, on Dumbarton Avenue between Congress and High Street in 1810. The school moved several more times before Mrs. Billings's death in 1826.

Site of Yarrow Mamout Residence

3330-3332 Dent Place, NW

Although almost unrecognized today, Yarrow Mamout was a prominent resident of early 19th century Georgetown. After purchasing his freedom from his Georgetown master, Mamout used one of his few possessions, a cart, to establish a successful hauling business. Investing his profits, he became one of the first depositors of the Bank of Columbia, and bought a house in Georgetown in 1800.

In 1819 Mamout sat for artist Charles Willson Peale, probably the most accomplished portrait painter in federal America. "I spent the whole day and painted a good likeness of him," Peale wrote. "Yarrow owns a House and lots and is known by most of the Inhabitants of Georgetown and particularly by the Boys who are often teazing him which he takes in good humor." Peale's portrait of Yarrow Mamout now hangs in the Peabody Collection of the Georgetown Public Library.

Yarrow Mamout was a unique citizen of his time who "lived through the American Revolution, acquired property, never gave up his Moslem religion, and lived to be over one hundred years old...."

Slave Quarters Site

3410 Volta Place, NW

Two small cottages at this address were once used as slave quarters. Local slave owners often provided living quarters for their slaves away from the main residence. These slaves performed skilled labor for the master and were frequently "for hire" to others. Usually the most minimal of shelter, the quarters were lofts, stables, alley shacks or a cottage.

Holy Trinity Church and Parish

36th Street between N and O Streets, NW
3515 N Street, NW (original church site)

Blacks have been parishioners at Holy Trinity Church from its beginning in 1787. For more than a century it was the only place that black Catholics in Georgetown could worship. In the early years black members had to stand in the center of the nave with those who could not afford to rent pews during church services. Later, they sat in an extension of the choir loft that was entered by a separate stairway.

Records from the early 1800s indicate that one of Georgetown's most prominent black Catholic families, the William Becrafts, belonged to Holy Trinity. A free person, Mrs. Becraft was the housekeeper for Charles Carroll of Carrollton, signer of the Declaration of Independence. Mr. Becraft was the chief steward at the Union Hotel. After teaching at Mrs. Billings School, daughter Maria established her own school on Dumbarton Street in 1820. Later, with the help of the clergy at Holy Trinity, Maria Becraft founded the first academy for black girls on 35th Street across from the Convent of the Visitation. She abandoned her teaching career in 1831 to take her vows as a Sister of Providence. Her death two years later ended a brief and illustrious career.

Epiphany Catholic Church

2717 Dumbarton Avenue, NW

The Epiphany Mission was organized by 350 black members of segregated Holy Trinity Church in 1924. They rented a property in eastern Georgetown at 1409 28th Street and subsequently purchased two lots on Dumbarton Avenue, the present site.

The first black priest to serve any Catholic Church in Washington was Epiphany's Father Chester C. Ball from 1952 to 1958.

Father Patrick Francis Healy, S.J., and Georgetown University

37th and O Streets, NW

The history of black American Catholicism begins with the Healy brothers. Father James Healy was the first black Catholic priest and bishop in America. His brother, Father Patrick F. Healy, became the first black Jesuit and the first black president of a major college in the United States. Born in Georgia in 1834 to an Irish father and a mulatto slave mother, Patrick Healy was educated by Quakers. In 1850 he received his bachelor's degree from Holy Cross College before entering the Jesuit order. After studying in Europe he returned to the U.S. in 1866 to teach at Georgetown College and eight years later became its president.

Father Healy is best remembered for his dedicated leadership in turning the small college into a major educational and spiritual center. His efforts expanded and strengthened the curricula of both the law and medical schools. Built during his tenure, the 1879 Victorian Healy Building dominates the Georgetown skyline.

Father Healy left his post in 1882, but returned in 1908 to the university's campus infirmary where he died. He is buried in the Jesuit cemetery on the grounds of the university.

Duke Ellington School of the Arts

35th and R Streets, NW

Named for one of Washington's most famous citizens, the Duke Ellington School of the Arts, a D.C. public high school, is a four-year pre-professional institution for training in dance, vocal and instrumental music, drama, and the visual arts. Entrance for Washington's gifted teenagers is gained through a rigorous audition process. However, Ellington places equal emphasis on its academic and arts curriculum. Almost 80 percent of the school's graduates continue their training at many of the nation's eminent schools such as Juilliard, Pratt Institute of Art, or Rhode Island School of Design.

Ellington occupies the former Western High School building on a hill overlooking upper Georgetown.

CHAPTER 15

Foggy Bottom and the Mall

Foggy Bottom Neighborhood

South of K Street and Pennsylvania Avenue,
between 17th and 25th Streets, NW

Originally a small fishing village laid out in 1768 as a seaport to rival Georgetown, the swampy and often unhealthy area of Foggy Bottom along the Potomac River was called Hamburgh. It was home to succeeding waves of ethnic and immigrant families. Many former slaves and free blacks moved here before the Civil War, while other contraband and destitute freedmen inhabited the abandoned Camp Fry barracks after the war. The building of Washington's gas plant in 1857 secured Foggy Bottom's future as a working-class neighborhood. Irish, Italian, and German families lived near their places of employment in a deteriorating neighborhood of industrial plants, the Heurich and Abner Drury breweries, and vacant lots. The enclave of Irish gas-house workers around 23rd Street quickly became known as Connaught Row.

By 1900 and for the next fifty years Foggy Bottom was filled with miserable slums, many occupied by impoverished black families. Now, thirty years after the onset of urban renewal, few blacks remain in the gentrified Foggy Bottom neighborhood.

St. Mary's Episcopal Church

728 23rd Street, NW

A historic landmark, St. Mary's Episcopal Church is an architectural jewel, designed by 19th century architect James Renwick. Renwick had previously enhanced Washington with his designs for William Wilson Corcoran's original Gallery of Art (now named the Renwick Gallery), the Smithsonian Castle building on the Mall, and the small chapel in Georgetown's Oak Hill Cemetery.

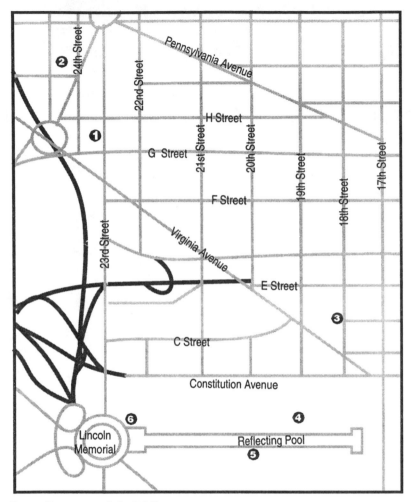

Foggy Bottom and the Mall
1. St. Mary's Episcopal Church
2. Snow's Court
3. Negro Mother and Child Sculpture
4. Future Site of the Black Patriots Memorial
5. Site of Resurrection City
6. The Lincoln Memorial

The first black Protestant Episcopal Church in the District, St. Mary's, like many other black churches in Washington, symbolizes the struggle for religious equality and dignity.

Twenty-eight black men and women met in 1867 to separate from the Episcopal Church of the Epiphany downtown and to form their own congregation. St. Mary's Chapel for Colored People would be free from the the discriminatory practices experienced at the Church of the Epiphany. The chapel building was secured through the efforts of Secretary of War Edwin Stanton. Epiphany's rector recalled that the secretary had mentioned that "there was a chapel attached to Kalorama Hospital [used during the Civil War], which was about to be taken down and sold for lumber. I asked him to give it to the Colored people for a church. He was pleased with the suggestion and offered to have it taken down carefully and rebuilt."

In 1873 the congregation gained its own black pastor, the Reverend Alexander Crummell. After a dispute over the property deed, Crummell left St. Mary's and led a majority of his congregation to St. Luke's Episcopal Church on 15th Street when that building was completed in 1879.

The remaining small congregation was able to hire the distinguished Mr. Renwick to design the impressive, brick church building at a cost of $15,000. Of particular interest in the interior are the handsome timber roof of the nave and the stained glass windows, one of which is from the Tiffany Studio and honors Secretary Edwin Stanton. Three others over the altar are from the famous Lorin manufactory in Chartres, France.

Snow's Court

Interior of block bounded by 24th, 25th, I and K Streets, NW

Snow's Court, the first inhabited alley in Foggy Bottom (c. 1860), housed more than 300 persons by 1892 and was one of nine such alleys in the neighborhood. Irish immigrants originally inhabited the four frame buildings and greenhouse built by *National Intelligencer* publisher C.A. Snow on his property in the interior of the block. By 1912 all residents were black except for one family that operated a small store in the court. Conditions in crime-ridden Snow's Court were among the worst in the city. Social workers were afraid to enter the large alley community. Reformer Charles Weller found a family of eight living in two rooms that he described as "filthy." In spite of the conditions, a sense of community grew among the inhabitants. One resident lived at six different addresses in Snow's Court. Each time she had moved away, she missed life in the alley and returned to a different home.

In 1953 Snow's Court became one of the earliest urban renewal projects in Foggy Bottom. Twenty-six century-old rowhouses that had accommodated 10 to 12 persons per home with no gas, electricity, or indoor plumbing were renovated into picturesque townhouses and sold for $14,750 each.

Negro Mother and Child Sculpture

Department of the Interior Courtyard
C Street between 18th and 19th Streets, NW

Hidden away in the inner courtyard at the Department of the Interior is a touching bronze sculpture entitled *Negro Mother and Child*, executed by sculptor Maurice Glickman in 1934 under the auspices of the Public Works of Art Project. The original plaster model is located at the Founders' Library on the Howard University campus.

Future Site of the Black Patriots Memorial

Constitution Gardens, The Mall

A Memorial to black Revolutionary War Patriots will be built on the Mall between the Lincoln Memorial and the Washington Monument, a reminder that African Americans were cofounders of our nation's independence. The first American to lose his life in the Revolution was a black man who had escaped slavery, Crispus Attucks. Over 5,000 African Americans, both slave and free, fought in most of the War's major battles including Bunker Hill, Saratoga and Yorktown, and were part of General Washington's troops at Valley Forge.

The Memorial, designed by black sculptor Ed Dwight and Washington architect Marshall Purnell, will consist of two curved sloping walls facing one another. The one, a curving 90-foot bronze sculpture, will begin with figures in bas relief—vaguely visible—representing the black patriots and their families. As the wall continues, the figures become more distinct, finally emerging as individuals, signifying the break from bondage. The opposing granite wall will feature a fragment of a poem by the contemporary poet and the first black woman poet in America, Phillis Wheatley:

In every human Breast,
God has implanted a Principle,
which we call love of Freedom;
it is impatient of Oppression,
and parts for Deliverance....

Aiming for a July 4, 2000 dedication, private funds of nearly $10 million for the Memorial are being raised by the Black Patriots Foundation and through the sale of commemorative coins produced by the U.S. Mint.

Site of Resurrection City

West Potomac Park, The Mall

"We will be here," declared the Reverend Ralph David Abernathy of the Southern Christian Leadership Conference (SCLC), "until the Congress and leaders of government decide they are going to do something about poverty, unemployment, and underemployment in the United States." In May 1968 Reverend Abernathy, successor to the slain Dr. Martin Luther King, Jr., as head of SCLC, opened Resurrection City, the Poor People's Campaign encampment around the Reflecting Pool on the Mall.

The nation's poor and unemployed came to Washington to demand jobs and programs to eradicate poverty in the country. Vowing not to leave until the Congress and political leaders addressed their problems, the demonstrators camped here in 600 plywood and canvas A-frame structures. Spread over most of this site's fifteen acres, Resurrection City was organized into neighborhoods and blocks around two principal streets named after King and Abernathy.

Providing necessary conveniences for nearly 3,000 camped residents was a staggering task. Campaign organizers supplied electricity, water, telephones, trash removal, sanitation, and sewage facilities. A local committee headed by Giant Food Store's Joseph Danzansky mobilized scores of churches, charitable organizations, and corporations to provide food, including one hot meal per day, cooked elsewhere and trucked into the community.

Calamity plagued Resurrection City. After a week of torrential spring rains the encampment oozed with ankle-deep mud; then an early beginning to summer brought sizzling heat and dust. These severe weather conditions were followed by a wave of violent incidents between the police and a few rowdy Resurrection City residents after a series of muggings and assaults on visitors and members of the press. The high point of the Resurrection City project was to be a giant Solidarity Day rally on June 19. Although a symbolic mule train carrying 100 poor people from Marks, Mississippi, finally entered the city shortly before the rally, the crowd of 50,000 was well below the organizers' anticipated goal. After a one-week National Park Service permit extension, Resurrection City was closed on June 24 as police and city workers swept through the Mall, dismantling the nearly deserted community. In contrast to the mood of hopefulness and optimism after the 1963 March on Washington, the aftermath of Resurrection City was one of disillusionment.

The Lincoln Memorial

Potomac Park, west end of Mall

Washington's pervasive segregation could not have been more dramatically illustrated than at the dedication of the Lincoln Memorial in May 1922. One of the principal speakers, Dr. Robert Moten, president of Tuskegee Institute, sat with other distinguished black guests in an all-Negro section, roped off from the main speaker's platform. American blacks were indignant.

On an extraordinary Easter Sunday afternoon in 1939 the national spotlight again focused on Washington's discrimination problems. Before 75,000 persons, contralto Marian Anderson presented a recital of operatic arias, spirituals, and patriotic music. She recalled that "the crowd stretched in a great semicircle from the Lincoln Memorial around the reflecting pool onto the grounds of the Washington Monument. I had a feeling that a great wave of goodwill poured out from these people, almost engulfing me."

Miss Anderson had accepted an invitation from Howard University to perform in concert. When the Daughters of the American Revolution (DAR) refused use of their Constitution Hall, the city's finest concert auditorium, an outraged community formed the Marian Anderson Citizens Committee. The committee requested the use of the large auditorium at white Central High School. The D.C. Board of Education granted one-time-only permission with the proviso that this concession was not precedent setting. Miss Anderson refused to perform under such degrading conditions. Public pressure continued after First Lady Eleanor Roosevelt resigned her DAR membership, and Secretary of the Interior Harold Ickes offered the Lincoln Memorial for the concert.

The day after the concert Mary McLeod Bethune wrote to Charles Houston, attorney for the citizens committee, that history would record the moving event, but "it will never be able to tell what happened in the hearts of the thousands who stood and listened.... I came away almost walking in the air. My hopes for the future were brightened. All fear has vanished. We are on the right track—we must go forward." Marian Anderson's Easter concert marked a turning point in the struggle for civil rights.

From that day citizens have come to the base of the monumental figure of President Lincoln to protest and voice their opinions. On August 28, 1963, planes, buses, cars and trains brought the largest crowd in history to the nation's capital. The March on Washington for Jobs and Freedom, sponsored by five major civil rights organizations—the Southern Christian Leadership Conference, NAACP, CORE, the Urban League, and the Student Non-Violent Coordinating Committee—was the most hopeful and optimistic event in the long struggle for equal rights. Thousands of citizens—black and white, farmer and congressman, student and elderly—marched up Pennsylvania Avenue to the memorial where they stood mesmerized as the young Reverend Martin Luther King, Jr. described his vision of an America free from racism: "I have a dream that my four little children will one day live in a nation where they will not be judged by the color of their skin but by the content of their character."

Selected Bibliography

BOOKS

African and African American Resources at the Smithsonian. Washington, D.C.: Smithsonian Institution, n.d.

Apidta, Dr. Tingba. *The Hidden History of Washington, DC: A Guide for Black Folks.* Second in a Series. Washington, D.C.: The Reclamation Project, 1996.

Anderson, Jervis. *This Was Harlem 1900-1950.* New York: Farrar Straus Giroux, 1981.

Baker Association. *Baker Handbook of Negro-Owned Businesses.* Washington, D.C. Metro Publications, 1947-1948.

Bancroft, Frederic. *Slave Trading in the Old South.* New York: Frederick Ungar Publishing Co., 1959.

Beale, Marie. *Decatur House and Its Inhabitants.* Washington: National Trust, 1954.

Bergheim, Laura. *The Look-It-Up Guide to Washington Libraries and Archives.* Osprey, Florida: Beacham Publishing, Inc., 1995.

Birmingham, Stephen. *Certain People: America's Black Elite.* Boston: Little, Brown and Co., 1977.

Borchert, James. *Alley Life in Washington 1850-1970.* Urbana: University of Illinois Press, 1980.

Brawley, Benjamin. *Negro Genius.* New York: Biblo and Tannen, 1966.

Brown, Letitia W. *Residence Patterns of Negroes in the District of Columbia, 1800-1860.* Records of the Columbia Historical Society, Washington, D.C. 1969-1970. 69-70 (June 1971), 66-79.

Brown, Letitia W., and Lewis, Elise M. *Washington From Banneker to Douglass, 1791-1870.* Washington, D.C.: Education Department, National Portrait Gallery, Smithsonian Institution, 1971.

_____. *Washington in the New Era, 1870-1970.* Washington, D.C.: Smithsonian Institution, 1971.

_____. *Free Negroes in the District of Columbia, 1790-1846.* New York, 1972.

Brown, William Wells. *The Rising Sun*. New York: Negro University Press, 1970.

Cary, Francine Curro. *Urban Odyssey: A Multicultural History of Washington, D.C.* Washington, D.C.: Smithsonian Institution Press, 1996.

Carpenter, John A. *Sword and Olive Branch: Oliver Otis Howard.* Pittsburgh: Pittsburgh University Press.

City Directories for the District of Columbia.

Christopher, Maurine. *America's Black Congregation*. New York: Crowell, 1971.

Clarke, Nina. *History of the Nineteenth-Century Black Churches in Maryland and Washington, D.C.* New York: Vantage Press, 1983.

Clark-Lewis, Elizabeth. *Living In, Living Out: African American Domestics in Washington, D.C., 1910-1940.* Washington, D.C.: Smithsonian Institution Press, 1994.

Collins, Kathleen. *Washingtoniana Photographs, Collections in the Prints and Photographs Division of the Library of Congress.* Washington, DC: Library of Congress, 1989.

Colored Professionals, Clerical, Skilled and Business Directory of Baltimore City. Baltimore: R. W. Coleman, 1913.

Cook, Patricia M. *"Like the Phoenix". The Rebirth of the Whitelaw Hotel.* Washington History Vol. 7, No. 1 (Spring/Summer 1995), 4-23.

Cosentino, Andrew J. and Glassie, Henry H. *The Capital Image: Painters in Washington, 1800-1915.* Washington, D.C.: Smithsonian Institution Press, 1983.

D.C. Department of Housing and Community Development. *LeDroit Park Conserved.* Washington, D.C., c.1979.

D.C. History Curriculum Project. *City of Magnificent Intentions: A History of the District of Columbia.* Washington: Intac, Inc. 1983.

Dyson, Walter. *Howard University: The Capstone of Negro Education.* Washington, D.C.: The Graduate School Howard University, 1941.

Edmonds, Helen G. *Black Faces In High Places: Negroes in Government.* New York: Harcourt Brace Jovanovich, 1971.

Ellington, Edward Kennedy. *Music is My Mistress.* New York: Da Capo Press, 1976.

Fausett, Arthur. *Black Gods of the Metropolis.* Philadelphia: University of Pennsylvania Press, 1944.

Federal Writer's Project. *Washington, City and Capital.* American Guide Series. Washington, 1937.

Fleming, G. James and Burckel, Christian E., eds. *Who's Who in Colored America.* Seventh Edition. Supplement. Yonkers-on-Hudson, New York: Christian E. Burckel & Associates, 1950.

Fleming, Walter L. *The Freedmen's Savings Bank.* Westport, Conn.: Negro University Press, 1970.

Foner, Eric. *Freedom's Lawmakers. A Directory of Black Officeholders During Reconstruction.* Revised Edition. Baton Rouge: Louisiana State University Press, 1996.

Forman, Stephen M. *A Guide to Civil War Washington.* Washington, DC: Elliott & Clark Publishing, 1995.

Gatewood, Willard B. *Aristocrats of Color: The Black Elite, 1880-1920.* Bloomington: Indiana University Press, 1990.

Goode, James M. *The Outdoor Sculpture of Washington, D.C., A Comprehensive Historical Guide.* Washington, D.C.: Smithsonian Institution Press, 1975.

_____. *Capital Losses: A Cultural History of Washington's Destroyed Buildings.* Washington, D.C.: Smithsonian Institution Press, 1979.

Gilbert, Ben W. *Ten Blocks from the White House, Anatomy of the Washington Riots of 1968.* New York: Praeger, 1968.

Gillette, Howard, Jr. *Between Justice and Beauty: Race, Planning, and the Failure of Urban Policy in Washington, D.C.* Baltimore: The Johns Hopkins University Press, 1995.

_____, ed. *Southern City, National Ambition. The Growth of Early Washington, D.C., 1800- 1860.* Washington, D.C.: The American Architectural Foundation and The George Washington University Center for Washington Area Studies, 1995.

Gilman, Michael. *Matthew Henson, Explorer.* New York: Chelsea House Publishers, 1988.

Green, Constance McLaughlin. *The Secret City, A History of Race Relations in the Nation's Capital.* Princeton, N.J.: Princeton University Press, 1967.

_____. *Washington: A History of the Capital, 1800-1950.* Princeton, N.J.: Princeton University Press, 1962.

Ham, Debra Newman, ed. *The African American Mosaic, A Library of Congress Resource Guide for the Study of Black History & Culture.* Washington, DC: Library of Congress, 1993.

Harris, Abram L. *The Negro As Capitalist: A Study of Banking and Business Among American Negroes.* Philadelphia: The American Academy of Political and Social Science, 1936.

Henson, Matthew A. *A Negro Explorer at the North Pole.* New York: Frederick Stokes, 1912. Reprint, Lincoln: University of Nebraska Press, 1989.

Herron, Paul. *The Story of Capitol Hill.* New York: Coward, McCann, and Geoghegan, 1963.

Haler, Andrew F. *The Twentieth Century Union League Directory, A Historical, Geographical and Statistical Study of Colored Washington.* Washington, 1892, 1896, and 1901.

Hine, Darlene Clark, and Brown, Elsa Barkley, and Terborg-Penn, Rosalyn. *Black Women in America, An Historical Encyclopedia. Vol. 1 & 2.* Bloomington & Indianapolis: Indiana University Press, 1993.

Holt, Thomas. *Story of Freedman's Hospital, 1862-1962.* Washington, D.C.: Academic Affairs Division, Howard University, 1975.

Hundley, Mary. *The Dunbar Story (1870-1955).* New York: Vantage Press, 1965.

Hutchinson, Louise Daniel. *The Anacostia Story: 1608-1930.* Washington, D.C.: Smithsonian Institution Press, 1977.

_____. *Anna J. Cooper: A Voice from the South.* Washington, D.C.: Smithsonian Institution Press, 1981.

Johnson, Haynes. *Dusk at the Mountain, The Negro, the Nation and the Capital.* New York: Doubleday and Co., 1963.

Jones, William H. *Recreation and Amusement Among Negroes in Washington, D.C.: A Sociological Analysis of the Negro in an Urban Environment.* Washington, 1927.

_____. *The Housing of Negroes in Washington, D.C.: A Study in Human Ecology.* Washington, 1929.

Junior League of Washington. *The City of Washington: An Illustrated History.* New York: Knopf, 1977.

King, Le Roy O. *100 Years of Capital Traction: The Story of Streetcars in the Nation's Capital.* np: Taylor Publishing Co., 1987.

Lee, Douglas, Meersman, Roger L., Murphy, Donn B. *Stage for a Nation: The National Theater, 150 Years.* New York: The American Press, 1985.

Lee, Richard M. *Mr. Lincoln's City: An Illustrated Guide to the Civil War Sites of Washington.* McLean, Va.: EPM Publications, Inc., 1981

Leska, Kathleen M., Babb, Valerie, and Gobbs, Carroll R. *Black Georgetown Remembered. A History of its Black Community from the Founding of "The Town of George" in 1751 to the Present Day.* Washington, D.C.: Georgetown University Press, 1991.

Lewis, David. *When Harlem Was in Vogue.* New York: Knopf, 1981.

_____. *District of Columbia: A History.* New York: W. W. Norton & Co., 1976.

Logan, Rayford W. and Winston, Michael R., eds. *Dictionary of American Negro Biography.* New York: W.W. Norton, 1982.

Logan, Rayford W. *Howard University, The First Hundred Years, 1867-1967.* New York: New York University Press, 1969.

Low, W. Augustus and Clift, Virgil A., eds. *Encyclopedia of Black America.* New York: McGraw-Hill, 1981.

Maddex, Diane. *Historic Buildings of Washington, D.C.* Pittsburgh: Ober Park Associations, Inc., 1973.

Major, Geraldyn. *Geri Major's Black Society.* Chicago: Johnson Publishing Co., 1976.

Manning, Kenneth R. *Black Apollo of Science, The Life of Ernest Everett Just.* New York: and Oxford: Oxford University Press, 1983.

McDaniel, George W., and Pearce, John N. Eds. *Images of Brookland: The History and Architecture of a Washington Suburb.* Center for Washington Area Studies, The George Washington University, 1982.

McFeely, Williams. *Frederick Douglass.* New York: W.W. Norton & Company, 1991.

McPherson, James M. *The Negro's Civil War: How American Negroes Felt and Acted During the War for the Union.* New York: Pantheon, 1965.

Mitchell, Mary. *Chronicles of Georgetown Life 1865-1900.* Cabin John, Md.: Seven Locks Press, 1986.

Morrison, Keith. *Art in Washington and Its Afro-American Presence: 1940-1970.* Washington Project for the Arts, 1985.

Natanson, Nicholas. *The Black Image in the New Deal. The Politics of FSA Photography.* Knoxville, Tennessee: The University of Tennessee Press, 1992

National Capital Planning Commission. *Shaw School Urban Renewal Area Landmarks.*

Newman, Debra L. *Black History: A Guide to Civilian Records in the National Archives.* Washington, D.C.: National Archives Trust Fund Board, 1984.

New Negro Alliance Yearbook. 1939.

The Negro in American History. Encyclopedia Britannica Educational Corporation, 1969. (3 volumes)

Oak, Vishnu V. *The Negro's Adventure in General Business.* Westport, Connecticut: Negro Universities Press, 1949.

Painter, Nell Irvin. *Sojourner Truth. A Life, A Symbol.* New York: W.W. Norton and Company, Inc., 1996.

Places and Persons on Capitol Hill: Stories and Pictures of Neighborhood. Presented by The Capitol Hill Southeast Citizens Association of Washington, D.C., 1960.

Powell, Ron, and Cunningham, Bill. *Black Guide to Washington.* Washington, D.C.: Washingtonian Books, 1975.

Pride, Armistead S., and Wilson II, Clint C. *A History of the Black Press.* Moorland-Spingarn Series. Washington, D.C.: Howard University Press, 1997.

Records of the Columbia Historical Society. Washington, D.C.: 1895-1980.

Robinson, Wilhelmina. *Historical Negro Biographies.* New York: Publishers Co., 1967.

Salk, Erwin A., comp., ed. *A Layman's Guide to Negro History. The First Comprehensive Bibliography of Books and Teaching Aids, Plus Listings of Major Events and Personalities in the United States.* New York: McGraw-Hill Book Company, 1967.

Salley, Columbus. *The Black 100. A Ranking of the Most Influential African-Americans, Past and Present.* New York: Citadel Press, 1993.

Savage, Beth L. *African American Historic Places.* Washington, D.C.: National Trust for Historic Preservation, 1994.

Schaefer, Christina K. *The Center. A Guide to Genealogical Research in the National Capital Area.* Baltimore: Genealogical Publishing Company, Inc., 1996.

Scott, Pamela, and Lee, Antoinette. *Buildings of the District of Columbia.* New York: Oxford University Opress, 1993.

Shepperd, Gladys B. *Mary Church Terrell: Respectable Person.* Baltimore: Human Relations Press, 1959.

Sherman. *Directory and Ready Reference of the Colored Population of the District of Columbia,* 1913.

Sherwood, Suzanne Berry. *Foggy Bottom 1800-1975: A Study in the Uses of an Urban Neighborhood.* Center for Washington Area Studies, The George Washington University, 1978.

Silver Jubilee Commemorating 25th Anniversary of First Eucharistic Sacrifice Celebrated March 14, 1943. Washington, D.C.: Our Lady Queen of Peace.

Simmons, William J., *Men of Mark: Eminent, Progressive and Rising,* Cleveland, 1887.

Smith, Kathryn S. and McQuirter, Marya. *A Guide to the Historical Resources of Shaw.* Washington, DC: The Thurgood Marshall Center for Service and Heritage. Funded by The Humanities Council of Washington, D.C. and The Dorothea deSchweinitz Fund of The National Trust for Historic Preservation, 1996.

Southern, Eileen. *The Music of Black Americans: A History.* New York: W.W. Norton, 1971.

Spradling, Mary Mace. *In Black and White.* Vol. I & II. Detroit: Gale Research Co., 1980.

A Study of Historical Sites in the District of Columbia of Special Significance to Afro-Americans. Prepared by the Afro-American Bicentennial Corporation, 1974. (Volumes I, II, and III)

Terrell, Mary Church. *A Colored Woman in a White World.* Washington, D.C.: Ransdell, Inc., 1940.

Thompson, Dolphin G. *A Picture Guide to Black America in Washington, D.C.* Washington, D.C.: Brownson House, 1976.

Thorpe, Earle E. *Black Historian: A Critique.* New York: William Morrow and Co., 1971.

Turner, Darwin. *Black American Literature.* Columbus, Ohio: Merrill, 1970.

Warner, William W. *At Peace With All Their Neighbors. Catholics and Catholicism in the National Capital, 1787-1860.* Washington, D.C.: Georgetown University Press, 1994.

Washington, DC, African-American Historical Attractions Guide, by the Washington, D.C. Convention and Visitors Center.

Waskow, Arthur I. *From Race Riot to Sit-In*. Garden City, NY: Doubleday, 1966.

Weeks, Christopher. *AIA Guide to the Architecture of Washington, DC. Third Edition*. Washington Chapter of the American Institute of Architects. Baltimore: The Johns Hopkins University Press, 1994.

Weller, Charles Frederick. *Washington, Neglected Neighborhoods, Stories of Life in the Alleys, Tenements & Shanties of the National Capital*. Philadelphia: John C. Winston, 1909.

Wolseley, Roland E. *The Black Press, USA*. Ames: Iowa State University Press, 1971.

Woodson, Carter G. *The History of the Negro Church*. Washington, D.C.: Associated Publishers, 1921.

Wurman, Richard Saul. *ACCESS Washington DC*. New York: Harper/Perennial/ACCESS Press Guide, 1996.

REPORTS, MANUSCRIPTS, GOVERNMENT DOCUMENTS, BROCHURES, and ARTICLES

1990 Memorial Dedication Booklet for the A. Philip Randolph Bust, Union Station

Addison Scurlock exhibition catalog. Corcoran Gallery of Art, 1976.

The Asbury Communicator, Vol. 11, Issue 5, September 1996. Lonise Fisher Robinson, Church Historian, Asbury United Methodist Church.

"Build-Grow" Sculpture, "Swan Column," "Branching Column," and Sculpture Garden by Richard Hunt. Wells Fargo Real Estate Group Press Release, September 18, 1992.

Fitzpatrick, Michael Andrew. *Shaw, Washington's Premier Black Neighborhood: An Examination of the Origins and Development of a Black Business Movement*. M.A. Thesis, University of Virginia, 1989.

The Local Aspect of Slavery in the District of Columbia, by Walter C. Clephane. Records of the Columbia Historical Society, Vol. 3 (1900), pg. 239.

National Archives and Records Service, General Services Administration. *Special List No. 34. List of Free Black Heads of Families in the First Census of the United States 1790.* Compiled by Debra L. Newman, 1973.

The Northern Shaw-Strivers Cultural Resources Survey, Phase II, Final Report. Traceries: Washington, D.C., August 1993.

Opening Convocation & Unveiling of Freedmen's Column. Howard University, September 22, 1989.

Pacifica, Michele F. *"Don't Buy Where You Can't Work". The New Negro Alliance of Washington.* 6:1 Washington History (Spring/Summer 1994), 66-88.

Washington Post. 25 July 1995; 25 January 1996; 1, 14 March 1996; 3 September 1996; 3 October 1996; 18 November 1996; 17, 30 January 1997; 3, 6, 9 February 1997; 24 April 1997;

Washington Times. 28 January 1993.

Wender, Harry S. *An Analysis of Segregation and Recreation in the District of Columbia.* Manuscript at Columbia Historical Society, 1949.

Index